NYC
AN OWNER'S
MANUAL

NYC

AN OWNER'S MANUAL

ARRIVING, SURVIVING, → THRIVING (A)(N)(D) THRIVING

IN THE GREATEST CITY IN THE WORLD

BY CAITLIN LEFFEL AND JACOB LEHMAN

UNIVERSE

First published in the United States of America in 2008

Universe Publishing, A Division of
Rizzoli International Publications, Inc.
300 Park Avenue South
New York, NY 10010
www.rizzoliusa.com

2008 2009 2010 2011 / 10 9 8 7 6 5 4 3 2 1

Distributed in the U.S. trade by Random House, New York

Printed in the United States of America

ISBN-13: 978-0-7893-1803-9

Library of Congress Control Number: 2008904973

Ⓒ Ⓛ: THIS BOOK IS **FOR MY FAMILY: ALEX, MATTHEW, MY FATHER, AND MY MOM.**

Ⓙ Ⓛ: **FOR MY PARENTS,** WHO HAVE HELPED ME GET BY IN THE TWO GREATEST CITIES IN THE WORLD.

ACKNOWLEDGMENTS

Thank you first to Kathleen Jayes, our editor, for her devotion to this book when there are so many others who need her. And thanks to Charles Miers at Universe Publishing, for believing in our NYC expertise from the very beginning.

It would have been impossible for us to write this book without insider information about places and things to do all over the city, and we owe a heavy debt to many New Yorkers who generously shared their tips about their neighborhoods, their activities, and their experiences in New York. Special thanks to: Alyssa Sheinmel and Barclay Bowen for all the honest info on buying apartments; David Wellner for sharing his favorite tennis courts, the great metaphor for Connecticut beaches, and much more; Peter DeFlorio for Upper West Side recommendations and roommate tips; Maryana Grinshpun for her endless patience; Juliette Cezzar for her Greenpoint texts and Gene Perelson for his Long Island City ones; Joanna Czech and Louis for their wonderful tour of Washington Heights; Matt Richards for setting us straight about Cobble Hill and Boerum Hill (and food in Astoria); Tracy Shafer for her mac 'n' cheese; Karen Ulrich, for details on small claims court and dry-cleaning horror stories; Joana Kelly for her relentless shrift; Jennifer Aslan for the eloquent story about when her car was towed; Marit Vagstad for her insight on running and the apartment hunt; and Peggy Schwartz for everything on Chelsea Piers and the North Fork. And a special thanks to Charlotte and Clara for being something to look forward to on writing days.

CONTENTS

INTRODUCTION

When I was growing up in New York City, my family had a blue Volvo station wagon that we kept in a garage a block from our apartment. That my family had a car was unusual among my friends—plenty of their parents didn't even have drivers' licenses. And that we kept our car in a garage rather than on the street made it seem like even more of a luxury, as we didn't have to abide by the laws of alternate side of the street parking. Of course, being New Yorkers, my parents didn't use the car to commute or go to the grocery store—in fact, I can't remember the car ever being used on a non-holiday weekday. Its purpose was for trips out of the city, mostly to visit family. One of the trips we took most often was to see my grandmother in Westchester, and that journey is engrained in my memory so strongly that I can remember every turn and landmark. There was an incredible billboard for Newport Lights that you could see from the Third Avenue Bridge, with neon lights that flashed different designs around the enormous cigarette box and an electronic ticker like the one in Times Square that spun headlines, Yankees' scores, and exotic sounding "Bulova time." There were the infamous squeegee men at the stoplight in front of the McDonald's getting off of the Major Deegan Expressway and Keith Haring's "Crack is Wack" mural that you could see from the FDR Drive. I would always keep my eyes fixed out of my brother's window the moment we got on the FDR because I didn't want to miss it. When there was no traffic, I'd usually just catch one of the more prominent details as the car whizzed by; when there was traffic, I'd try to process the entire picture: the skull, the dollar bill, and all the writhing bodies on top of one another. I still do.

Because I grew up here, I have always thought of New York City first and foremost as a place to live. The same city that is home to Broadway, the Statue of Liberty, and the Met is also where people run errands, host dinner parties, and take their children to Little League. The former attractions may make New York City a destination, but the latter activities are what make it home to me. In a way, it's like being the child of a movie star, in that my birthplace gets a lot of attention and special treatment, but my relationship with this city is completely normal—or at least it seems that way to me—because it's the only home I've ever known.

There's a familiar adage that goes, "New York is a nice place to visit, but I wouldn't want to live there." As a native New Yorker, I can't even imagine what it's like to visit this city, but I can see why people might be turned off by the idea of living here. The common gripes about miniscule and astronomically expensive apartments, the noise, and the crowds, can make it hard to see how this flashy, action-packed, mega-super-metropolis could feel like home. And this isn't something that is true only for newcomers—one can live in this city for years and still feel like an outsider sometimes. While Jacob and I both love New York (and celebrated it in our first book, *The Best Things to Do in New York*), we recognize that it's not always an easy place to live. So we decided to write something to and for our fellow city dwellers who have chosen to make New York their home. If *Best Things* was a love letter to NYC, then this book is a bit more of an exposé. We share intimate details, are harsh when we need to be, and are honest about absolutely everything.

As a well-functioning team of native and non-native (Jacob originally hails from London), we see this city as an equalizer. We're all on these streets together, and while there are staggering differences in interests, income, and experience with city living, no one lives a perfect New York life because there is no one perfect New York life. At its core, this book is a map of NYC living that starts with finding an apartment; carries on with profiles of different neighborhoods and tips for navigating everything from the city bureaucracy to the best ways to get around; and ends with ways to have fun: making friends, playing sports, going out, and even getting out of town. Along the way we've marked the route with shortcuts, landmarks, things to avoid, and plenty of places where you can branch off the beaten path if you choose. In some parts of the book, when we want to demystify certain city-specific experiences, we tell you exactly what to do or where to go. But in other parts, we've just outlined the landscape, shown you the options, and tried to steer you away from the pitfalls that each of us has experienced on occasion.

Full disclosure: I wrote my part of the last section of this book in LA. It was February, not a particularly inspiring time to be in New York, and back at home I had been struggling to find more to say about the city. Surprisingly—ironically—I immediately started to have more observations about New York than I had had in a while. Most palpably, I could feel New York in a way that I hadn't been able to while I was there, like I could touch something that I had been wrapped in for a long time. I realized I had only been thinking about the inside of the city—the rules, the details, the nuances—and had forgotten what the outside felt like: the kinesis on the streets, the everyone-all-piled-up-on-top-of-each-other sensibility, and most importantly, how in New York, you are never alone or far away from anything. I tried to channel a little Joan Didion and incorporate these transcoastal thoughts into my writing, while looking at the mountains and canyons and strip malls.

Of course, being in LA made me appreciate little, specific things, too. Being able to go to dinner without a reservation is nearly an impossibility, I discovered, in a place where everyone drives everywhere, and streets aren't crammed with restaurants block after block after block. The disconnectedness of LA—the flip side of having more space, more distance—seemed downright uncivilized to me, and the practice of structuring one's schedule around traffic ebbs and flows (dinner at 4 or 10:30 p.m.; refraining from visiting people who live a few neighborhoods away, etc.) seemed like a violation of a basic right. In the middle of a city that did not allow one to travel independently or at will, I could see clearly New York's unique permissiveness for spontaneity and autonomy, its glorious urban messiness, and the sexy, intimacy-breeding proximity to everyone and everything. It's this mix that makes living in New York so intoxicating.

This city belongs to everyone, but there's a piece of it that belongs only to you. We hope this book helps you find it and enjoy it.

—Caitlin Leffel, May 2008

PART

1

FINDING A PLACE TO LIVE

The New York City real estate market is a topic of legend, full of nuance and completely idiosyncratic. For some it's a sport, for others, a hobby, for still others an all-consuming passion; only very few can say that they think of their apartment as just a place to live. But if you're going to live here, then you'll have to involve yourself with this fickle beast at some point. If you are a true tycoon, by all means, jump in, sit back, and enjoy the ride. But for the rest of us, our advice is this: get in and get out of the hunt as quickly as you can.

No matter how long or short a time you're planning to stay in New York, you will have to find a place to live at some point. If you will be renting, you should consider whether you want to look for a rent-regulated apartment, what type of landlord (individual or corporate) you want, and if you'll need a roommate—or several of them. If you're buying, you will have to consider whether you want a co-op or condo, if you want to buy an existing apartment or new construction, and how much work you would be willing to put into it. Whether you are renting or buying, you'll also be considering neighborhood, type of building (old or new; full-service or little- to no-service; loft, brownstone, or high-rise), and of course, how much you can spend. Below, we'll give you an overview of all of these items, along with a few other considerations that you may not have thought of before.

RENTING VS. BUYING

If you are planning on renting, the first step is to tell everyone you know that you are looking for a new place. Don't just spread the word to people living here; cast your net widely to relatives and friends all over the country—and the world. One person we know from Minnesota found her first apartment in New York through an uncle—who lives in San Diego. Turns out he knew someone who was going to be moving out of his apartment on the Upper East Side right around when she needed to move in. She got in touch with the guy moving out, who put her in touch with the landlord; she ended up staying in that apartment for three years. With the number of people moving around the city at any time of the year, chances are pretty good that you can hook up with someone who's got what you're looking for (or what you'd happily consider) just by word of mouth. This bit of networking can be well worth the effort; in addition to saving on brokers' fees (which typically range from one month's rent to 10 percent of the total annual rent), this friend also saved an untold amount of time cruising ads and pounding the pavement. Send an e-mail to everyone you know and ask them to forward it to anyone they know in or out of New York who might have some leads. The wider your search is, the more options you are likely to have, and the more likely it is that you'll find something that lines up with what you want.

If you can't find something from word of mouth, there are a couple of other routes to explore. You can look through listings or go directly to a broker. In a sense, these routes actually overlap, because as you look through listings, you will inevitably be weeding through postings from brokers. The main reason to avoid a broker is to avoid paying fees, but it means you'll have to work a little harder. Two of the best sources for rental listings, Craigslist and backpage.com, which runs the *Village Voice* classifieds, have search options that allow you to look only for no-fee and by-owner rentals (though beware that some "owners" are actually people who are "representing" the landlord, who may be brokers). The *New York Times* online real estate listings are a great resource when you are starting to look and want to know what is available in certain areas and what kinds of prices apartments go for; but we don't know anyone who has actually found an apartment there, whether to rent or to buy. Some newspapers still print classifieds, but they're pretty obsolete, and much harder to search through.

Buying an apartment in New York is a very different game from renting, and what you will be buying will most likely not be a simple piece of land with a freestanding structure on it. In fact, if you are buying into a co-op building, as many New Yorkers do, when all is said and done (and paid . . . and paid), you won't actually "own" any physical land at all—you'll own shares in a corporation that owns the building.

Apartments for purchase fall into two categories, co-ops and condos. There are more co-op buildings than condo buildings in New York City, although the number of condos has been growing. In general, you tend to get a little more space for your money in a co-op, but you must be approved by the building's board, submit an extensive collection of financial statements and personal information called the "board package," and agree to the co-op's specific "house rules." These rules vary from building to building, but usually govern what can and can't go on in any common spaces, including noise in the lobby, elevators, stairwells and hallways; storage in the basement; laundry facilities; procedures for garbage and recycling; and roof or balcony access if there is any. In addition, they can also extend to the apartment itself: the type and number of pets permitted; guidelines for carpeting (some buildings mandate a certain amount of carpeting in each apartment to muffle sound); and restrictions on the types of appliances that can be installed (garbage disposals, for instance, which were banned in the city until 1997 are still off-limits in many co-ops, especially older ones). One set of house rules we looked at covered everything from appropriate dress in the lobby to prohibitions on noise to exactly which types of air conditioners can be installed in a unit. If you have strange (or a large number of) pets, play a loud musical instrument, can't live without a garbage disposal, or like to walk around your lobby barefoot without a shirt on, a condo might be a better choice. On top of this, some may find complying with the requirements of the board package intrusive and sufficiently off-putting. As one recent co-op buyer explained to us: "Buying into a co-op is not for the modest. You pretty much have to be willing to disclose everything."

In a condo, the buyer actually owns his property and pays a common charge to cover maintenance of shared areas. While there are still far fewer condos than co-ops in the city, many new buildings are condos, and those often come with more amenities, including gyms and concierges. Condos are typically more expensive, and the buyer's reward is ostensibly more control over his or her property. (And they are also easier to sell, since the incoming tenants don't have to go through as vigorous a vetting process.) Condos do have boards, however, and while they are still less stringent then those of co-ops, it's not as if you can just show up with an eight-foot iguana and a harpsichord and move in. Most want to discourage owners from renting out their units, and like co-op owners, want to ensure a certain character in the building, whatever that may be. Bottom line: If you're looking for complete autonomy for you and your reptile musical protégé, buy a house or start looking a lot farther upstate. Being a home owner in New York City still means you have to get along with everyone else.

⟶ Tips for the First-Time Buyer ⟵

- **BE PATIENT.** As a first-time buyer, you'll need to do a lot of homework. Before you start looking at places to buy, start looking at places that are actually for sale. The *New York Times* has an excellent and well-designed search tool on its real estate site that also has neighborhood profiles, mortgage calculators, and other useful features (though as we mentioned earlier, you shouldn't expect to find your place on it). Get an idea of what apartments are like in different neighborhoods, what kinds of buildings there are, and the prices.

- **FIND A BROKER YOU LIKE.** Most buyers go through brokers, as there is no cost to the buyer (both the buyer's and seller's broker are paid through the sale by the seller). The broker will do everything from finding apartments that fit your criteria to helping you make an offer to guiding you through the mechanics of the closing. As a first-time buyer, having an experienced professional on your side is, of course, especially important. You will be relying on your broker a lot, so make sure he or she understands what you are looking for. Open houses can be a great place to meet brokers.

- BE FLEXIBLE . . . This applies to everything from how broad an area to look in to dealing with a closing date that changes at the last minute (a not-infrequent occurrence that may require you to figure out some last-minute accommodations).

- . . . UNTIL THE FINAL WALK-THROUGH. People may try to tell you that certain things aren't worth noticing on the walk-through, especially in new construction. Don't listen to them. If something's not right, get it fixed before you move in. Once you move in, it's your problem.

A NOTE ON NEW CONSTRUCTION

There are a lot of new apartments in New York City these days; in many neighborhoods all over the boroughs, it's hard to walk more than a block or two without seeing a new building going up. New construction can either be a completely new building or an older building (sometimes even a landmarked one) that's been gutted and reconfigured into apartments. It's easy to see why a buyer would be seduced by these apartments: nothing has been used or lived in by anyone but you, and if you buy during the building phase, you may get to make choices on colors, finishes, and appliances. Many of these new buildings are also condos, so they offer the same benefits of "true" ownership of your unit. And if you're buying in the building phase, you'll never have to go through any sort of approval process.

But there's a bit of a dark side here. Construction projects in New York rarely finish on time, and the completion date that the developer gives can be weeks or even months off. When you finally are allowed to move in, often parts of the building (or even things in your apartment) may not be totally finished, and features and amenities that were promised initially either haven't yet been completed—or in some cases, never are. In addition, there are also some fees and taxes that are usually covered by an existing apartment's previous owner that you as the buyer will have to swallow.

If you are buying into new construction, research the reputation of the developer and management company. Have their projects been completed on time, and if not (well, *when* not), how has the company handled the situation? As much as you can, familiarize yourself with building codes and make sure the engineers and developer are not cutting corners. Be wary of the developer's move-in date, and be prepared for set-backs and delays, which may mean staying where you are, finding an interim rental with a flexible move-out date, or bunking with a friend with a comfortable couch who owes you a favor. The later you buy into the project, the more likely it is that the completion date will be accurate. Try to make sure the building is at least close to being finished before you close on an apartment.

RENT CONTROL AND RENT STABILIZATION

Aside from public and subsidized housing, there are two types of rentable apartments in New York: market-rate and rent-regulated. The difference between market-rate apartments and those that are rent-regulated is that rent amounts (and increases) in market-rate apartments are determined by the landlord, whereas in rent-regulated apartments, there are limits set by the state.

Rent-regulated apartments encompass both rent-controlled and rent-stabilized units. But before you get excited about the words "rent-control," slow down. While rent-controlled apartments do still exist here, *vacancies* in them do not, because according to the current laws, rent-controlled units that become vacant (and are not passed on to family members) are put on the market at market-rate and do not remain rent-controlled. So unless you have a family member who loves you enough to pass on his or her $500-a-month multi-bedroom rent-controlled apartment, rent-stabilization is the only way to save on rent in a government-regulated kind of way.

A rent-stabilized apartment, however, is a realistic option: about a million apartments in the city are rent-stabilized, a hundred thousand of which typically have vacancies in a given year, according to the New York City Rent Guidelines Board. In a rent-stabilized apartment, the percentage that a rent can be raised each year is fixed and regulated, unlike in a market-rate apartment, where the increase in rent between leases is at the landlord's discretion. In addition, tenants in rent-stabilized apartments are guaranteed by law the option of lease renewal (with the regulated rent increases) at the end of their previous lease (which is not true in market-rate apartments), and they have certain prescribed rights that individual landlords of non-stabilized buildings may not provide, such as subletting. (Landlords of rent-stabilized apartments are required by law to offer both one- and two-year lease options. The two-year lease option guarantees the percentage increase that the tenant will face in the second year, which can significantly benefit the tenant. Because the rent increases in stabilized apartments are not fixed but are determined by the board each year, the two-year lease determines that you will only face the percentage increase stated in the lease in the second year, even if the board-dictated increase is greater.) Tenants also benefit from certain mandated building services, and—though we hope it never comes to this for you!—it's more difficult to be evicted from a rent-stabilized apartment than a market-rate apartment. (Actually, it's pretty difficult to get evicted from anywhere, even if you haven't been paying your rent. Not that we're encouraging you not to! See page 163 for more on eviction.) Rent-stabilized apartments all have rents below $2,000 per month; once an apartment's rent exceeds that, the apartment can be deregulated. These apartments are typically found in buildings of six or more units, most built before 1974. However, there are exceptions to these rules, so if you are set on finding one of these apartments, the New York City Rent Guidelines Board has a list of buildings with rent-stabilized units in them; you should verify this with the landlords and managing agents. If you are using a broker, you can also ask him or her if they have any listings in buildings with rent-stabilized units.

While rent-stabilized apartments are typically not luxury properties (though there are actually some that have been kept rent stabilized for tax purposes), there's not anything sketchy about living in one, at least as specifically pertains to being rent stabilized. Caitlin lived in a rent-stabilized apartment for two years. She didn't specifically seek out a rent-stabilized apartment initially—actually, she'd never heard of rent stabilization before—she just couldn't resist taking a look at an apartment in Chelsea where a bedroom rental was going for less than $700 a month (her roommate paid a bit more for the larger bedroom). During their tenancy, they successfully negotiated a brand-new refrigerator and stove from the management company, endured some noisy neighbors and a few mice when the apartment above them was being renovated, had plumbers and exterminators visit the apartment as needed, and were once temporarily made homeless for one week in February when the boiler broke (for which they demanded and received a reduction in rent)—in short, pretty much par for the course for a New York City rental experience, except that their rent went up less than $300 total over two years.

Visit the New York City Rent Guidelines Board web site at www.housingnyc.com for more information on rent stabilization, and to see a complete list of rent-stabilized buildings in each borough.

⟶ A Brief History of Rent Control and Rent Stabilization ⟵

Rent-control and rent-stabilization laws have existed in other cities and states, but they are best known in and most frequently associated with New York City. Rent-regulation laws—first rent control and later rent stabilization—were initially developed as temporary economic relief measures, but have existed here continuously in various forms since 1943, longer than anywhere else in the country. To very much simplify their incredibly complicated history, the reason that they've lasted so long is that the city's housing market and its public housing programs have never been able to provide an adequate amount of affordable housing for residents on their own. Shocking.

Rent control was introduced in the U.S. during World War II by President Roosevelt as the Emergency Price Control Act, a temporary federal policy that instituted price controls in the country's housing market to curb wartime inflation. After the war, this act was allowed to expire, and was replaced by another federal rent-regulation act that kept rent controls on buildings built before February 1, 1947, but exempted buildings built from then on. Still with us?

Things started to get complicated in 1949, when Congress passed on to individual states the authority to institute and set any rent regulations. While much of the rest of the country eventually allowed rent regulation to go the way of ration cards and other wartime provisions, in New York, it stuck, though the powers that be have been tinkering with the formula every decade or so since then. (At the time that the authority on rent regulation was passed down to the states, 85 percent of the housing units covered in New York State were located in New York City, and the majority of the state's rent-controlled and rent-stabilized housing has always been here.) Since then, authority on setting the rent guidelines has passed from the state to the city and back to the state; at various times, individual residential units have been controlled, decontrolled, and controlled again; and stipulations regarding income caps, building sizes, and construction dates have been continually introduced, revised, and done away with. Rent control came to be seen as unnecessary and even detrimental in good economic times, but revoking the laws altogether—and sending apartments that had been kept at World War II–era rents up to market rate—stirred up a host of other problems. In the 1960s, there was a trend toward de-control, but the pendulum shifted back later on in the decade because of economic problems brought on by the Vietnam War. In 1969, in response to the rapid rise of inflation—and what was generally seen as the poor economic impact of rent control—rent stabilization was introduced. Rent stabilization is a type of rent control, but instead of actually fixing rent at a certain amount, it caps the amount rent can go up each year. Since 1969, rent-stabilization has been replacing rent control, and some rent-controlled apartments have been turned into rent-stabilized apartments when they are vacated.

Rent control is controversial, in theory and in practice. If you've ever taken an introductory economics class, you may remember that rent control tends not to get such a good rap from economists. Their argument is that rent control creates a price ceiling that adversely hurts both landlords and tenants, stifles growth, deters investment, and artificially manipulates the balance of supply and demand in the housing market. On the other hand, defenders claim that it provides affordable housing when a free market has shown that it can't. But for now, at least, that point is moot. The trajectory that rent control has taken since the 1960s would take up much more space than we think would be helpful to devote to it here, but the most important thing to understand is that rent control is no longer in effect, and rent stabilization is. The only rent-controlled apartments that exist are ones that have been lived in continuously since before July 1, 1971. Once these apartments are vacated by their original tenants (or immediate family members), rent control will cease to exist . . . unless they decide to bring it back again.

SUBLETS AND LEASES

Of New York's 8.5 million residents, more than 65 percent are renters—a statistic that reflects both the city's tough housing market and its fluid and mobile population. People come and go in New York with alarming frequency, and those that stay are likely to move up, down, or around a great deal during their time here. As neighborhoods evolve and as house prices rise and fall around the five boroughs, knowing when, where, and how to move from place to place is vital to living happily.

While going after a permanent place to live has its advantages, the first recourse of many newcomers to the Big Apple is to sublet. While people who rent an apartment usually sign a lease that binds them legally to live there for a set period (whether it's six months, a year, or two years), subletters can often move into places on a monthly or even weekly basis. The city's network of sublets works both ways, giving newcomers a place to stay while they look for a more permanent home, and allowing renters who are leaving town or moving into a new place to recoup the rent they would have wasted on an empty space.

Finding a sublet is a great deal easier than finding a place to lease. Besides the fact that people can often find a sublet through word of mouth, many of the ads posted on Craigslist are for sublets, and Sublet.com is a helpful web site devoted entirely to finding temporary rooms around the city. Making arrangements to sublet a place is much simpler, too: rental prerequisites such as deposits, guarantors, and even contracts are on the whole treated with less seriousness, and deals are made directly between you and the owner or another tenant of the place, so there are rarely any fees involved.

So what's the catch? Only that in subletting rather than leasing a place you sacrifice some of the longer-term security that you would enjoy as a full-time tenant. Sometimes tenants who advertise rooms to sublet do so without giving the landlord notice and therefore without permission, which can count as a breach of their tenancy agreement. You can be asked to leave as quickly and easily as you are allowed to move in and if you're subletting a room in an apartment that you're sharing with others, it's likely that one of the other residents will remain a principal tenant in the eyes of the landlord, which can impede a subletter's authority when it comes to issues affecting the state of the building.

If you're looking to sublet a room or an apartment, it's wise to make sure you understand exactly what the relationship is between you, the landlord, and any other tenants. If you're taking over somebody else's lease, it's a good idea to find out what the status of his or her deposit is—if you're required to give a deposit yourself, make sure it's understood that you're only liable to lose it on account of damages incurred during the period of your stay, and not for any problems that began during your predecessor's tenure. (Take some photos when you move in!) As with any other kind of rental, read any contracts carefully and be sure everything is above board.

→ The Pros and Cons of Subletting ←

When brokers and contracts are not involved, try to be a careful judge of character and use your discretion when it comes to subletting a room. A friend of ours rented a place from a tenant who was forbidden to sublet by contract, and had told the landlord before leaving for a trip abroad that his sister was going to look after the place while he was away. The subletter arrived to find strict written instructions as to her new "identity" and spent three very difficult months trying to conceal her real name from everybody in the building.

One of the advantages of subletting is that you can often find a room in an expensive part of town for a reasonable price—with most people looking to rent for six months or a year or two, short stays of anywhere from two weeks to three or four months can be real bargains. Another friend who moved to New York from San Francisco managed to spend seven months hopping from a balcony apartment in Chelsea to a corner room in Soho and a studio in Dumbo before finally settling for a more realistically priced home in Queens. Just don't let yourself get too attached to that loft in Tribeca, or the basement room you end up leasing in Hell's Kitchen will feel like a real step down.

CONTRACTS AND TENANCY ENTITLEMENTS

For anyone who didn't go to law school, the complex terminology of a landlord's contract can be baffling. The apparent gravity of signing a lease is enough to make even the simplest and most generous contracts seem confusing and frightening. Committing your name to dates, deposits, and details is a difficult thing to do whatever the circumstances, and the more you invest in a place financially and emotionally the more care you'll want to take to make sure things are done right. Take the time to learn a few basics of New York tenancy laws, though, and you may assuage some of the anxiety that accompanies the act of putting pen to paper. It's up to you as the tenant to make sure you understand what your contract stipulates, and as frequently as not it's within your power to influence, however trivially, the terms and conditions of your lease.

By New York State law, which differs in regard to tenancy entitlements only in minor detail from those elsewhere, every landlord is obliged to offer certain minimum standards in the living conditions of their tenants, and an adherence to these standard conditions will be bound by any contract. These range from obvious necessities such as working windows and functioning utilities to subtler requirements such as peep holes in doors or the minimum temperature of a building's heating. Sometimes these requirements will be spelled out in a lease, and sometimes the details will simply be references to parts of broader state legislation. The first thing to know is that every letter of the law is easily accessible through the city's official sources, and you can find out exactly what you're entitled to either online or by calling 311 and visiting citizens' advice bureaus. The second thing to know is that in the unlikely event of a landlord failing to maintain those standards, you are entirely within your rights as a tenant to complain and, if need be, to take legal action to restore them.

On the whole, serious problems between landlords and tenants in New York are relatively few and far between. There are gripes and battles here and there— everybody knows somebody whose landlord never did fix that boiler, or whose bathroom window never quite closed properly—but thanks to the strictures of the law and the competitive health of the real estate market, standards in the city's more accessible neighborhoods are high. Perhaps the most common fear among long-term tenants is that personal circumstances might change and that they might want or need to break the lease by moving out early. But with clear communication and a little luck, even that can be less of a nightmare than expected—helping a landlord find a replacement who will pay higher rent or simply relying on a landlord's capacity to empathize can pay off, and often a tenant might not even lose his or her deposit if things can be worked out adequately.

The issues tenants have most often arise from conditions in contracts that are specific to a building or to a landlord's personal whim, and it's here again that honesty, communication, and a little tact and savvy can make all the difference. Provisions in contracts designed to prevent one neighbor's noise from bothering another, for example, frequently come in the form of a clause that requires tenants to cover a certain percentage of their floors with rugs or carpeting. But before you wave good-bye to your beautiful hardwood floors, make the effort to talk to your downstairs neighbors, think realistically about the kind of racket you're likely to make, and work out whether or not that's really going to be an issue big enough to worry about. Rules stipulated by a landlord regarding a tenant's subletting of an apartment, or the sharing of an apartment with someone whose name isn't on the lease, may not always be as firm or nonnegotiable as the cold print on the contract might suggest, so if those are things you know will come up during your tenancy, be honest with your landlord and ask whether or not they have to be followed to the letter.

Whatever your situation, the most important thing to do before you sign any contract is to take stock of yourself and what you want from your place, and to make sure your agreement will complement that. If you're a musician and you need to be able to make noise, make sure the agreement makes no provisions that will inhibit you from doing that. If you have a pet, find a building where pets are allowed instead of signing a contract that specifies otherwise, hoping never to be discovered. However much talking things through with landlords and neighbors can help you assess the reality of a situation, it's better to be safe than sorry, and knowing exactly what you're putting your name to beforehand can save months of grief down the line.

Remember that tenancy laws are in place to protect everyone who needs them—landlords and tenants—and for the most part common sense and decency will prevail. But whether you're renting a room on a month-by-month basis or signing a two-year lease, handling the legal side of things is an important necessity. The New York State Attorney's web site is a helpful source for information on tenants' rights and more: www.oag.state.ny.us/realestate/tenants_rights_guide.html

ROOMMATES

At some point during your NYC career, it may be necessary for you to find one or multiple roommates. It may be because the friends you currently live with are ready to move on, and you have spaces to fill in your current apartment; or you may be the one who needs to move. Looking for a room in an apartment with roommates, rather than an apartment of your own has the added bonus of helping you avoid the broker-Craigslist–pavement-pounding tango. And often it comes with other perks, such as couches, microwaves, and shower curtains.

The best way to find a roommate is, not surprisingly, that same electronic version of word of mouth that we described earlier in the section on finding an apartment, albeit with a little more discretion in the "To" field. You will probably want to limit the recipients to people you know well and are likely to have other friends with whom you would get along, as the e-mail will (hopefully) be forwarded on. If you are looking for a space in an apartment (and proposing yourself as a potential roommate), don't forget to mention how quiet and considerate you are. If you are looking for roommates to fill a room (or rooms) that will be vacated, be sure to mention the price, utilities, move-in date, information about the apartment's common amenities (kitchen, bathroom, living room, etc.) and any non-negotiable specifications (pets and smoking being probably the two biggest). If this doesn't get results, try Craigslist.

Living with a roommate in New York City isn't so different from living with roommates in other places . . . except that it's New York City. You'll likely be sharing extremely close quarters with this person, and your room may be lacking four walls, a closet, a door—or more than one of the aforementioned. We'd love to say think carefully about whom you'd like to live with before signing the lease, but given how quickly apartments turn over (and how quickly one often needs to move from one apartment to the next), sometimes that's just not practical. Better advice: be open-minded, and go for it. Some roommates are no fun but make great stories later on; other roommates turn into great friends. Caitlin moved into an apartment with a girl from Virginia who was as wary of shacking up with a Yankee as Caitlin was living with a Southerner. Now she's one of Caitlin's best friends, three years after they moved out of the apartment.

You can also pick your roommate (or mates) first, then look for an apartment together. The number of roommates you have will make a big impact on your living situation. If you're looking for a place with a single roommate, there are options of varying degrees of niceness in pretty much every neighborhood; however, many have awkward layouts, with bedrooms that differ drastically in size, and unless you want to pay a lot more, count on sharing a bathroom. With a larger group (four or more roommates), you can usually save some money, but four-bedroom apartments are harder to find, and consider the complexity of getting everyone to agree on a place, not to mention the inevitable hassle of replacing the roommates as they move out—the more roommates you have, the more often you'll have to be coming up with replacements. Three, interestingly, seems to be a good number to work with. As the inhabitant of a criminally reasonable three-bedroom apartment with a full roof garden on West 72nd Street put it: "With two people, you're looking at a lot of converted one-bedrooms, which can be chopped up really awkwardly. With four, you'll probably be looking at a lot of lofts where you'll have to put up walls yourself. With three, you're more often looking at true three bedrooms, and you can have the option of one bathroom or two."

Before you embark on your stint of cohabitation, a wise roommate will set up a little financial structure, unromantic as it sounds. Here are some things to address:

REMEMBER WHO PAID THE SECURITY DEPOSIT, OR HOW IT WAS DIVIDED: It would be a shame to live with a person peacefully for years, then have a friendship-ending falling out over a security deposit that both of you remember paying.

COME UP WITH A WAY TO DIVIDE THE RENT THAT ALL ROOMMATES ARE COMFORTABLE WITH: The person with the biggest and nicest room should pay more, of course, but figuring out exactly how much the difference should be can take some negotiating.

MAKE A SYSTEM FOR PAYING BILLS: What's covered in your rent will be different in every building, so you may be responsible for electricity, heat, or other charges in addition to the rent. Those bills will likely fluctuate every month (heat is higher in the winter; electricity will be higher in the summer if you have an air conditioner), so it's usually a good idea to split each bill, in the interest of fairness. Telephone, Internet, and cable are all things you'll have to decide on together, and can be tricky. If one roommate doesn't want cable and the other does, will the person who doesn't want to pay for it never be allowed to watch TV? Consider fairness—and then consider that you have to live with this person. If there's a service you need that's non-negotiable, be prepared to pay for it and look the other way if your roommate occasionally uses it.

DEFINE WHAT IS SHARED: This area is a minefield of potential petty disagreements. If you're living with someone, you're probably going to share certain commodities, and if you're always the one buying the toilet paper, it can eat away at you. If you can, figure out a way to talk about things like whether you're okay with sharing food in the fridge, toothpaste, paper towels, cleaning products, cooking staples, etc. This task is only slightly less annoying than fighting a parking ticket, and may seem unnecessary if you've never lived with anyone before. But trust us—what is normal and reasonable is never exactly the same from person to person, and nothing brings out those differences more poignantly than living with someone in a small space.

SHAPE UP AND SHIP OUT

Whether you're renting, buying, or squatting in a friend's windowless attic while you wait for something to come up, chances are you're going to be bringing things with you. In a city of multi-story walk-ups, awkward stairwells, eccentric apartments, and narrow hallways, finding an affordable and reliable way to move is as important as finding the right place to move into. And in a city with such a mobile population, the market for movers is vast and varied. It should go without saying that anybody moving to New York from out of state will probably need to make arrangements with national operators to ship the contents of his or her old home to the bare floors of the new one. But there are myriad options for the great many tenants and homeowners who are in constant rotation within the five boroughs and the tristate area.

To find the movers that are right for you, take the time to explore what's out there: hundreds of companies are listed in the Yellow Pages, and a simple search for movers on the Internet or on Craigslist will yield hundreds more. And don't forget to ask around—everybody who's moved in the city will have hearty recommendations and hard-earned warnings about which firms they'd use and which ones they'd never use again. There are ostensibly three strata of moving company in New York: major firms with fleets of trucks; smaller companies with a more local concentration; and man-in-a-van or amateur operations. The larger companies are for the most part the most expensive, the smaller operations are cheaper, and the men-in-vans the most easily arranged—but when reliability, efficiency, and professionalism are priorities, it pays to keep looking until you find the right balance between price and security.

Two companies dominate the higher end of the moving market in New York: Shleppers and Moishe's. Like Bloomberg's parks, you're never more than a few hundred yards from one of their trucks—at least, sometimes it seems that way—and their armies of experienced staff make them the most popular choices for residents with entire households in transit. While they do handle smaller jobs and will work anywhere in the five boroughs, these companies and others this size are better reserved for families and inhabitants of the city's more spacious residential neighborhoods.

The best way to find smaller moving firms is to investigate the area you're moving to. Telephone directories will list companies that are located nearby, which is often an advantage both in cost and in reliability, if only because you might be able to go and arrange the move in person. They will have a good idea of the best ways to navigate the neighborhood and will also know what kind of building you'll be moving into, which saves time and helps ensure the movers make the right preparations. It's also a good idea to ask around in the area—people in your new building or down the block might have invaluable advice for someone moving into the neighborhood.

Beyond Google and the Yellow Pages, the most valuable sources for small-time movers are Craigslist and the city's many lampposts. While trawling online postings and tearing off telephone numbers might not seem the most glamorous methods, the reality is that the smallest local operations are often the quickest, easiest, and cheapest ways of moving house within the city, particularly for lighter households. The people that advertise in the streets and in the "services" pages of Craigslist are for the most part amateur movers moonlighting outside of regular jobs, which means they may neither be licensed movers nor offer insurance; but what they lack in professionalism or association with a larger company they are likely to make up for with flexibility, affordability, and unparalleled local knowledge.

Of course, you can always choose to do the job yourself. There are U-Haul outposts all over the five boroughs, from which you can rent any kind of vehicle from minivans to trucks for as long as you'll need, and if you and your friends can handle the labor it can be much cheaper than hiring a moving firm to do the job for you. And for those who travel light, Zipcar is another viable option. The company's cars are all over the city and can be rented online easily and affordably for short periods of time, so if you only have enough stuff to fill a town car or a people carrier, they're a useful compromise between renting a truck and taking a cab. You may also need packaging materials or other movers' supplies; if begging for cardboard boxes at your local stores or scavenging your neighbors' recycling won't do the trick there are more professional options all over the city. If you go with U-Haul, you should be able to rent equipment from them, too, but shops such as Mail Boxes Etc., the Container Store, and even UPS stores sell boxes and bags of every size, shape, and durability, as well as tape, twine, bubble wrap, and marker pens. And if your local hardware store doesn't carry them, places such as Home Depot or Lowe's sell tools, dollies, ramps, and larger crates, to help you shift heavy objects.

Whoever you go with, there are a few important things to consider. Moving house always requires a lot of thought, but moving within New York has its own particular demands. If you're unsure about a moving company, if you wish to make a complaint about a firm, or if the worst happens and you need to make a claim against your movers, you can call either the State Department of Transportation (1-800-786-5368), with which licensed movers must be registered, or the city's 311 service for advice and information on consumer affairs.

Top Five Moving Tips

① Make sure you know the specifics of your two locations. It'll be vital in determining the speed and cost of the job to ensure movers know what floor you're on, what kind of building it is, how many flights of stairs there are, what parking limitations there might be, and any potential difficulties with doors or hallways. Some leases even prohibit moving in and out on certain days or at certain times, too.

② Take the time to find the right way to move for you. If you're going to do it yourself, make sure you have everything you need, from dollies to wrapping cloth. If you're going to hire a firm, obtain estimates from as many companies as you can before choosing one that seems both reasonable and reliable.

③ Always agree on a price before the move, and be aware that some smaller companies might employ "freelance" movers who will try to talk you into a different deal. Consider how much you should tip, and also know that many movers only take cash or certified checks in payment.

④ Establish before the move whether you or the movers will pack up everything. If you're going to do it yourself you'll need to leave yourself time enough and make sure you have the right supplies to wrap and protect things properly. And if the movers are going to do it, you need to make sure they know that before they turn up.

⑤ Make sure you understand whether or not your belongings will be insured during the move, and if not, how you can arrange for them to be covered. It might be worth carrying your most delicate or valuable items with you, if not for their security then for the sake of your nerves.

And What's Your Day Job?

There are two camps from which moonlighting movers tend to emanate: artists, musicians, or writers looking to make money outside of their fields; and construction workers, part-time emergency-service workers, or professional movers looking for more work outside of their regular shifts. Essentially this means that you can choose between a group of skinny artists willing to schlep anything to support their work, and a van full of huge men who could lift twice as much in half the time if they wanted to.

Anybody with an artistic bent might like to patronize their peers, and amateur moving services staffed by artists will always announce their backgrounds in postings online or on flyers in the street. However noble the intention of supporting artists, though, it's best not to let a patron's sympathies interfere with common sense. A team of young amateurs can take a long time to finish a heavy job, which can cost a lot if rates are hourly, and some firms have no qualms about asking a client to kick in and help when things are going slowly. When Jacob hired an "artists' moving collective" to help him move into a fifth-floor walk-up uptown, he ended up carrying as much as one of the sculptors-for-hire and still paying full price for the job.

By the same token, a moving firm operated by people more familiar with manual work will underline their speed and efficiency but make fewer claims about treating your belongings with sensitivity. Jacob moved downtown a year later and used a firm staffed by construction workers and part-time firefighters, and although they broke two speakers and a mirror frame, the job took half as long and cost a third less. When they discovered the staircase was too narrow, two of the men even contrived to swing an oversized armchair in through a window from the roof above. The more you have to move and the heavier it is, the more sense it makes to have sheer physical force on your side.

If you're not going to go with a big firm, it's a good idea to find out the background of your moonlighting movers. Check out their testimonials and references if they're advertising online, and don't be afraid to ask questions if you're just calling a number. Whatever and wherever you're moving, there's someone appropriate to help.

CAST OF CHARACTERS

My building could be a sitcom." Not a sentiment we're unfamiliar with; any living situation in New York City has a potential for comedy, tragedy, and drama. Of course, you'll have neighbors no matter where you live, but in NYC, you'll probably have more of them, plus a super, and possibly landlord, doorman, or other kinds of building staff. Combine the unpredictable dynamic between this group of characters with the close quarters you're all residing in, and the dramatic possibilities are endless.

If you're lucky, you'll find a person or a small group of friendly normal people who you'll come to know and genuinely like. Lots of people have lovely relationships with the people they know from their buildings, and in the best cases, these people provide a warm, safe community for one another in the big, bad city. Caitlin's father's car recently escaped an uncertain future because a neighbor he bumped into tipped him off that the garage they both kept their cars in had suddenly lost its lease and was about to be demolished. For better and for worse, no matter where you live in this city, you're never living on your own.

Following is a short guide to the people you should know:

SUPERS

WHERE YOU'LL FIND THEM: In the common areas of the building, or basements. Buildings with more than nine units are required to have either a live-in super or a 24-hour super residing within one block of the building. You'll have an easier time finding the super when you need him if he lives in the building. Nevertheless, how much you see and get to know the super depends on how big the building is and how often you call him (if you call him at all).

CHARACTER SYNOPSIS: The job of a super varies from building to building, but it almost always involves organizing tenants' trash and recycling for pickup; maintaining common areas such as the lobby and basement; keeping the sidewalk outside of the building clear of snow, ice, water, and debris; and some amount of handiwork. One thing to note is that in rental buildings, the super actually works for the landlord, so the landlord will be reluctant to pay for another repairman to fix something in your apartment if he or she thinks the super can do it. So the handier the super, the better.

YOUR ROLE: Be nice, polite, and patient. Follow the building's rules about trash and recycling, use of the common spaces, and hallway clutter. If your super does any in-apartment repairs, you may want to offer a tip. (Some supers will refuse, and others may not be allowed to accept. But it's best to offer, at least the first time.) Always tip around Christmastime.

LANDLORDS

WHERE YOU'LL FIND THEM: In smaller buildings and townhouses, the landlord may be an individual who lives near, or even in, the building. In large buildings with many units, the landlord may be an office rather than a single person, and even in smaller buildings in areas where one landlord owns more than one property, the landlord may have an office with many people working for him or her.

CHARACTER SYNOPSIS: According to the official *New York State Tenant's Rights Guide*, a landlord is required to provide an apartment that is "livable, safe, and sanitary"; his or her objective is to do this as cheaply as possible. This covers basic things including heat and hot water, insect extermination, and repairs to door locks and smoke detectors, and some odd-seeming regulations about mirrors in elevators. (The guide is available online at www.oag.state.ny.us/realestate/tenants_rights_guide.html.)

YOUR ROLE: Choose your battles, but when you do need something fixed or replaced, be a pest—in the nicest possible way. A delicate combination of persistence and politeness got Caitlin multiple repairs and several new appliances in a single apartment over a two-year period. Also, landlords treat good tenants better than bad ones, so pay your rent on time, with checks that do not bounce. When you move in, expect to pay a security deposit of one month's rent, but know that anything more than that is illegal. When you move out, leave the apartment as clean as possible, and then send a request to the landlord or management company for your security deposit. If your landlord is part of a management company, know that it may take a little legwork to get it, but the check will come, eventually. And by the way, you have to pay your last month's rent—you can't just have them use the security deposit to cover it.

DOORMEN

WHERE YOU'LL FIND THEM: In the building lobby or outside the door, usually in a smart-looking uniform.

CHARACTER SYNOPSIS: Doormen will greet you at the door each time you enter and leave the building, direct your visitors up to your apartment, and keep suspicious characters from getting in. In some buildings, doormen also run the elevators. Though their specific duties vary by building, most doormen will accept packages, dry cleaning, and groceries, and many also distribute the mail. We've even heard of doormen in buildings who, for a tip, will move cars parked on the street. One thing to remember—doormen know what magazines you get, what you have delivered (and from what companies), who visits you, and what kind of people you bring home at night. They also probably know when you are sick, when you've been away, and if you have a baby, they'll be one of the first people to see it when you bring it home. So there's a kind of one-sided intimacy between you and your doorman that you may want to keep in mind.

YOUR ROLE: Unlike a super, this is a person (or people) who you'll have daily interactions with for as long as you live in the building, so developing a relationship with him is inevitable. It should go without saying that you want it to be a good one; it's just plain good manners. The trickier part for people who aren't used to having this kind of service where they live is what's required on your part. Think of your doorman as you'd think of a neighbor whom you happen to see a few times every day. You could just walk past him from the beginning, but you can save yourself years of awkward moments by taking some time when you first move in to introduce yourself and get used to greeting him as he greets you. A relationship will develop from there; you'll probably come to greet him by name, and chat about the weather or the Yankees from time to time. Always tip around Christmastime.

UPSTAIRS NEIGHBORS

WHERE YOU'LL FIND THEM: Uh, directly above your ceiling.

CHARACTER SYNOPSIS: No matter who they are or how many of them live there, upstairs neighbors all have one thing in common: they'll be loud, at least some of the time. Even if they don't have crazy parties, lots of pets, or play instruments, sometimes walking around can reverberate down to your apartment in a strange and maddening way.

YOUR ROLE: If the noise is particularly egregious or going on late at night, you could of course try talking to them. Banging the ceiling with a broomstick is a lot of work, with little payoff—trust us, we've tried it. (For more on official noise complaints, see page 123.) If you decide to cross the floor-to-ceiling divide, try to conjure up as much grace as your punchy, sleep-deprived self will allow for. Think karma. Which brings us to . . .

DOWNSTAIRS NEIGHBORS

WHERE YOU'LL FIND THEM: Underneath your feet.

CHARACTER SYNOPSIS: Not surprisingly, essentially the opposite of upstairs neighbors. Your downstairs neighbors can hear you walking, moving furniture, doing jumping jacks, or whatever—especially if you have a wood floor. Moreover, water from an apartment can actually leak below without your knowing it, which is a great setup for a dramatic denouement between the angry bottom tenant with water damage and blissfully unaware you.

YOUR ROLE: Collateral damage in apartment buildings tends to go top down, so in this case, you're more likely to be the one confronted. For things like water damage, there can be a gray area about who caused the problem, so beware, and pray that your downstairs neighbors are at least normal enough to have a civil conversation. If noise is the issue, don't wear shoes in the apartment—or get rugs to muffle the sound.

OTHER TENANTS

WHERE YOU'LL FIND THEM: In the lobby, mailroom, hallway on your floor, lounging on the shared garden or roof (if you have one), in the elevator with you (again, if you have one).

CHARACTER SYNOPSIS: They could, of course, be anyone, and this being New York, any and all means of eccentricity have the possibility of being represented in your tiny communal abode. Nearly everyone we know has stories about a crazy cat lady, an elevator hog, a hallway chatterbox, or a neighbor who doesn't bathe. To these gems we say, grin and bear it, and don't let it dissuade you from striking up a conversation with the reasonable-looking characters. It will make elevator rides (or walks up the stairs) less awkward, and having a neighbor or two who you are friendly with can come in handy if you get locked out, when you go away, or if a pipe suddenly bursts in your apartment. Neighbors with kids can be fun on Halloween if there's trick-or-treating in your building, and if you're really lucky, you'll have a Girl Scout who is selling cookies knock on your door at least once.

YOUR ROLE: How well you get to know your neighbors depends on how much effort you put into meeting them, but it also depends on the building, to some degree. Some buildings are quite social and host Christmas parties and other mixers; in other buildings, particularly co-ops, tenants may get to know one another a bit from the co-op board or from attending board meetings. In still others (particularly rentals), there will be such a high turnover of tenants that it may be hard to get to know anyone. Whatever situation you have, it is useful to make friends with a neighbor or two if you can and to stay on good or neutral terms with the rest of them.

MAILMEN

WHERE YOU'LL FIND THEM: At the front door, in the lobby, the hallway, the mail-room, or wherever mailboxes are found, if you're lucky; halfway down the block only thirty seconds after ringing your bell to deliver a package if you're too slow.

CHARACTER SYNOPSIS: Evasive but indispensable, often grumpy but seldom mali-cious, mail carriers are the messengers of joy to some, the harbingers of doom to oth-ers, and a lifeline to the outside world for others still. Every block has a regular carrier, and every carrier has a time and style of delivery that you will come to know as inti-mately as he or she knows your subscriptions and bill-payment habits.

YOUR ROLE: Anger a mailman and you will pay for it as long as you are a known resident at the address; befriend a mailman and you will reap the rewards. Getting to know your mail carrier is a smart move for several reasons. Intercepting a letter to a former tenant and letting your carrier know he or she is no longer at your address can prevent years of unwanted mail collecting in your box waiting to be returned to sender. Catching your carrier with a package too large to fit in your box and explaining that it's okay to leave it under the stairs in the hallway can save hours waiting in line to pick it up at the post office (if you ever even find the notes letting you know delivery had been attempted). If you live in a walk-up, friendship with a carrier and the right kind of holiday season gift can yield spectacular results, and you might find your bigger packages already waiting for you at your door. And best of all, on those rare occasions when you come home to find your carrier mid-delivery, you can stop and ask, in full confidence that he or she knows your name by now, "Anything for me?"

THE PEOPLE ACROSS THE WAY

WHERE YOU'LL FIND THEM: On the opposite side of your street, around the corner, through a courtyard, or right next door, at an angle. These are the people whose apart-ments you can easily inadvertently look into from your own.

CHARACTER SYNOPSIS: You may never know. You may, however, get a good sense of their decorating tastes or eating habits, depending on the position of your view.

YOUR ROLE: We're not suggesting that you buy a telescope to check them out *Rear Window*–style; the point is that your windows may be so close together that you won't be able to avoid it. Just try not to stare when people are in the room, and by all means, avoid eye contact. Also, if you can, consider the sightlines when you set up your furniture. In Caitlin's apartment, her living-room setup has the awkward arrangement of having the television next to a window, giving her a direct view of another apartment's kitchen every time she watches TV. (Fortunately, the apartment seems to be occupied by a constantly revolving cast of NYU students; looking at the same person you don't know for many years is much weirder.)

THE NEIGHBORHOOD GUIDE

Whether you are arriving for the first time, or you know you want to move as soon as your current lease is up, equally important a consideration as price, size, and number of roommates is where your apartment is located. Some people will happily take a grungy place in a super-desirable neighborhood; others will jump on a cheap and spacious apartment despite the fact that the neighborhood is still evolving; still others will end up in a certain neighborhood not because or despite its reputation but because of certain amenities, such as proximity to parks, a particular subway line, or because it's within walking distance of work. But all would agree that it's better to know what a neighborhood is really like before you sign the lease—a task that requires more subtle research than determining what's included in the monthly rent, or measuring each place's real square footage. We've toured the neighborhoods for you, and come up with profiles of twenty-two popular neighborhoods, covering location (where it is and what it is most convenient and inconvenient to), amenities (parks, shops, restaurants, bars), and character (homogenous or diverse? casual or ultra chic? kid-, dog-, or student-friendly?).

Our criteria in determining which neighborhoods to cover were: convenience (subway accessibility and reasonable proximity to Manhattan); ample available housing to rent and buy; and desirability for a newcomer. We've also included a few neighborhoods that don't quite fit these criteria, but that we still feel are worth knowing about. These are neighborhoods that seem to be on the brink of becoming newcomer-desirable but aren't quite there yet (lots of construction, amenities starting to trickle in) or are convenient places to live but don't have a ton of available housing or a lot of extra charm.

BEFORE YOU LOOK

Finding a neighborhood is a bit like shopping for an outfit for a special occasion; as you try things on, it's easy to be seduced by features and fancy trims, or alternatively be tempted to buy something that seems brainlessly practical. Before you make your decision, we suggest you take a good long look in the mirror to see which neighborhood fits you best. Here are some things to consider:

WHAT YOU NEED FROM YOUR NEIGHBORHOOD: Truthfully, you could probably plop down in any neighborhood and do just fine for a time. But if you want to enjoy living in the city—and that's what this book is about, after all—you should try and pick a place that will accommodate at least the most important parts of the lifestyle you already have. If you have a dog, for instance, living near a park with a dog run should be a priority. If you have a car, you may want to look at neighborhoods that have easier access to bridges and drives, and investigate street parking (much easier in some places than in others) or buildings with nearby garages. No laundry in the building? See how far the nearest coin-operated laundry is, and consider how much the walk to it is going to annoy you. If you cook, think about how you'll get to the supermarket or Greenmarket (if there is one), or find out if Fresh Direct delivers to the zip code. If you don't cook, scrutinize the take-out and delivery options, and make sure their offerings and hours mesh with yours. Everyone has his or her own particular needs, and certain amenities are bound to be more important to you than others. As much as you can, imagine what you need your neighborhood to offer and only consider ones that have these things.

WHAT YOU DO AND WHERE YOU GO: No matter how much you love your neighborhood, you will need to leave it from time to time. If you have an office to be at every morning, for instance, consider how close or far you'd like to be from it. Close proximity to work means convenience, being able to sleep in a little, and not having to experience the ugliness of a morning subway commute. On the other hand, you might find that being as far away as possible either from work or the bustle of the city helps you sleep at night and live life with a clearer perspective.

WHAT YOU'LL PAY FOR AND WHAT YOU CAN LIVE WITHOUT: Put aside the location and neighborhood for a second, and take a good look at what you're working with. A doorman is a luxury, but if you work at home and get a lot of packages, it's a luxury you may want to consider paying more for, lest you risk spending half your life in maddening pursuit of the UPS guy with your papers/proofs/samples/etc. If you garden, head for the outer boroughs where yard space is more plentiful, or look for buildings in the city with healthy roof access. If you're a cyclist in a walk-up, a bike room or area in the basement isn't a must, but remember how many flights of stairs you will be carrying your Cannondale after a 60- or 100-mile ride.

A NOTE ON THE BRONX AND STATEN ISLAND

Caitlin's mother, who grew up in a suburb of NYC, used to say that she transferred from a college in upstate New York to Wagner College on Staten Island because she wanted to be in New York City—and then transferred back upstate to a different college after a year because she realized that Staten Island wasn't New York City. She was wrong, of course—to the chagrin of the Staten Island contingent that wants to secede from the city altogether. But as a place for a young adult new to New York City, Staten Island, as well as the Bronx (and areas of Queens and Brooklyn that aren't near any subway lines, or are past the last stops), can still seem as remote from the things that make New York City what it is—Central Park, the Brooklyn Bridge, the shops, restaurants, theaters, and galleries, and the boundless energy of the subways—as Buffalo is.

In the Bronx, though certain areas are experiencing some revitalization, public housing dominates the landscape in many neighborhoods, and amenities like supermarkets, restaurants, gyms, and coffee shops can be few and far between. There are also some well-established residential ethnic enclaves that a newcomer to the area would likely find isolating, and areas like Fieldston and Riverdale are geographically and characteristically closer to the true blue suburbs of Westchester County. The Bronx is also comparatively remote mass-transitwise. Only six subway lines have service in the Bronx, and three of them (the 4, 5, and 6) run along the same line through Manhattan. Depending on how far out you are, it can take almost an hour to get to Midtown. Going downtown, or to Queens or Brooklyn, will take much, much longer.

Staten Island's remoteness is even more obvious, proclaimed most prominently by the absence of subways altogether. Ferry and bus service are the options, but mass transit doesn't have the proud mainstream currency that it does in other boroughs; having a car is the norm. It's also much more family-focused. More than half of the borough's residents are married couples, a significantly higher percentage than any other borough; and less than a quarter of the borough's residents live alone. While there are plenty of newcomers and new homeowners each year (there is a growing Russian community, for instance) the demographics and geography translate to a self-contained and isolated part of the city, geared toward families and couples.

Though we didn't include any neighborhoods in these boroughs in our neighborhood guide as places to live, we absolutely do not discourage you from going to visit them. Both boroughs have interesting attractions that aren't dangerous or backbreakingly remote. The Bronx boasts the New York Botanical Gardens, the Italian (well, today primarily Albanian) mecca of Arthur Avenue, and City Island, the city's very own fishing village, with boats, marinas, and plenty of good greasy fish shacks. In addition to museums and a beloved minor-league baseball team, as the rural borough, Staten Island's got a bunch of great outdoor destinations, including beaches and the Greenbelt, a 2,500-acre urban forest with hiking trails, playing fields, and enough nature and wildlife to keep you sated until your next trip outside of the big city.

THE NEIGHBORHOODS

MANHATTAN

CHELSEA AND THE MEATPACKING DISTRICT

IN BRIEF: Gentrification has been the big trend in the city for more than a decade, and arguably no neighborhoods in Manhattan have gentrified as dramatically as the area on the west side between 14th Street and Penn Station. Starting in the 1990s, these two neighborhoods benefited (or were cursed, depending on your point of view) by a perfect storm of location and situation: the opening of the walking path and stretches of park along the Hudson River; the scarcity of storefront space in Soho, which inspired an influx of art galleries into industrial buildings in the West 20s; and the arrival of a few high-fashion pioneers to the farthest reaches of 14th Street, an area that few besides those buying wholesale meat had ever stepped foot in before. The aboveground park being built atop the Chelsea Highline on Tenth Avenue, opening in sections starting in late 2008, will introduce another major desirability factor into the mix.

Today, both neighborhoods have a unique mix of cutting-edge cool, residential appeal, and an eclectic assortment of inhabitants, both old and new. Chelsea, once known primarily as a gay (and strictly male) *quartier*, also encompasses the new gallery district (and all of the restaurants and bars built around it), several public and subsidized housing complexes, and the Fashion Institute of Technology. The Meat-packing District, for better or worse, is the quintessential portrait of modern gentrification. From a distance, you'd think you were looking at an old-fashioned industrial neighborhood, but between the jutting scaffolds and uneven cobblestone, you're more likely to find signs for high-end fashion designers than steak or beef. (Is the fact that famously vegetarian designer Stella McCartney has her store here an ironic coincidence or a statement?) But though buildings seem to be put up, torn down, and gutted on a daily basis, both neighborhoods are still a little rough around the edges in places, particularly west of Ninth Avenue, east of Seventh Avenue, and north of 23rd Street. But that's part of the area's signature charm—so enjoy it while it lasts.

LOCATION: Chelsea extends up the west side of the city from 15th Street to Penn Station, with 23rd Street as the main artery; the Meatpacking District is a smaller square below the western part of it (starting roughly where Hudson Street and Ninth Avenue intersect) down about four blocks to Gansevoort Street (which is just below Little West 12th Street). In contrast to the nearby West Village, both neighborhoods have excellent subway access, and the proximity to Penn Station (one stop away from the A at 14th Street and Eighth Avenue; the 2,3 at 14th Street and Seventh Avenue; and the C or E at 23rd Street and Eighth Avenue) and the West Side Highway make getting out of the city a cinch. One other notable feature about Chelsea is the relative abundance of mini-storage facilities around Eleventh Avenue, so unlike many city residents, those who live in the neighborhood will not find their tennis rackets and ski accoutrements out-of-reach.

LIVE THERE FOR: CHELSEA MARKET. While the neighborhood notably lacks a nearby Greenmarket, this indoor marketplace offers some consolation. What it doesn't have in fresh-off-the-farm offerings, it compensates for with boutique bakeries, cafés and restaurants, and gourmet food shops. And it's a much more pleasant place to shop than a Greenmarket in the winter. **IMMENSE CONVENIENCE.** With the subway stations on 14th and 23rd streets at every avenue between Sixth and Eighth, and Penn Station mere minutes by subway, we can't overstate the convenience factor for this neighborhood. Tribeca, the East Village, Brooklyn, the Theater District, Central Park, and the Upper West Side are all easy trips from anywhere; the Upper East Side is about the only place in Manhattan that's a challenge to get to.

Chelsea Market, 75 Ninth Avenue, between 15th and 16th streets, www.chelseamarket.com

KEEP LOOKING: IF YOU WANT QUIET NIGHTS. While there are plenty of quiet blocks (especially the farther north you go), this neighborhood is a lot of people's playground—actually, a lot of different playgrounds—at many times of the day and night. From the clubs in the West 20s and around 14th Street; trendy shops, cafés, and restaurants in the Meatpacking District; and the perennially rowdy scene on Eighth Avenue, there's a different kind of liveliness at every corner, all the time.

EAT: The blistered peppers, fried chickpeas, and other delectable small plates at popular tapas joint Tía Pol are a major draw. There's always a line during normal dining hours, but it's worth a wait, or try to eat at an off time. There's also a spin-off on Ninth Avenue called El Quinto Pino; the food is different, but the crowds are the same. When you want to eat right away, there's easy brunch and bistro fare at Le Grainne Café and even easier coffee, smoothies, and snacks at the quirky Paradise Café.

Le Grainne Café, 183 Ninth Avenue, at 21st Street, (646-486-3000) www.legrainnecafe.com

Paradise Café, 139 Eighth Avenue, at 17th Street, (212-647-0066)

El Quinto Pino, 401 West 24th Street, at Ninth Avenue, (212-206-6900)

Tía Pol, 205 Tenth Avenue, between 22nd and 23rd streets, (212-675-8805) www.tiapol.com

DRINK: There's no shortage of gorgeous places to imbibe, especially around the Meatpacking District, but most of the better-known options are exclusionary, perennially mobbed, and shockingly expensive. A sweet antidote to the attitude and the velvet ropes is a trip to the Half King, a neighborhood veteran with a literary bent. When you want to avoid people altogether and enjoy an evening at home, a personal recommendation from the lovely and helpful staff at Chelsea Wine Vault is the way to go.

Chelsea Wine Vault, 75 Ninth Avenue, between 15th and 16th streets (in the Chelsea
**   Market), (212-462-4244) www.chelseawinevault.com**

The Half King, 505 West 23rd Street, at Tenth Avenue, (212-462-4300) www.thehalfking.com

SHOP: Jeffrey was a Meatpacking pioneer and is still a place to pick up an impossibly cool souvenir (if you can afford it). On 17th Street between Sixth and Seventh are three less-cutting-edge stores worth checking out: Housing Works and Angel Street thrift stores are great for clothes, furniture, and other secondhand treasures, and Pippin has vintage jewelry and furniture in two side-by-side storefronts.

Angel Street Thrift Shop, 118 West 17th Street, between Sixth and Seventh avenues,
**   (212-229-0546) www.angelthriftshop.org**

Housing Works, 143 West 17th Street, between Sixth and Seventh avenues,
**   (212-366-0820) www.housingworksauctions.com**

Jeffrey, 449 West 14th Street, between Ninth and Tenth avenues, (212-206-1272)
www.jeffreynewyork.com
Pippin Home and Vintage Jewelry, 112 and 112½ West 17th Street, between Sixth and
Seventh avenues, (212-206-0888) www.pippinvintage.com

HEAR/SEE CHELSEA IN: The Hotel Chelsea is a bastion of cultural folklore, where artists, musicians, and writers, have famously flocked to, stayed, lived, and died. The hotel appears in work all across the spectrum of pop culture; "Chelsea" is in so many song titles that it's hard to keep them all straight. For the full effect, you could make a mix with Bob Dylan's "Sara," Nico's "Chelsea Girls," Joni Mitchell's "Chelsea Morning," Leonard Cohen's "Chelsea Hotel #2," anything by Patti Smith (she lived here with Robert Mapplethorpe), and...Bon Jovi! (His song "Midnight in Chelsea" is actually about Chelsea in London, but part of the video was filmed here.) Or try a Hotel Chelsea triple feature of Warhol's *Chelsea Girls, Sid & Nancy,* and *The Professional.*
Hotel Chelsea, 222 West 23rd Street, between Seventh and Eighth avenues, (212-243-3700)
www.hotelchelsea.com

EAST VILLAGE

IN BRIEF: Steeped in some of the city's most colorful cultural history, the East Village was famously a mecca for both artists and immigrants well into the twentieth century, and a melting pot where Polish restaurants and Yiddish theaters long coexisted with beatniks, artists, and punks. Despite the loss of old-neighborhood stalwarts such as CBGB, DoJo, and the Second Avenue Deli (now relocated to Murray Hill), the neighborhood clings to all of the counterculture it can, and wears its history proudly, and visibly. Fans of both Ginsberg and *Rent* make pilgrimages to Tompkins Square Park, while long-time residents romanticize the days of squatters and syringes.

But there's more to the East Village than nostalgia. Zoning is strict, so there isn't as much new construction as there is in many other Manhattan neighborhoods. And unlike the West Village, the pretty, leafy side streets here are lined not with beautiful but unattainable brownstones but modest five- and six-story apartment buildings. If you've dreamed of living in a quirky railroad flat with a police lock and a bathtub in the kitchen, look no further.

LOCATION: The East Village is bounded by 14th and Houston streets on the north and south, and west to east from Third Avenue to Avenue D. The northwestern part of the 'hood is right next to Union Square, so that part of the neighborhood enjoys a nice combination of convenience and residential charm. Subway access gets a little dicey (well, pretty much non-existent) the deeper you go, and the F and V at Second Avenue and Houston Street are the only options on the southern end. But if you spend a lot of time in Brooklyn, the L train along 14th Street offers easy access to Williamsburg (Bedford Avenue is the next stop after First Avenue), and other Brooklyn neighborhoods via the G transfer at Lorimer-Metropolitan.

LIVE THERE FOR: MOVIE THEATERS. An interesting logistical feature of the East Village is its proximity to many (and many different kinds of) movie theaters. If a movie is out, chances are you can catch it here, either at the multiplexes at Third Avenue and 11th Street and Union Square; the artier venues like the Landmark Sunshine and Anthology Film Archives; or the idiosyncratic Village East Cinema on Second Avenue and 12th Street, the former Yiddish theater that shows an unusual combination of off-beat independents, thoroughly mainstream movies, and the odd revival. In addition, the Angelika, the Quad, and Cinema Village are all within walking distance of the neighborhood. **ALL THINGS JAPANESE.** Though you won't find it marked in any guidebook, the area around St. Mark's Place is an indisputable Little Japan. There is the thoroughly Asian Sunrise Mart and vaguely Asian M2M Mart, plus plenty of hole-in-the-wall sushi and *robataya* joints, particularly around St. Mark's Place and Cooper Square. But it's the ramen joints that have gotten the most attention. Momofuku Noodle Bar is supposedly a must, but we've never had the patience to wait in line to get in . . . **VEGETARIAN (AND VEGAN) FOOD.** Spartan, greasy, trendy, ethnic—vegetarians, take your pick. There are so many that we can't even name them all, so here are a few of our personal favorites. For fast food, there's Curly's, a vegetarian diner that is about as unhealthy as this kind of food gets. Viva Herbal holds the rare distinction of being legendary among foodies as well as those with dietary restrictions: it is the only pizza place we know of where a gourmand, a vegan, a celiac, and someone who keeps kosher could happily share a pie. Angelica Kitchen is the grand dame of Manhattan's vegetarian restaurants and is everything that vegetarian food should be (including delicious!), but when the line is too long or the prices seem too steep, the Organic Grill has a similar menu at a sizable discount, and there's never a wait for a table. (And unlike Angelica, they deliver.) For something less crunchy, there's Counter Restaurant and Wine Bar, and Pukk, a stylish yet ridiculously cheap all-vegetarian Thai place.

AMC Loews Village 7, 66 Third Avenue, at 11th Street, (212-982-2116)

Angelica Kitchen, 300 East 12th Street, between First and Second avenues, (212-228-2909)
  www.angelicakitchen.com

Anthology Film Archives, 32 Second Avenue, between 1st and 2nd streets,
  (212-505-5181) www.anthologyfilmarchives.org

Counter Restaurant and Wine Bar, 105 First Avenue, between 6th and 7th streets,
  (212-982-5870) www.counternyc.com

Curly's, 328 East 14th Street, between First and Second avenues, (212-598-9998)
  www.curlyslunch.com

Landmark Sunshine Cinema, 143 East Houston Street, between First and Second avenues,
  (212-358-7709) www.landmarktheatres.com

M2M Mart, 200 East 11th Street, at Third Avenue, (212-353-2698)

Momofuku Noodle Bar, 171 First Avenue, between 10th and 11th streets, (212-777-7773)
  www.momofuku.com

Organic Grill, 123 First Avenue, between 7th Street and St. Mark's Place, (212-477-7177)
  www.theorganicgrill.com

Pukk, 71 First Avenue, between 4th and 5th streets, (212-253-2741) www.pukknyc.com

Regal Cinemas Union Square Stadium 14, 850 Broadway, between 13th and 14th streets,
  (212-253-6266)

Sunrise Mart, 29 Third Avenue, near 10th Street, (212-598-3040)

Village East Cinema, 181-189 Second Avenue, at 12th Street, (212-539-6998)
  www.villageeastcinema.com

Viva Herbal, 179 Second Avenue, between 11th and 12th streets, (212-420-8801)

KEEP LOOKING: IF YOU HAVE AN AVERSION TO YOUNG PEOPLE. Three universities have facilities in the East Village and Union Square area: New York University, the New School, and the School of Visual Arts. In addition to the several enormous high-rise dorms, there are plenty of students living in other buildings around the area (both university-owned and not), all using the neighborhood's services (gyms, delis, supermarkets, banks, etc.). Expect to get carded a lot, no matter your age, and if you live anywhere near a dorm, consider taking a holiday the last week in August every year, when the students are moving in, and they and their parents are double- and triple-parking their SUVs on every block. Many local businesses take NYU's "campus cash," which can make you feel like you are living on a college campus. It's no surprise that students are always lined up for $3 wine at Trader Joe Wine Shop, conveniently located in the building that also houses NYU's Palladium dorm; and the salad bar and prepared food area at the local Whole Foods is like a school cafeteria nine months of the year. Also, **THE GREEN SPACE IS A LITTLE SPARSE.** While both Tompkins Square Park and Union Square Park don't have a whiff of their former drug-dealer-infested incarnations, neither is particularly peaceful or lush, at least as compared to a lot of other city parks. Also, the East River waterfront hasn't gotten the same sprucing up as the Hudson, and crossing over the FDR drive is an obstacle.

EAT: Arepas! Sloppy, juicy, spicy, and sweet, the arepas at Caracas are sleazy food in the best possible way. These overstuffed corn bread pockets are delicious, inexpensive, a little greasy, and satisfying. The storefront closer to First Avenue is where you order for takeout; if you want to eat in, you'll go to the arepa bar two doors down. To call the dining area cramped is a gross understatement (this is probably one of the narrowest restaurants in the city), but this really isn't the kind of meal you'll want to linger over. (They also deliver, but in our opinion the arepas should really be eaten as soon as they come out of the kitchen.) For more of a cloth-napkin dining experience, Hearth is a rare upscale restaurant that is neither stuffy nor trendy. It's an excellent choice for when a visiting relative wants to take you out to dinner.

Caracas, 93½ East 7th Street, between First Avenue and Avenue A, (212-529-2314); Caracas
    to Go, 91 East 7th Street, (212-228-5062) www.caracasarepabar.com
Hearth, 403 East 12th Street, at First Avenue, (646-602-1300) www.restauranthearth.com

DRINK: Given that the rest of the area is a bit of a college bar scene, Bar Veloce is an excellent neighborhood standby. This wine bar has good panini and wines by the glass, and it is perfect whether you're planning to meet someone or go solo (If you find yourself there too many nights in a row, you can switch it up with Spanish wine and tapas next door at Veloce's fraternal twin, Bar Carrera.) The fresh juices at Liquiteria are well worth their shocking prices. If carrots, beets, and kale are your thing, you'll be in paradise; if not, the pineapple-pear-ginger combination called the Royal Flush is great for first-timers.

Bar Carrera, 175 Second Avenue, between 11th and 12th streets, (212-375-1555)
    www.barcarrera.com
Bar Veloce, 175 Second Avenue, between 11th and 12th streets, (212-629-5300)
    www.barveloce.com
Liquiteria, 170 Second Avenue, at 11th Street, (212-358-0300) www.liquiteria.com

SHOP: While many NYC neighborhoods have great indie boutiques scattered about, 7th Street between Second Avenue and Avenue A is great for browsing without a particular destination in mind or a specific thing to buy. It is filled with an eclectic assortment of one-of-a-kind stores selling interesting housewares, handmade goods, adventurous fashion, secondhand and vintage pieces, and cheesy clothes and accessories. We're particularly partial to Outlet 7, a permanent boutique that sells expensive designer clothes at sample-sale prices; and the small-scale housewares store, Tiny Living (see page 114 for more info). Just around the corner on 6th Street is a charming eco-chic boutique gominyc. The prices might freak out the Birkenstock set, but the clothes and accessories will convince even the most hardcore fur-and-reptile-skin-loving fashion plate that eco-friendly fashion is not an oxymoron.

gominyc, 443 East 6th Street, between First Avenue and Avenue A, (212-979-0388)
www.gominyc.com

Outlet 7, 117 East 7th Street, between First Avenue and Avenue A, (212-529-0766)
www.showroomseven.com

Tiny Living, 125 East 7th Street, between First Avenue and Avenue A, (212-228-2748)
www.tinyliving.com

READ THE EAST VILLAGE IN: *Downtown* by Pete Hamill. And, of course, Allen Ginsberg's epic *Howl*.

GREENWICH VILLAGE

IN BRIEF: Greenwich Village—aka, "the Village"—is the Times Square of downtown in that it's a central hub with a lot of action and entertainment that stays up very, very late. Most of the noise can be attributed to NYU, which, though it has sprawled into Union Square and the East Village, is centered in this neighborhood, around Washington Square Park. While the street that faces the park on the north is full of lovely townhouses (many owned by the university), east, west, and south are full of big university buildings, and the streets below the park and surrounding it (Thompson, Sullivan, Macdougal, and LaGuardia Place) are the university's version of a college town, with lots of rowdy restaurants and bars, coffee shops, and casual shopping. Macdougal Street is the fake-ID capital of the city, both for procuring and using. Eighth Street and Bleecker are both reliably rowdy, while Broadway and Sixth Avenue are amenity-laden, but also feel a bit mall-ish, albeit in a slightly left-of-mainstream way. Each has an Urban Outfitters, American Apparel, Ricky's drugstore, and several Starbucks. Still, they're useful places to pick up a cheap outfit or a pair of cool sneakers.

Beneath the din, the neighborhood has some pretty, quiet patches. The blocks between Fifth and Sixth avenues from 9th to 13th streets have some West Villageesque brownstones, and lower Fifth Avenue has echoes of its tony uptown version, with dignified doorman buildings full of longtime Village gentry. Though much of the counterculture that the Village used to host has been diluted and gentrified, there are still some vestiges of the music-coffeehouse culture of the 1950s and 1960s, like Café Wha and the Village Vanguard, and even some of the cleaning up has produced some worthy additions to the culture scene. An excellent example of this is the IFC Film Center, which the cable channel redeveloped out of what had been a sketchy movie theater. The dilapidated building was cleaned up, and the film selection has been kept edgy enough that even hardcore hippie holdouts can't help but admit that it's an improvement.

Café Wha, 115 Macdougal Street, between Bleecker and West 3rd streets, (212-254-3706)
   www.cafewha.com

IFC Film Center, 323 Sixth Avenue, at West 3rd Street, (212-924-7771) www.ifccenter.com

Village Vanguard, 1787 Seventh Avenue South, between 11th and Perry streets,
   (212-255-4037) www.villagevanguard.com

LOCATION: Greenwich Village extends from 14th Street down to Houston Street, roughly from Broadway to Sixth Avenue, in between the East Village and the West. The western boundary is particularly blurry; streets start breaking out of the grid and begin to twist and turn, but you'll know it when you see it. When things start looking quaint and distinguished, you know you have crossed over into the West Village.

LIVE THERE FOR: THE CENTRAL LOCATION. Greenwich Village is the most centrally located of downtown neighborhoods, and it's an easy walk from here to a number of desirable destinations: Union Square, Soho, Chelsea, and the Meatpacking District, as well as the East and West villages. When you do need to take a subway, the West 4th Street station is a hub for the A, C, E, B, D, F, and V; there's also the 1 train at Christopher, and the N and R at 8th Street and Broadway. **CHEAP RESTAURANTS AND BARS.** This being major NYU territory, it is also the land of happy hours and cheap eats. Right around Washington Square you'll find a large selection of bargain-priced eating and drinking outlets, often best frequented after 10 p.m. The Hummus Place is a favorite of the authors, because you can still get fresh-out-of-the-oven pitas to go with your hummus, falafel, or foul, well into the evening.

The Hummus Place, 99 Macdougal Street, between Bleecker and West 3rd streets,
   (212-533-3089) www.hummusplace.com

KEEP LOOKING: IF YOU LIKE TO SPEND A LOT OF TIME IN YOUR APARTMENT. There's plenty of cheap housing here—especially between semesters—but much of it is small, in ancient walk-ups. In addition, any apartment that faces Macdougal, Sixth Avenue, or 8th Street is bound to get a lot of noisy late-night foot traffic. **IF YOU WANT A PARK TO RELAX IN.** Washington Square Park, the neighborhood's only open space, is no longer gritty, but with all due respect, it's still not a great park for getting a breath of fresh air (particularly in its current state; at the time of publication, it's undergoing a massive renovation that has torn up everything except the playgrounds). Plus, it's pretty much the NYU undergrad quad, with everything that suggests. The pickup basketball at the courts on Sixth Avenue and West 4th Street is great to watch, but there's no breathing room there either.

EAT: Village meets all the prerequisites for a perfect neighborhood restaurant: good bistro food, a cozy bar area with dining booths, a huge dining room (so reservations are never needed), and even a tiny outdoor dining terrace in the front. You can eat cheaply, decadently, and reservations-free at Alta, if you can limit yourself to a few of the restaurant's long list of delicious tapas. If not, the splurge will be worth it. (If you really must have it all, you can get one of everything on the menu for $350.) Insomnia Cookies delivers to much of downtown, but only at its store on West 8th Street can you get the cookies fresh out of the oven. There's nothing fancy about these cookies—white chocolate macadamia is the craziest flavor offered—but for ninety cents, there are few treats more satisfying anywhere in the city. And while delivery hours don't start until 8 p.m., the retail store is open from 9 a.m. to 3 a.m. every day.

Alta, 64 West 10th Street, between Fifth and Sixth avenues, (212-505-7777)
    www.altarestaurant.com

Insomnia Cookies, 50 West Eighth Street, between Sixth Avenue and Macdougal Street,
    (877-63-COOKIE) www.insomniacookies.com

Village, 62 West 9th Street, between Fifth and Sixth avenues, (212-505-3355)
    www.villagerestaurant.com

DRINK: The best bars in the Village are the ones that have been there the longest, the kinds of places that could best be described as "haunts." There are plenty to choose from around Waverly, Washington Place, and West Third Street; you'll know you have stumbled on a good one if it doesn't look like the décor has been touched since the 1960s. Vol de Nuit is not quite as divey as some of the stalwarts, but it's good to know about, especially if you're into beer—there's a large selection of imported beers, some well-known, some obscure, all Belgian. (You can complete the experience with a plate of *moules frites*.) When you are in the mood for something prettier, try The Dove, a sweet parlorlike lounge with reasonably priced cocktails that is perfect for an intimate rendezvous.

The Dove, 228 Thompson Street, between Bleecker and West 3rd streets, (212-254-1435)

Vol de Nuit, 148 West 4th Street, at Sixth Avenue, (212-982-3388) www.voldenuitbar.com

SHOP: Broadway Panhandler is a wonderland of kitchen gadgets, cookbooks, and cooking accoutrements. If you are a stifled home cook whose kitchen is too small to hold even a lemon zester, consider taking in one of the masterful in-store demos. Ludivine is one of the best places in the city for French fashion. It carries mostly cool French designers like Vanessa Bruno and Claudie Pierlot, as well some international labels that are popular in Paris but hard to find here. Prices are not cheap, but the store does honor the French tradition of seasonal sales, and you can find excellent deals in January or July. Greenwich Letterpress is a rare gem. In addition to doing custom letterpress, it has preprinted cards, stationery, and journals, plus baby clothes, some home accessories, and other pretty, unusual things. This is a great place to get a unique gift, as well as the card and wrapping to go with it.

Broadway Panhandler, 65 East 8th Street, between Broadway and University Place,
   (212-966-3434) www.broadwaypanhandler.com

Greenwich Letterpress, 39 Christopher Street between Waverly Place and Seventh Avenue,
   (212-989-7464) www.greenwichletterpress.com

Ludivine, 172 West 4th Street, between Jones and Cornelia streets, (212-336-6576)
   www.boutiqueludivine.com

HEAR GREENWICH VILLAGE IN: "Blowing in the Wind" and "Positively Fourth Street." Bob Dylan started his music career in Greenwich Village, writing protest songs, playing at clubs, and drinking at bars with aging beatniks and young hippies. Dylan allegedly wrote "Blowing in the Wind" in one afternoon in 1962 at a club on Macdougal. The song was the first track on his second album, *The Freewheelin' Bob Dylan*, whose cover featured a picture of Dylan and his girlfriend, Suze Rotolo, walking by their apartment on 4th Street. Later, after Dylan left the Village and the folksong crowd, he wrote "Positively Fourth Street," a response to criticism from his Village crew that he was selling out.

HELL'S KITCHEN

IN BRIEF: What's in a name anyway? Like Red Hook, now referred to by realtors as Columbia Heights, this sprawling neighborhood on the west side of Manhattan that earned its moniker thanks to decades of vice and crime has long since outgrown its name and these days is also known as "Clinton," at least among real estate agents. Covering a vast expanse of the west side and blurring into such a wide range of districts, it's difficult to imagine that Hell's Kitchen could maintain a singular identity. But with a surprisingly large population and innumerable options for eating, drinking, and entertaining, it gets by as a self-sufficient residential neighborhood with a character all its own.

As clean as Manhattan is these days, the past is rarely forgotten altogether, and the history of the neighborhood remains a major factor in its appeal—or otherwise—to potential inhabitants. Throughout the nineteenth century and much of the twentieth century, Hell's Kitchen was a crime-ridden gangland whose major draws ranged from sleazy houses of ill repute to the supper clubs and speakeasies of the Prohibition era. Remnants of this shady past remain, to the pleasure of some and the chagrin of others, in the clusters of sex stores and the characteristic dive bars that are dotted around the area.

But, like Murray Hill across town, Hell's Kitchen thrives on what has traditionally been a transient crowd. That it is so populous a residential area can come as a surprise even to lifelong New Yorkers, some of whom might only see the neighborhood as a dilapidated annex of Times Square and Midtown West. Home to much of the Theater and Garment districts, it was long considered a popular roosting spot for wandering thespians and artists who took advantage of the cheap rents kept in check by the neighborhood's reputation. These days, the more pleasant (and more expensive) residential blocks between Ninth Avenue and the river are surprisingly quiet and feel like a dirtier version of Chelsea. And in certain pockets of the neighborhood there is a real sense of community found in weekly flea markets and in stores and bars that have survived in the area for decades.

LOCATION: Hell's Kitchen is among the largest neighborhoods in Manhattan, stretching from the northernmost point of Chelsea in the 30s to 59th Street, on the west side between Eighth Avenue and the Hudson River. The neighborhood shares its borders with several distinct areas, from the pristine sophistication of Chelsea to the touristy bustle of Midtown and Times Square and up to Lincoln Center and the beginnings of the Upper West Side. Physically, it's one of Manhattan's most varied districts, ranging from the piers alongside the river to concrete high-rises uptown, smaller rows of townhouses in the middle, and grungy theater and office buildings to the east. Being so close to so many different neighborhoods, Hell's Kitchen also takes a little character from each, leaving it a gritty but habitable amalgam of what's around it.

LIVE THERE FOR: THE ACTION. If your life is in the city, it makes sense you should live there, too. Hell's Kitchen has become a popular place to live for people whose jobs take them to Midtown or Flatiron, and the neighborhood's residential buildings are divided between larger apartments and smaller studios that cater to the remnants of the thespian and media crowds.

KEEP LOOKING: IF YOU NEED URBAN RESPITE. What makes Hell's Kitchen unique is its relentlessly urban atmosphere. It's impossible to forget you're in the middle of one of the biggest cities in the world. The avenues are large and busy, it still draws a pretty rowdy crowd at night, and you really have to travel to get away from the city grime.

EAT: Hell's Kitchen's proximity to Times Square and the Theater District means it absorbs a fair amount of nightlife traffic, and a broad range of options for eating exists across the neighborhood. As well as the classic American fare of the Film Center Café, there's the Delta Grill, a spirited Southern-style restaurant with a Mardi-Gras theme "where Hell's Kitchen meets the French quarter." Its sizzling Southern macaroni and cheese is the crispiest and the richest in the city.
Delta Grill, 700 Ninth Avenue at 48th Street, (212-956-0934) www.thedeltagrill.com
Film Center Café, 635 Ninth Avenue at 45th Street (212-262-2525) www.filmcentercafe.com

DRINK: Rudy's is the only bar in Manhattan that gives away hot dogs to its loyal regulars. A longstanding favorite of the area, Rudy's has a courtyard out back that fills up in the summer months, an unchanging jukebox of classic rock and soul music, red leatherette booths, and bar prices that keep falling as the night goes on and the bartenders get happier. And the hot dog machine keeps rolling on.
Rudy's Bar and Grill, 627 Ninth Avenue, between 44th and 45th streets, (212-974-9169)

SHOP: Hell's Kitchen is by no means a shopper's destination, and while there are treasures here and there they mostly take the form of eclectic outposts of neighboring industries—props warehouses and fabric stores leaking over from the Theater and Garment Districts. But the weekly flea market that occupies 39th Street between Ninth and Tenth avenues is one of the best in the city. Less pretentious than its cousin in Chelsea and much more affordable than the haughtier antiques markets farther up the west side, the market is a great place to find odds and ends you never knew you wanted, from eccentric furniture to vintage clothes, bicycles, and books.
Hell's Kitchen Flea Market, 39th Street, between Ninth and Tenth avenues (Saturdays and Sundays), (212-253-5343) www.hellskitchenfleamarket.com

SEE HELL'S KITCHEN IN: *West Side Story*, the toughest look at immigrant gang warfare in New York City ever to be set to catchy showtunes and played out in swanky theaters only a few blocks from the streets where it all went down. Hell's Kitchen has also been the backdrop for several movies including *In America* and *State of Grace*, and has been visited by such icons of American fiction as Ayn Rand's Gail Wynand and Brett Easton Ellis's villainous Patrick Bateman.

MURRAY HILL AND KIPS BAY

IN BRIEF: If we were to sum up each NYC neighborhood in a single word, Murray Hill (and the adjoining neighborhood of Kips Bay) would be . . . "practical." This centrally located, reasonably priced, amenity-laden area lacks almost nothing but character (and good shopping, but we'll get to that). If you can live without the glitz and grit found elsewhere, you'll be rewarded with a relatively hassle-free existence.

The landscape here is a mish-mash where big-city behemoths tower over a little bit of West Village–style intimacy. On the avenues are vast apartment complexes with plenty of retail amenities underneath them, which nearly eclipse the sweet townhouses on the side streets. Of the complexes, the Kips Bay Towers between 30th and 33rd streets on First and Second avenues offer your best shot of real-estate cachet, for a killer price. Designed in the 1960s by I. M. Pei, the two-building 1,118-unit complex originally called Kips Bay Plaza was one of the city's first residential real-estate projects by a famous architect in the city; the exposed concrete offers an anachronistic architectural counterpoint to the sleek name-brand architect glass boxes along the Hudson River—in a retro-French-housing-project kind of way.

Green space exists, but it's similarly unglamorous. Despite proximity to the East River, there's no pleasant waterfront to speak of, and the only city park, St. Vartan's, is practically on top of the Queens-Midtown Tunnel (and because it's got the only playground in the neighborhood, it tends to be pretty packed with strollers). Instead, locals find their respite in the well-kept gardens and public plazas of the apartment buildings and complexes. Knowing that you're twenty feet away from a Food Emporium may detract from the ambience, but on the plus side, these spaces are often cleaner, quieter, and less frenzied than many parks. A word to the wise, however: be careful where you sit. When you're relaxing on a building's property, benches are fair game but sitting on the steps is considered loitering, and building staff people don't like loiterers—as one of your authors learned the hard way when doing her research!

LOCATION: Given their central Manhattan location, these two neighborhoods prove that New Yorkers pay a premium for cool; you can find rentals and places to buy for less than what you'd pay for a fourth-floor walk-up in many trendier neighborhoods much farther afield. Located just south of Grand Central, this area is within walking distance of the businesses of Midtown, the charms of Gramercy, and the shops and restaurants of Flatiron. When you want to leave the city, the FDR Drive and Metro-North are right there.

Like a lot of east side neighborhoods, the subway access isn't the best (just the 6 on Lexington Avenue), but given how many things can be reached on foot, this is less of an issue in this neighborhood than those farther north, and if you can make it to Grand Central, the shuttle and 7 train can help you get to the west side. Crosstown buses are never pleasant, but the buses up First Avenue and down Second Avenue are surprisingly speedy (especially if you manage to find an express). And hey, if you hang on long enough, you may even see the Second Avenue subway. (At press time, scheduled completion date was still many years away.)

Planning on a summer share in the Hamptons? You'll shave 20 to 30 minutes off your travel time by living so close to the Queens-Midtown Tunnel.

LIVE THERE FOR: SAFETY, CONVENIENCE, AMENITIES, ETC. This neighborhood caters to the residential. No matter where you live, you won't have to walk far to get to a real supermarket (not an oversized deli or a gourmet food shop), drugstore, dry cleaner, movie theater, deli, gym, bookstore, nail salon, or hospital. There will never be a San Gennaro Festival, Gay Pride Parade, or a crowd waiting for a midnight screening of *The Rocky Horror Picture Show* on your block. There will never be a line for cupcakes at your bakery, or nightclubs pouring out in front of your door. The visible presence of uniformed police officers—the police academy is nearby—helps keep the peace in this already peaceful place. In short, this is not a hard place to live.

KEEP LOOKING: IF YOU WANT GOOD PEOPLE-WATCHING. Checking out local color and passersby can be fun and inspirational, and NYC offers some of the best places to do this in the world. This neighborhood is not one of them. Corporate is the weekday uniform, with an increased presence of sweats and gym clothes at night. The major weekend looks are defined by wet hair and college logos; the great fashion faux-pas would be wearing Duke colors to a UNC bar.

EAT: In between a lot of bland-looking eateries with run-of-the-mill salads and burgers, there are some under-the-radar treasures, especially in the realm of ethnic food.

In addition to the Indian restaurants on the strip of Lexington Avenue known as "Curry Hill," on Third Avenue in the 20s, there's Bamiyan, an Afghani restaurant, Turkish Kitchen, and East, which boasts one of the city's few sushi conveyor belts. These are the kinds of places more commonly found in the outer boroughs that people love to post about on the city's many foodie blogs—no-frills, middling service, with food that is authentic and properly spiced. An overall good rule of thumb in this neighborhood is the older and dingier looking the place, the better the food. When you do crave something a little more posh, there is the lovely bistro and *fromagerie*, Artisanal. And while they aren't hip, Josie's and Better Burger serve tasty, healthy, reasonably priced food, and may come in handy if you develop a taste for kebabs and fondue.

Artisanal, 2 Park Avenue, at 33rd Street, (212-239-1200) www.artisanalbistro.com

Bamiyan, 358 Third Avenue, at 26th Street, (212-481-3232) www.bamiyan.com

Better Burger, 565 Third Avenue, at 37th Street, (212-949-7529) www.betterburgernyc.com

East, 366 Third Avenue, between 26th and 27th streets, (212-889-2326)

Josie's, 565 Third Avenue, at 37th Street, (212-490-1558) www.josiesnyc.com

Turkish Kitchen, 386 Third Avenue, between 27th and 28th streets, (212-679-1810)
www.turkishkitchen.com

DRINK: At the bars of Murray Hill, you won't find a lot of style, but you won't find $20 cocktails either. If it's atmosphere you're after, though, try Rodeo Bar; it is proudly referred to as "NYC's longest-running honky tonk." If you really need a comfy couch and a pomegranate mojito, there is always the W Hotel on 39th Street. No cute coffee shops or cafés around but Lite Delights has a respectable juice bar, with friendly hours (it's open from 7 a.m. to 11 p.m. every day).

Lite Delights, 456 Third Avenue, between 31st and 32nd streets, (212-679-2114)

Rodeo Bar, 375 Third Avenue, at 27th Street, (212-683-6500) www.rodeobar.com

W New York (The Tuscany), 120 East 39th Street, between Park and Lexington avenues,
(212-686-1600) www.starwoodhotels.com

SHOP: Just to the south of the official boundary between Murray Hill and Gramercy are a couple of excellent thrift shops. At the Vintage Thrift Shop, novice vintage shoppers and those weary of the Housing Works madhouse will snap up treasures like Eames chairs and $3 Heath ceramic plates that aren't already marked with a SOLD tag. That the clothes are hit-or-miss is par for the course, but make sure to go in the back where you can find some seriously vintage vinyl (*Porgy & Bess* anyone?) and mint-condition *Playboy* magazines from the 1960s. (FYI: it's closed on Saturdays.)

Once you enter Murray Hill proper, pickings are seriously slim, with not even a

Banana Republic as far as the eye can see. Rodeo Wares, a strange little boutique connected to the Rodeo Bar (see page 53), gets points for gumption and an excellent selection of cowboy boots, though we'd guess that any real cowboy might be suspicious of a place that sells $60 Michael Stars T-shirts. There are also a couple of overpriced boutiques that might be good for a sparkly top in a pinch—but beware that the clothes are much more cheaply made than their price tags would suggest.

Rodeo Wares, 379 Third Avenue, at 27th Street, (212-683-0319) www.rodeobar.com

Vintage Thrift Shop, 286 Third Avenue between 22nd and 23rd streets, (212-871-0777)

SEE MURRAY HILL IN: The comedy/burlesque shows hosted by drag-king performer, Murray Hill, aka "Mr. Showbiz," aka "the hardest working middle-aged man in show business." For information on upcoming shows, visit www.mrmurrayhill.com.

NOLITA, CHINATOWN, AND LITTLE ITALY

IN BRIEF: Over the last decade, Nolita has evolved quickly from a bona-fide element of Little Italy into its own animal, a trendy residential haven above Chinatown and Little Italy, neighborhoods that for many decades have been the preserve only of families constituting two of New York's most famously impenetrable ethnic enclaves. For the few that can live there—it's a small neighborhood, and rents are high—Nolita serves as both a perfect downtown home and an invaluable refuge from the crowds that surround it. Streets lined with independent boutiques, eclectic cafés, and expensive bars and restaurants have attracted a young and trendy crowd. Of the three neighborhoods, though, it's the best candidate for living in. Real estate in Little Italy and Chinatown is dominated either by local etiquette that keeps places "in the family," or by Italian and Chinese realtors, who can be very inaccessible to non-Chinese or Italian speakers. The spaces themselves are smaller, too, and the noises and smells of the markets mean these neighborhoods are not for the faint of heart. They're great places to have nearby though, so if you live in Nolita, you can have the culture and commotion when you want it.

Over nearly two centuries of history, changing rates (and laws) of immigration have seen the area between Chinatown and Nolita evolve from the hub of Italian-Irish gangland to the fractured district it is today, comprising a small Italian enclave, a contained hipsterish neighborhood, and one of the most densely populated Chinatowns in America. Where once there was Five Points, nineteenth-century Manhattan's most notorious slum, there is now Columbus Park at the heart of Chinatown. The buildings throughout these three neighborhoods bear the markings of this transient heritage—you might find a vintage clothing store in a tenement building with the name of a defunct Italian business engraved above the door and Chinese decorative elements adorning the façade.

LOCATION: Nolita is one of Manhattan's smallest and most clearly contained neighborhoods, bounded on the north by Houston Street, on the east by the Bowery, on the south by Broome Street, and on the west by Lafayette Street. The shops and lofts of Soho lie immediately to the west, the touristy strips of Little Italy and the frenetic activity of Chinatown to the south, Houston Street and Noho to the north, and the expanse of the Lower East Side to the east. Centered around the bucolic St. Patrick's Old Cathedral, Nolita's narrow, café-lined streets retain a relatively peaceful, European feel, and its location amid some of Manhattan's liveliest and busiest neighborhoods encourages a fierce and rewarding local loyalty.

Little Italy—an increasingly little area centered around Mulberry Street and extending a little along Kenmare, Grand, and Broome streets—is one of the city's busiest tourist districts, a neon parody of its former self, lined with restaurants and food stores whose proclamations of Italian heritage are more important than their quality, and as such don't hold much appeal for new residents. Chinatown, on the other hand, is still expanding. Roughly contained by Lafayette Street and the curve of the Bowery and stretching from Broome Street down to a few blocks south of Canal Street, it is an expanse of busy streets, shops, restaurants, and fresh-food markets that remains one of New York City's most flavorful districts. People crowd the streets all day every day, the variety of foods on sale at the hundreds of indoor and outdoor markets is extraordinary, and the sounds of Chinese dialects fill the air.

LIVE THERE FOR: **THE FOOD, THE SHOPPING, AND THE FUN.** The ever-changing landscape of Nolita's boutique-lined streets is enough to keep even the most hardened shopaholics content, and there is a young designer's market in the school beside St. Patrick's Old Cathedral every weekend. The high-end stores of Broadway and Soho and two of Manhattan's coolest independent cinemas—the Angelika and the Landmark Sunshine on Houston Street—are only a few blocks away. A handful of the city's nicest bars and restaurants are in Nolita, and living close to Chinatown and Little Italy means you're within walking distance of some of the best cooking and the most authentic markets and delis in the city. And if you ever do get bored with what's on your doorstep, the neighborhood's location and plethora of nearby trains means you can be anywhere from Chelsea to Williamsburg in a matter of minutes.

KEEP LOOKING: IF YOU NEED YOUR SPACE. Nolita, Chinatown, and Little Italy are among Manhattan's busiest neighborhoods and are popular with both tourists and locals throughout the year. While Nolita is much quieter than the neighborhoods that surround it, the apartments are small and it's not as peaceful as more solidly residential areas downtown such as Chelsea or the West Village—there are enough bars and restaurants to keep people coming and going all night.

EAT: With its own mix of restaurants and literally hundreds more in Chinatown and Little Italy, Nolita is one of the best-fed neighborhoods in Manhattan. Café Habana and Café Gitane remain Nolita's most popular eateries. Habana is the liveliest joint on the block, a spicy Cuban restaurant with a take-out window next door popular for grilled corn and fresh lemonade; Gitane is a stylish French café with tables outside, great coffee, and a Mediterranean menu. Xicala is a charming and quiet tapas bar, happily overlooked by most in its spot between Nolita and Chinatown. But beside one another on Elizabeth street are the neighborhood's best: Lovely Day, a fun and cozy bar with delicious Asian food and comfy leatherette booths; and Peasant, a rustic, candlelit Italian restaurant with communal tables, great atmosphere, and a hearty and meaty menu.

Everybody in the city has a favorite restaurant in Chinatown. Peking Duck House, Joe's Shanghai, and Hop Kee are among the best, and cover the full spectrum from exquisitely prepared and expensive whole ducks to the city's most popular soup dumplings to the tastiest, greasiest, and cheapest pork fried rice in town. And while the restaurants on the main drags of Little Italy's Mulberry and Grand streets can be more show than taste, L'asso and Lombardi's each stakes a justifiable claim to serve the city's best pizza.

Café Gitane, 242 Mott Street, at Prince Street, (212-334-9552)

Café Habana, 17 Prince Street, at Elizabeth Street, (212-625-2002)

Hop Kee, 21 Mott Street, at Mosco Street, (212-964-8365)

Joe's Shanghai, 9 Pell Street, between Doyers Street and Bowery, (212-233-8888)
   www.joeshanghairestaurant.com

L'asso, 192 Mott Street, at Kenmare Street, (212-219-2353) www.lassonyc.com

Lombardi's, 32 Spring Street, between Mott and Mulberry streets, (212-941-7994)
   www.firstpizza.com

Lovely Day, 196 Elizabeth Street, between Prince and Spring streets, (212-925-3310)

Peasant, 194 Elizabeth Street, between Prince and Spring streets, (212-965-9511)
   www.peasantnyc.com

Peking Duck House, 28 Mott Street, between Mosco and Pell streets, (212-227-1810)
   www.pekingduckhousenyc.com

Xicala, 151 Elizabeth Street, between Kenmare and Broome streets, (212-229-0599)

DRINK: Shebeen on Mott Street serves the best lychee martinis in the city—that won't seem like such a spurious claim once you've tried one—and Epistrophy, its immediate neighbor, is a lively and cozy Italian wine bar with tables outside in the summer.

Epistrophy, 200 Mott Street, between Spring and Kenmare streets, (212-966-0904)

Shebeen, 202 Mott Street, between Spring and Kenmare streets, (212-625-1105)

SHOP: McNally Robinson on Prince Street is one of New York's greatest bookstores. There are two floors of well-chosen books, from bestsellers and art monographs to substantial nonfiction, reference, and children's sections, and plenty of comfy leather chairs and stools to sit around and browse on. The store attracts interesting authors for readings and book-signing events, stocks a great selection of magazines and journals, and has one of the neighborhood's best cafés to boot. It's a wonderful place to while away an afternoon and an invaluable source for anyone downtown who has neither the time nor the inclination to travel up to Barnes and Noble or the Strand at Union Square. Just don't make the mistake of settling down in the café with a book you haven't paid for.

The neighborhood's other shopping gems are trendy boutiques that range from secretive outposts of major names to younger independent stores—a new one of which seems to pop up every few weeks. Ralph Lauren, Paul Frank, Charlotte Ronson, and NIKE iD stores, for example, coexist relatively unobtrusively alongside the uniquely charming Mayle and the cute and decorative Lyell.

Charlotte Ronson, 239 Mulberry Street, at Kenmare Street, (212-625-9074)
    www.charlotteronson.com

Lyell, 173 Elizabeth, between Spring and Kenmare streets, (212-966-8484)

Mayle, 242 Elizabeth Street, between Houston and Prince streets, (212-941-7210)

McNally Robinson, 52 Prince Street, between Lafayette and Mulberry streets,
    (212-274-1160) www.mcnallyrobinson.com

NIKE iD, 255 Elizabeth Street, between Houston and Prince streets, www.nikeid.com

Paul Frank, 195 Mulberry Street, between Spring and Kenmare streets, (212-965-5079)
    www.paulfrank.com

Ralph Lauren RRL, 242 Mott Street, at Prince Street, (212-343-1934) www.ralphlauren.com

SEE NOLITA, CHINATOWN, AND LITTLE ITALY IN: While the busy streets of Little Italy and Chinatown are familiar locations for countless films set in New York, the St. Patrick's Old Cathedral on Prince Street between Mulberry and Mott streets has been a part of some seminal moments on the silver screen. It's inside St. Pat's that Michael Corleone becomes godfather at his nephew's christening and in the beautiful church-yard that Johnny Boy dances around the car to "Mickey's Monkey" in Martin Scorsese's *Mean Streets*.

SOHO AND TRIBECA

IN BRIEF: Soho and Tribeca are among the areas of New York whose characters have changed the most dramatically over the course of time. Built in the mid- to late nine-teenth century as the commercial and industrial zones of the city as it grew north-ward from what we now know as the Financial District, these two neighborhoods consist largely of beautiful great warehouses and factories constructed along cobbled streets, many of which survive today. Architecturally, they are among New York's most important neighborhoods, containing among other treasures almost all of the city's 250 celebrated cast-iron buildings — until its rebranding in the 1970s, Soho was known as the "Cast-Iron District."

It was in the 1970s, a century after their construction and decades after the indus-tries they housed had become redundant, that Soho and Tribeca began to change into what we see today. With the city in recession and the historic buildings protected from an unsentimental local government, artists moved into the area and transformed the huge industrial spaces into lofts, studios, and galleries. Until the 1980s, when money flowed back into the city and rents skyrocketed, these neighborhoods were occupied for the most part by squatting artists and writers, and became infamous as the lawless and messy heart of the New York art scene.

In the last twenty years, property prices and the potential for commercialization have forced the artists farther and farther out into Brooklyn and beyond, and these two neighborhoods have become business and shopping districts — and the exclusive and expensive homes of New York's rich and famous. While Tribeca has kept a quiet distance from the majority of the downtown crowd — and has suffered economically since September 11, 2001 — it is filled with upscale restaurants, bars, and stores, is home to some of the city's largest and most beautiful loft apartments, and proudly hosts local icon Robert De Niro's celebrated Tribeca Film Festival. And Soho has become downtown New York's most tourist-happy neighborhood, a prized destina-tion for shopping, eating, and drinking, an inimitable set for movies and TV shows, and an icon of the city's status.

LOCATION: It's all about the capitals here. Soho, abbreviated from "south of Houston," lies between Houston and Canal streets and runs roughly from Broadway at its easternmost edge to Sixth Avenue at its westernmost. In among the concrete, tarmac, and tourist-trapping storefronts are wide, cobbled pedestrian streets, iron-fronted industrial buildings, and some of the prettiest blocks in the city. The heart of downtown Manhattan, Soho is within easy walking distance of Chinatown, Little Italy, Nolita, Noho, Tribeca, Washington Square Park, and the West Village, and is well served by the A, C, E, N, R, W, and 6 trains along Prince and Spring streets.

Soho's quieter neighbor Tribeca earned its own acronym by occupying the "Triangle Below Canal Street." Tribeca's borders are loosely defined by Sixth Avenue to the east, Canal Street to the north, Chambers Street to the south, and West Street bordering the Hudson. Tribeca is far enough out of the way for it to remain relatively quiet, in spite of its being bisected by some of the west side's largest highways and routes to New Jersey. Although Soho, Chelsea, Chinatown, the West Village, and the Financial District are within easy walking distance, getting somewhere farther across town takes either time and effort or a hefty cab fare.

LIVE THERE FOR: THE MOST BEAUTIFUL APARTMENTS IN THE CITY. For most people, Soho and Tribeca are about shopping: Soho for designer boutiques and department stores, Tribeca for an eclectic range of antique and contemporary furniture shops. But for anyone lucky enough to live here, the living spaces themselves are the stars of the neighborhoods. Although the days of low rents for gigantic artists' lofts are pretty much gone, apartments in the older buildings make for beautiful homes, with inordinately high ceilings, spectacular pillars of iron and steel, and vast windows—austere remnants of an industrial past that make the most of those precious New York commodities, space and light. And for the kind of money you'll be paying, you can rest assured that the buildings are maintained to a higher standard than elsewhere in the city.

KEEP LOOKING: IF YOU LIKE TO HAVE SPENDING MONEY LEFT AFTER YOU'VE PAID YOUR RENT. Not only are rents higher in these two neighborhoods than in the rest of Manhattan, but everything around you is expensive too, from upscale bars and restaurants to high-end shops and "delis" that would pass for gourmet markets in other parts of town. While this may sound like heaven for those that can afford it, it's important to understand just how inflated prices are in this part of the city before you fall irrevocably in love with it. And if you're looking to live in Soho, know that during the daylight hours at least you'll be sharing your neighborhood with throngs of tourists 365 days a year.

EAT: Although much of Soho caters primarily to the tourist crowd, who will pay too much for anything as long as it's within walking distance of the Prada store, there are gastronomic truffles here and there that are worth sniffing out. Barolo on West Broadway is a high-end Italian restaurant with a magnificent and romantic courtyard that puts the cramped backyards of other downtown "gardens" to shame. And within walking distance of one another on Sullivan Street are the delicious fresh pastries of the Sullivan St. Bakery, the amazingly fresh fish of Soho's Blue Ribbon Sushi, and the bright and healthy flavors of Yoghurt Place II.

Tribeca is the stomping ground of longtime resident chef David Bouley, whose local culinary empire has endured for more than twenty years through the financial and spiritual damage of September 11. Both his eponymous restaurant, Bouley, and Danube, his Austrian café, remain two of downtown Manhattan's finest places to eat, and the Bouley Bakery and Market is a truly unique experiment in combining every element of cuisine from shopping to cooking. The neighborhood is also the home of native New Yorker and local hero Robert De Niro, and his restaurant, Nobu, is another highlight of the city's culinary scene. Among the first upscale restaurants to bring sushi to the city when it opened nearly fifteen years ago and one of the few that still manages successfully to mingle Asian and western styles and flavors, Nobu remains popular among New York's glitterati and is hard to get into for the rest of us—but it's worth the effort, and if you can't get a reservation you can always head to its informal sister restaurant, Nobu Next Door.

Barolo, 398 West Broadway, between Spring and Broome streets, (212-226-1102)
   www.nybarolo.com
Blue Ribbon Sushi, 119 Sullivan Street, between Prince and Spring streets, (212-343-0404)
   www.blueribbonrestaurants.com
Bouley, 120 West Broadway, at Duane Street, (212-964-2525) www.davidbouley.com
Bouley Bakery and Market, 130 West Broadway, between Duane and Thomas streets,
   (212-608-5829) www.davidbouley.com
Danube, 30 Hudson Street, at Duane Street, (212-791-3771) www.davidbouley.com
Nobu and Nobu Next Door, 105 Hudson Street, between Franklin and North Moore streets,
   (212-219-0500) www.noburestaurants.com
Sullivan St. Bakery, 73 Sullivan Street, between Spring and Broome streets, (212-334-9435)
   www.sullivanstbakery.com
Yoghurt Place II, 71 Sullivan Street, between Spring and Broome streets, (212-219-3500)
   www.yoghurtplacenyc.com

DRINK: The Room on Sullivan Street is one of the best bars in Soho, a small but cavernous place with a cozy bar in one room and a host of couches and tables in the next. The Room is intensely dark, the music is loud and atmospheric, and the selection of beers and wines is deliberately surprising, including a range of fruit beers and specials such as pumpkin ale. It's remarkable for being one of the few bars in the neighborhood that is neither a glitzed-up neon cocktail lounge nor an overpriced dive.

And while there are plenty of bars to choose from in Tribeca, to make a change we thought we'd turn our back on alcohol and reach for something more refreshing. Soda Shop on Chambers Street is a true old-school shake shack, using authentic recipes and wholesome ingredients to create a full menu of nostalgic sodas, from triple-thick milkshakes to fresh-fruit smoothies, ice cream floats, and enigmatic egg creams. On top of the drinks menu, the tiles and stained glass will make you feel like you're back in the days of the Cast-Iron District.

The Room, 144 Sullivan Street, between Houston and Prince streets, (212-477-2102)
   www.theotherroom.com
Soda Shop, 125 Chambers Street, between West Broadway and Church, (212-571-1100)
   www.sodashopnewyork.com

SHOP: Soho's got the best and the worst of the city's street shopping. Because of the high volume of shopper's foot traffic, its streets are equally coveted by vendors as storefronts are by retailers. But it's not a meritocracy, and the lucky vendors who have scored spots on streets like Prince and Spring are a mixed bag. (Vendors have their tables in the same spots on regular days and at the same times so repeat customers can find them easily.) A favorite are the handmade limited-edition printed T-shirts from fluxproductions. You can find them being sold by their creator at a table on Prince Street most weekends from noon to 6 p.m.

A welcome new addition to Soho's main drag along Broadway is the city's only branch of the Japanese design chain MUJI. With products that range from simple clothing and accessories to furniture, office supplies, stationery, and stereo equipment, MUJI is something of a tastemaker for the modest urbanite. Like a better-dressed IKEA, MUJI covers a broad spectrum of home design, from watches to cushions and diaries, all flavored with a quiet and uniquely Japanese simplicity. But if humble and modest isn't your thing, head down to Opening Ceremony, one of the city's best-kept fashion secrets, on Howard Street. As well as an imported line from Top Shop in the UK, the store stocks some of the most interesting independent and high-end designers for both men and women, and is far enough off the beaten Soho track to avoid the overcrowding of Broadway and Spring Street.

And as the quiet retail capital of Manhattan's interior design scene, Tribeca is a wonderful, if expensive, place to scout around for furniture and home décor ideas. Even if you can't afford the new or vintage pieces at the Urban Archaeology showroom on Franklin Street, you can learn more about contemporary taste and antique design in an hour or two here than you could in a lifetime at Crate and Barrel. And for slightly more affordable designs in a more contemporary palette, try Room on Duane Street.

fluxproductions vendor table, Prince Street between Greene and Wooster streets, www.fluxproductions.etsy.com.

MUJI, 455 Broadway, between Grand and Howard streets, (212-334-2002) www.muji.com

Opening Ceremony, 35 Howard Street, between Broadway and Crosby, (212-219-2688) www.openingceremony.us

Room, 182 Duane Street, between Greenwich and Hudson streets, (212-226-1045) www.roomonline.com

Urban Archeology, 143 Franklin Street, between Hudson and Varick streets, (212-431-4646) www.urbanarcheology.com

SEE SOHO AND TRIBECA IN: Everything from *Hannah and Her Sisters* and *Unfaithful* to Cycle 10 of "America's Next Top Model."

UPPER EAST SIDE

IN BRIEF: If New York City were one big family, the Upper East Side would be the rich and eccentric grandmother from the old country. With a heritage that includes the earliest Astor estate and the city's densest enclaves of middle- and eastern-European immigrants, the neighborhood encompasses some of the city's grandest architecture and its most prestigious cultural institutions. It's only in the last ten or fifteen years that the Upper East Side has become a residential neighborhood accessible to anyone outside of the age-old circles of wealthy dynasties and European enclaves. Since the rise of Brooklyn as a cheap stronghold for commuters, however, prices have fallen in the area, and these days the easternmost parts of the neighborhood are affordable enough for a whole new generation of twenty- and thirty-something Midtowners. The west half of the neighborhood remains one of the swankiest parts of the city, and with just cause: Museum Mile, on Fifth Avenue alongside the park, boasts the Metropolitan Museum of Art, the Frick Collection, the Cooper-Hewitt Design Museum, the Museo del Barrio, and the Neue Galerie, among others. Between the posh attractions near Central Park and the homelier and more ethnically flavored streets farther east, the neighborhood is on the whole a pleasant and quiet part of town.

LOCATION: Starting at the Lincoln Memorial in Grand Army Plaza, at 59th Street and Fifth Avenue, and extending north until it bleeds into East Harlem in the 100s, the Upper East Side is one of the largest neighborhoods in the city. It covers a greater area than the Upper West Side, stretching across nine broad avenues at its widest point from Central Park to the East River. Despite its size and its nature as one of the denser commuter areas, the Upper East Side is poorly served by the subway, with only the 4, 5, and 6 lines running up- and downtown beneath Lexington and Park avenues. The city has promised to establish a much-needed Second Avenue subway line, which would have a huge impact on the area east of Third Avenue where home prices are currently lower because of its relative inaccessibility. But until that happens—if it ever really happens—people make do with a walk to the green line and with the MTA's decent bus coverage of the neighborhood.

LIVE THERE FOR: THE PARK, THE RIVER, AND THE HIGH BROWS. Between the walkways along the East River and the proximity of Central Park, Upper East Siders have two of the most pleasant and archetypal New York recreations within easy walking distance. Everybody in the city comes to the park once in a while, but for uptowners it's a weekly or even daily presence, and the John Finlay Walk that runs along the East River from the 70s to the 90s is a happy scene of joggers, dogwalkers, and romantics huddling on the benches overlooking Roosevelt Island and the expanse of Queens and the Bronx to the north. And if its bucolic pastimes aren't enough for you, the Upper East Side is of course also home to a disproportionate number of the city's cultural institutions, from the many treasures of Museum Mile on Fifth Avenue to Gracie Mansion, the galleries and department stores of Madison Avenue, and enough of Woody Allen's shooting locations to keep you amused for a lifetime.

KEEP LOOKING: IF YOU BELIEVE YOUTH AND SKILL OVERCOME OLD AGE AND TREACHERY. The Upper East Side has a strong older demographic, even with some of the residential streets farther east that are cheap enough to attract younger commuters and Midtowners. Although there's a strong frat-house presence, especially in the diners and bars along Second Avenue in the 70s and 80s, the neighborhood as a whole wears its heritage on its sleeve, and the majority of its amenities, from apartments to restaurants and shops, skews to an older, richer, and more garish crowd than anywhere else in the city.

EAT: True to the neighborhood's European pedigree, the Upper East Side has some of the best delis in the city. Wurstmeisters Schaller & Weber have a café and bar on Second Avenue where you can indulge in a wide variety of delicious sausages and giant glasses of beer, with a patio on the sidewalk in true mittel-European style. Café Sabarsky, the Austrian restaurant within the Neue Galerie, is a fantastic place for a continental breakfast or an afternoon coffee and pastry. And Etats-Unis, one of the city's best French restaurants, has a small and considered dinner menu that includes the best chocolate cake we've ever tasted (ask for it early in your meal; they bake it to order) and a companion bar directly across 81st Street where you can eat the same dishes in a less formal setting.

Café Sabarsky, 1048 Fifth Avenue, between 85th and 86th streets, (212-288-0665)
    www.cafesabarsky.com
Etats-Unis, 242 East 81st Street, between Second and Third avenues, (212-517-8826)
Schaller & Weber, 1654 Second Avenue, at 86th Street, (212-879-3047)
    www.schallerweber.com

DRINK: With a curious mix of frat-house dives and swanky hotel and museum bars, the Upper East Side is an unlikely drinking destination, and is worth exploring for the odd surprise. Doc Watson's is a popular example of the former, with red-and-white checked tablecloths and pitchers of beer; the bars at The Carlyle and the Plaza Athénée are splendidly over-the-top and occasionally glamorous examples of the latter (Woody Allen still plays The Carlyle with his jazz band every week).

Café Carlyle, 35 East 76th Street, between Madison and Park avenues, (212-570-7189)
    www.thecarlyle.com
Doc Watson's, 1490 Second Avenue, between 77th and 78th streets, (212-988-5300)
    www.docwatsons.com
Hôtel Plaza Athénée, 37 East 64th Street, between Madison and Park avenues,
    (212-734-9100) www.plaza-athenee.com

SHOP: Everybody knows the Upper East Side is a top destination for department stores and designer boutiques, from Bloomingdale's and Barneys to Prada, Dolce & Gabbana, and Miu Miu, among hundreds of others. But the Upper East Side is also prime book country, with a few of the city's finest bookstores dotted along Madison Avenue. The magnificent Ursus Books occupies a beautiful space above the bar at The Carlyle, and has the best (and an expensive) range of new, used, and rare art and architecture books. Crawford Doyle is a little-known but amazingly well-stocked new bookstore on a quiet stretch of Madison Avenue with equally good ranges of illustrated books and new and classic fiction and poetry titles. And the Corner Bookstore is one of the city's most beloved independents, a small shop with a noble and diverse selection that hosts great readings and events for local authors throughout the year.

Barneys, 660 Madison Avenue, between 60th and 61st streets, (212-826-8900)
   www.barneys.com

Bloomingdale's, 1000 Third Avenue, between 59th and 60th streets, (212-705-2000)
   www.bloomingdales.com

Corner Bookstore, 1313 Madison Avenue, between 92nd and 93rd streets, (212-831-3554)

Crawford Doyle, 1082 Madison Avenue, between 81st and 82nd streets, (212-288-6300)

Dolce & Gabbana, 660 Madison Avenue, between 60th and 61st streets, (212-249-4100)
   www.dolcegabbana.com

Miu Miu, 831 Madison Avenue, between 69th and 70th streets, (212-249-9660)
   www.miumiu.com

Prada, 841 Madison Avenue, at 68th Street, (212-327-4200) www.prada.com

Ursus Books, 981 Madison Avenue, at 76th Street, (212-772-8787) www.ursusbooks.com

SEE THE UPPER EAST SIDE IN: Any Woody Allen movie you care to name. Woody Allen, longtime resident of the Upper East Side and still regularly heard blowing the clarinet at The Carlyle, is also the neighborhood's most faithful chronicler. Many of his most memorable movies feature locations in the area's beautiful aristocratic townhouses, the east side of the park, and the iconic architecture of Fifth and Park avenues where many of his characters committed murders, held witty dinner parties, and had calamitous and romantic affairs. The most famous location of all, perhaps, is the bench on the East River where Woody and Diane Keaton sat together in *Manhattan*, in Sutton Place Park near the 59th Street Bridge.

UPPER WEST SIDE

IN BRIEF: New Yorkers can be territorially contrarian and 'hood-proud, but no matter where they're from, few would dispute that the Upper West Side seems like a nice place to live. For those who venture above 23rd Street only to go to the dentist, the rivalry between the neighborhoods on either side of the park might seem to be missing the point—they're both uptown—but not only do they vary tremendously in character, the Upper West Side has several distinct logistical advantages over the Upper East. On both sides, prices become reasonable the farther away from Central Park you go. The difference on the Upper West Side is that once you get into the middle (around Broadway), you're only two blocks from Riverside Park. On the Upper East, you have to go farther—at least three blocks (to Lexington)—to find reasonable prices, and though there's the lovely Carl Schurz Park on the East River, that's still as many as five long avenue blocks away. Those avenue blocks also come into play for subway access: on the Upper East Side, you are as far from the subway as you are from Lexington Avenue; on the Upper West, you've got more subway lines, on more avenues.

Some of those avenues (Columbus, Amsterdam, and Broadway) can be ugly, as are the major cross streets (72nd, 86th, and 96th), but they are useful. There is no shortage of chain stores and big boisterous restaurants; however, there is a shortage of interesting boutiques, and intimate, charming restaurants.

In terms of culture, Lincoln Center is the anchor of the local art scene, offering everything from opera and the Philharmonic to dance, film, theater—and even the circus. Much of the complex is undergoing renovations, scheduled for completion by the complex's 50th anniversary in 2009. Farther uptown, Symphony Space has more theatrical and music performances, readings and other literary events, and films.

LOCATION: The Upper West Side officially starts at Columbus Circle, and covers everything from Central Park West to the Hudson River. In terms of transportation, the 1, 2, and 3 offer easy access to Midtown, Penn Station, and Tribeca; the B and D opens up Greenwich Village and the Lower East Side, and the A and C cover the West Side from Soho to Washington Heights. For express-train junkies, there's no better place to be. The A train makes no stops from 59th to 125th streets, and can also get you down as far as Canal Street very swiftly; the 2, 3 at 72nd and 96th streets are also useful for those who can't stand the excessive stops of the 1 train. Brooklyn and Queens, however, are a long trip.

LIVE THERE FOR: DANCE. Though the neighborhood's not lacking in any of the performing arts, the Upper West Side is unrivaled in its offerings for dancers (current, aspiring, or dabbling). Lincoln Center is home to the New York City Ballet, one of the country's most prestigious ballet companies, and the American Ballet Theatre splits its seasons between the Metropolitan Opera House and City Center, just south of the Upper West Side on 55th Street. Also bordering the neighborhood is the new home of the revered Alvin Ailey American Dance Theater, the largest facility devoted entirely to dance in the country. The area also has a ton of places where less accomplished dancers can take classes. Steps on Broadway offers many different kinds of dance, plus pilates, yoga, and more; the Lucy Moses School at the Kaufman Center, offers adult ballet. **PARKS.** Green spaces tend to get better the farther uptown you go, and the Upper West Side is flanked by two excellent examples: Central and River-side parks. Both are big, green, and have lots of sports and recreation amenities (playgrounds, playing fields, baseball diamonds, tennis courts, etc.) — giving neigh-borhood residents the opportunity to do outdoor activities they love conveniently. When was the last time you ever heard of anyone playing tennis in the East Village?

Alvin Ailey American Dance Theater (The Joan Weil Center for Dance), 405 West 55th Street at Ninth Avenue, (212-405-9000) www.alvinailey.org

American Ballet Theatre, Metropolitan Opera House, Columbus and Amsterdam avenues, between 62nd and 65th streets, (212-477-3030) www.abt.org

Central Park, 59th to 110th streets and Fifth to Eighth avenues, (212-310-6600) www.centralpark.com

Lucy Moses School at the Kaufman Center, 129 West 67th Street, at Broadway, (212-501-3360) www.kaufman-center.org

New York City Ballet, Lincoln Center, Columbus and Amsterdam avenues, between 62nd and 65th streets, (212-870-5570) www.nycballet.com

Riverside Park, 72nd to 158th streets, along the Hudson River, (212-690-7485) www.nycgovparks.org

Steps on Broadway, 2121 Broadway at 74th Street, (212-874-2410) www.stepsnyc.com

KEEP LOOKING: IF YOU HATE SMALL CHILDREN. The Upper West Side has long been a haven for urban families, and though children are on the rise all over the city, this neighbor-hood has a well-established family-friendly vibe. If you're going to live in an apartment building, expect to be approached at your door for raffle ticket and, walk-a-thons, and on Halloween. **IF YOU'RE NOT A BUS PERSON.** Though getting north and south is a cinch on the subway, if you're going east-west, you'll have to take the bus. The cross-town bus scene during school drop-off and pick-up times is a minefield of backpacks, soccer cleats, and science projects wielded at knee height. Travel at your own risk.

EAT: While restaurants are plentiful and a take-out-and-delivery culture prevails, good, reasonably priced haunts that you'd want to become a regular at are hard to come by in this neighborhood. It's said that this is changing, but it remains to be seen if some interesting newbies will stick it out. Until then, here are a few stalwarts. Café Luxem-bourg is what Balthazar and its dozens of imitators wish they were: an old-timer with a boisterous atmosphere, comfy-but-not-worn-out banquettes, and good bistro food. Another perk: its generous hours. Also good to know about if you are craving a big meal after hours is Big Nick's. At any time of day or night (it's open 24 hours), you can get pretty much anything there (the menu is nearly thirty pages long). Saigon Grill has been plagued by some nasty labor issues, but if your conscience will allow it, you can partake in the excellent Vietnamese food of this longtime neighborhood favorite. It has some of the best deals in the city, and unlike many places with a brisk take-out business, this location is actually pleasant to eat in (there are also locations in Greenwich Village and on the Upper East Side, but your authors think this one is the best). The sweet-and-sour soup is addictive—but know before you order it that it comes in a vat large enough to feed an entire low-rise apartment building. Last but not least, Telepan would be a standout in any neighborhood—but in any other neighborhood, it would probably lose its lovely well-bred feel. For the true neighborhood experience, forget reservations and eat in the bar area.

Big Nick's Burger and Pizza Joint, 2175 Broadway, at 77th Street, (212-362-9238)
   www.bignicksnyc.com

Café Luxembourg, 200 West 70th Street, at Amsterdam Avenue, (212-362-9337)
   www.cafeluxembourg.com

Saigon Grill, 620 Amsterdam Avenue, at 90th Street, (212-875-9072)

Telepan, 72 West 69th Street, between Central Park West and Columbus Avenue,
   (212-580-4300) www.telepan-ny.com

DRINK: Dives handily outnumber cute little wine bars in this neighborhood. The neighborhood post-college bar scene is thriving, and varied. Like country music? Head to Yogi's. Board games? Dive 75. Beer pong? Jake's Dilemma. Bourbon Street is as much of an institution as a dive bar could be; go for 1980s music and fifty-cent beers.

Bourbon Street, 405 Amsterdam Avenue, between 79th and 80th streets, (212-921-1332)

Dive 75, 101 West 75th Street, at Columbus Avenue, (212-362-7518) www.divebarnyc.com

Jake's Dilemma, 430 Amsterdam Avenue, between 80th and 81st streets, (212-580-0556)
   www.nycbestbars.com

Yogi's, 2156 Broadway, at 76th Street, (212-873-9852)

SHOP: The Upper West Side doesn't have many boutiques, but a useful local one-off is the Town Shop, which has been providing NYC ladies with unmentionables of all kinds for over a century. Prices aren't particularly cheap, but you'll get a lot for your money (it is known for its bra-fitting services). If you have no idea what kind of undergarment to wear with a particularly complex clothing item, the staff there will figure it out. Roam is a store that wouldn't stand out Carroll Gardens or the East Village—and we mean that as a compliment. Although charming, independently owned boutiques are a dime a dozen in other hoods, they are harder to come by on the Upper West, and this one is a big local asset when you need something like a hostess gift or a pretty letterpress card. (And if we were giving out awards, Roam would get one for its nice, reasonably priced jewelry selection.) Complimentary cookies, juice, and Hershey's Kisses put the finishing touches on the welcoming atmosphere. The UWS also has the city's only outpost of the chain apothecary Bluemercury, which beats Sephora for cosmetics and body products any day if only for the generous take-home freebies staffpeople shower you with if you make a purchase. If you are shopping for sweets, the old-fashioned, no-frills Levain Bakery is bit of a neighborhood secret, and more than one local told us (well, whispered is more like it) that their cookies are the best in town. That is perhaps debatable, but the size is not—each cookie weighs almost half a pound!

Bluemercury, 2305 Broadway, at 83rd Street, (212-799-0500) www.bluemercury.com

Levain Bakery, 167 West 74th Street, between Columbus and Amsterdam avenues,

(212-674-8080) www.levainbakery.com

Roam, 488 Amsterdam Avenue, between 83rd and 84th streets, (212-721-0155)

Town Shop, 2273 Broadway, between 81st and 82nd streets, (212-787-2762)

www.townshop.com

SEE THE UPPER WEST SIDE IN: *You've Got Mail* is the most obvious cinematic love letter to the neighborhood, with Upper West Side character practically dripping off of every shot. But this quintessentially New York neighborhood has played a role in many quintessential New York productions. The Dakota alone has made an indelible mark all over pop culture, with references to it found everywhere from rock songs to the *Baby-Sitters Club*. The worst, of course, is that it was the place where John Lennon was shot; the best is *Rosemary's Baby,* featuring Mia Farrow's shocking pixie cut, psychedelic 1960s witchcraft, and super-campy dream sequences.

The Dakota, Central Park West and 72nd Street

WASHINGTON HEIGHTS

IN BRIEF: The phrase "best-kept secret" was repeated by each and every one of the Washington Heights residents who spoke to us about their neighborhood. Buffered by its relative distance on the compact island of Manhattan, this stretch between the West 160s and 180s at first appears to be out-of-the-question remote and other-boroughly. But the numbers can be deceiving: thanks to the swift A train, it only takes thirty to forty minutes to get to Columbus Circle, Port Authority, or Penn Station.

There's more to the secret than convenience. Gorgeous, full-service pre-war buildings with incredible views of the Hudson line the avenues west of Fort Washington, and there's not a high-rise condo development in site. (Due to the uneven topography and lack of vacant space to develop, there probably won't ever be.) As for the neighborhood, a glance across the quaint commercial strips on 181st and 187th streets will tell you that the neighborhood is changing—something that long-time residents feel unanimously ambivalent about. On one hand, neighborhood veterans are wary of development, commotion, and other nuisances not previously found in this part of the city. ("It's starting to get hard to park on the street," one woman sighed.) On the other hand, they're all for the sushi, pedicures, and Pilates. Nowhere else in the city have we heard such warm feelings expressed for the opening of a Starbucks.

In truth, there are two Washington Heights. East of Fort Washington Avenue is the city's biggest Dominican enclave, and English-speakers are a distinct minority. If you don't speak Spanish, it's not easy to buy a sandwich (an empanada or a bowl of *habichuelas con dulce* is an easier find), let alone find a place to live. West of Fort Washington, you'll find a more diverse mix of students and Orthodox Jews (it's home to Yeshiva University's main campus), a Russian and Polish population, parks, families, dogs, and a quiet residential feel.

The newcomers may well provide the bridge between the two worlds, as they drive a need for English-speaking businesses and services—and encourage existing businesses to reach out across the geographic and linguistic divides. (Case in point: Caitlin was given a neighborhood tour by Louis, a bilingual hairdresser who formerly worked at an upscale Upper East Side salon; he had recently been hired by the owner of a Dominican salon on Cabrini Boulevard, where he sees both English- and Spanish-speaking clients.) Starbucks don't just appear out of nowhere—for better or worse, there are bound to be a few more chain outlets to come (a UPS store and a sparkling Chase Bank have already appeared). In the meantime, locals are taking advantage of this renaissance to colonize the commercial hubs with some specialty businesses and attractions—and their neighbors are embracing them. When Caitlin visited, everyone was talking about Washington Heights's first art gallery, K.B. Gallery, which had opened the night before in a sunny ground-floor spot on Riverside Drive with breathtaking Hudson views. The reception had been overflowing with curious and supportive neighbors who, according to the owner, celebrated its arrival "by going through seven cases of wine."

LOCATION: In terms of topography, Washington Heights encompasses Manhattan's highest point, and the area is noticeably hilly. Parks abound, so take your pick. For running, there are the river views from the secluded path along the Hudson. There's a sweet little park on Fort Washington Avenue right outside the 181st Street subway entrance, which is popular with local families. In addition, at the neighborhood's northern border is Fort Tryon Park—recently revitalized by several neighborhood foundations—and the Cloisters.

The A and the 1 trains are great for getting anywhere on the west side; the easy commute between Lincoln Center and the Theater District probably accounts for some of the area's recent colonization by artists and performers. The east side is a more strenuous trip, and Brooklyn might as well be in Connecticut (actually, it's probably easier to get there). For car owners, it's a cinch to get to New Jersey from the George Washington Bridge (at 175th Street), or the Bronx and Westchester (from the Henry Hudson Parkway). FYI: Even though going downtown on the A train is easy-peasy, most people around here have cars.

LIVE THERE FOR: BEAUTIFUL APARTMENT BUILDINGS. Even though the prices aren't dirt cheap, you'll get a lot for your money, both in terms of space and service. Castle Village—an elegant five-building complex perched above the river's edge—is the neighborhood Gold Coast, but there are also plenty of desirable options that are a bit more modest, including many pre-war conversions. Marble fixtures, elevators, and amenities are the norm here.

KEEP LOOKING: IF YOU NEED A GYM AND A MOVIE THEATER. A health club, a movie theater, a bookstore, and a toy store topped the list of things residents were still eager to see in the gentrification boom. The latter two are probably not far away; if you're dying to open an independent bookstore, this would be the neighborhood to do it in. The gym and the movie theater are a bit trickier, as they require large storefront spaces that the neighborhood doesn't seem to have room for—as evidenced by the narrow footprints of most of the stores. For now, order your books online and try Hudson Pilates, a sweet studio with very reasonable group mat and reformer classes and private sessions, and scenic runs along the river.
Hudson Pilates, 836 West 181st Street, at Pinehurst Avenue, (212-740-7178)

EAT: Frank's Market plays the part of a Garden of Eden perfectly (if you don't know what we're talking about, see page 170), complete with an olive bar and generous free samples from the bakery counter. Hispaniola is a popular dinner spot with an eclectic menu. If you're a smoker, don't miss Fumée, the tiny attached cigar bar. Even if you're not, it's worth holding your breath to peek in to see the walk-in cigar room and a members' lounge straight out of a Cary Grant movie. There's even a barber's chair where men can get a straight-razor shave in between smokes. Washington Heights may still be lacking a few amenities, but tofu and organic groceries aren't among them now that there's a branch of the health-food chainlet Karrot. For a green meal you can feel doubly good about, try New Leaf Café. Proceeds from this elegant restaurant go toward revitalization projects for Fort Tryon Park.

Frank's Market, 807-809 West 187th Street, near Fort Washington Avenue, (212-795-2929)

Hispaniola and Fumée, 839 West 181st Street, at Cabrini Boulevard, (212-740-5222)
  www.hispaniolarestaurant.com

Karrot, 854 West 181st Street, at Cabrini Boulevard, (212-740-4417)

New Leaf Café, 1 Margaret Corbin Drive, in Fort Tryon Park, (212-568-5323)
  www.nyrp.org/cafe

DRINK: Compared to most of the small storefronts around here, Cabrini Wines looks like a superstore. Locals love this place for maintaining a good selection in all price ranges, from the finest of the high-end to affordable and drinkable. It also does neighborhood delivery. No Parking was the neighborhood's first official gay bar and remains the official capital of the growing gay scene. But gay and straight of all races and ethnicities still mingle at Bleu Evolution and Monkey Room, especially in their shared melting pot of a backyard. Even though everyone's psyched about the Starbucks, Emilou's is the place to go if you want your coffee served with some neighborhood gossip.

Bleu Evolution, 808 West 187th Street, at Fort Washington Avenue, (212-928-6006)
  www.bleuevolutionnyc.com

Cabrini Wines, 831 West 181st Street, at Pinehurst Avenue, (212-568-3290)
  www.cabriniwines.com

Emilou's, 287 West 181st Street, between Pinehurst Avenue and Cabrini Boulevard,
  (212-795-2312)

Monkey Room, 589 Fort Washington Avenue, at 187th Street, (212-543-9888)

No Parking, 4168 Broadway, between 176th and 177th streets, (212-923-8700)

SHOP: Along with manicures, massages, and the best care your face can get, Sava Spa also serves as the neighborhood's one upscale boutique. In addition to the requisite skin-care products, you can also pick up high-end jewelry, hair accessories, clothing, paper goods, and more. Some items are made by Sava clients; all are hand-picked by the spa's fashionable owner, Joanna Czech. Her offerings will more than hold you over until your next trip down to Barney's. Even if blinis and smoked fish aren't your thing, Moscow on the Hudson is worth a visit, if only for the fascinating juxtaposition of this

Russian grocery in between a Starbucks and a Dominican deli.

Moscow on the Hudson, 801 West 181st Street, at Fort Washington Avenue, (212-740-7397)

Sava Spa, 211 Pinehurst Avenue, at 187th Street, (212-543-0888) www.savaspa.com

READ WASHINGTON HEIGHTS IN: *Wild Cowboys: Urban Marauders and the Forces of Order*, a Williams College sociology professor's account of the nearly two years in the early 1990s that he spent with the local Washington Heights police investigating violent crimes committed by a dangerous drug ring called the Wild Cowboys.

WEST VILLAGE

IN BRIEF: The West Village probably doesn't need much of an introduction. Not only does it top many people's list of neighborhoods they'd most like to live in, but unlike Manhattan's other gold coasts (yes, the West Village is most definitely a gold coast, even though it's downtown), this neighborhood is also a destination for people who don't live here—for dining, shopping, and those famous Magnolia cupcakes. Wandering the genteel streets trying to find a restaurant on Perry, Charles, Cornelia, or Jane, it's hard not to be seduced by the West Village.

Let's dissect that charm a little bit. There are historic brownstones and townhouses on unusually quiet side streets. There are large amounts of literary, cultural, and even Revolutionary War–era history. There is distance from hubs like Union Square—but not too much—and proximity to the river. There are wonderful restaurants, as well as great shopping and beautiful people to watch. It's a pretty picture, and if you live here—even in a fourth-floor walk-up rental on Bleecker—you get to be a part of it.

So presuming that you won't be inheriting a townhouse anytime soon, those walk-ups can be your way in. The West Village borders NYU and the New School, so there are a decent number of modest rentals right in the thick of things, just west of Sixth Avenue. (Tip: try looking in May and August.) A step above that are some nice-but-not-extravagant buildings on the blurry boundary between Greenwich Village and the West Village, around Christopher, Grove, and West 10th streets, between Sixth and Seventh avenues. The farther west you go, the fewer apartment buildings there are and the pricier things become.

This ascent happens fast, and it's easy to see on Bleecker Street. Between Macdougal and Christopher, it's casual and almost college-townish; west of there is like Madison Avenue South. Hudson Street is a bit more pleasant to shop and socialize on—less high fashion, and more casual hangouts, independent boutiques, and even a regular grocery store. It has the appealing feel of being both neighborhoody and populist at the same time, and can be a good reminder of the one thing that all West Village residents have in common: loving the West Village.

LOCATION: The West Village is bound by Sixth Avenue on the east and the Hudson River on the west, and like the East Village, 14th Street on the north and Houston Street on the south.

One of the most charming of the West Village's charming features is how its streets elegantly break out of the Manhattan grid, gently meandering away from Sixth and Seventh avenues toward the river; a good test for how well you know the neighborhood is if you can recite the order of the east-west streets from 14th Street to Houston. The farther east you are, the less likely you are to get lost, and the closer you are to public transportation. The West 4th Street station has a lot of good local and express possibilities; there's also the Christopher Street station for the 1 train, and on 14th Street, the L train. Greenwich Village, Tribeca, and the Meatpacking District are within walking distance, as is Hudson River Park. There's another teeny-tiny little park at the western end of Bleecker Street that attracts a lot of babies and dogs. For getting out of the city, there's the West Side Highway and the Holland Tunnel.

LIVE THERE FOR: GETTING AWAY FROM THE CHAINS. Deep in the West Village, you'll have the privilege of being spared the blight of Dunkin' Donuts and Duane Reade. Cool kids in the neighborhood get their prescriptions filled at Bigelow (also see page 181), where they can also pick up fancy European skin and body products.
Bigelow, 414 Sixth Avenue, at Ninth Street, (212-533-2700) www.bigelowchemists.com

KEEP LOOKING: IF YOU SPEND A LOT OF TIME IN DIFFERENT NEIGHBORHOODS. Deep in the West Village, walks to the subway can be long. Beautiful, but long. **IF YOU LIKE TO DRESS "CASUALLY."** The West Village has both impossibly chic members of the fashion police and outright gawkers right off the *Sex and the City* tour bus. You can still go out for milk and a paper in your sweatpants, but you probably wouldn't want to.

EAT: The best West Village restaurants are also tiny. If you can't get into perennially packed places like The Spotted Pig, The Little Owl, or Perilla, the owners of Snack Taverna will find a place to squeeze you in and make you feel like a regular. Resist the temptation to fill up on mezze as mains are equally scrumptious. (The restaurant delivers, too.) The beloved no-reservation, BYOB Tartine often has a line outside, but thanks to how closely the tables are packed in this tiny room, it actually goes quite quickly. It has a long menu with something for everyone, and one of the few places we can think of where it's truly pleasurable to be bumping elbows with your neighbors at the next table.

The Little Owl, 90 Bedford Street, by Grove Street, (212-741-4695) www.thelittleowlnyc.com

Perilla, 9 Jones Street, by West 4th Street, (212-929-6868) www.perillanyc.com

Snack Taverna, 63 Bedford Street, at Morton Street, (212-929-3499)

The Spotted Pig, 314 West 11th Street, at Greenwich Street, (212-620-0393)
     www.thespottedpig.com

Tartine, 253 West 11th Street, at West 4th Street, (212-229-2611)

DRINK: The White Horse Tavern is a drinking establishment as famous for its literary history as its longevity. Opened in 1880, it was just a regular pub until writers, artists, musicians, and beatniks started congregating there in the 1950s. Dylan Thomas, James Baldwin, Bob Dylan, Hunter S. Thompson, and Norman Mailer have all put in time here; and they say this is the place where the idea for the *Village Voice* was hatched. The coffee shop Joe now has several locations in Manhattan, but the one on Waverly Place is the original, and the only one that carries, from time to time, Amy Sedaris's homemade cupcakes. A lot of coffee bars in the city make excellent espresso drinks, but no one makes them prettier than Joe.

Joe, 141 Waverly Place, at Gay Street, (212-924-6750) www.joetheartofcoffee.com

The White Horse Tavern, 567 Hudson Street, at 11th Street, (212-243-9260)

SHOP: The West Village part of Bleecker Street is like a mini–Madison Avenue, full of posh designer stores (Marc Jacobs and Ralph Lauren take up a half-dozen storefronts between them) and upscale boutiques (Intermix, Olive & Bette's). But our money is usually on Greenwich Avenue, a renegade of a street that runs diagonally between 13th Street and Eighth Avenue and 8th Street and Sixth Avenue. The retail offerings here are fairly quirky as well, and it is also far less crowded on weekends than Bleecker. The original location of the hip travel store Flight 001 is here, and it remains the best source in the city for ingenious travel accessories (alarm clocks, guidebooks, passport holders, FAA-approved carry-on liquids). Its luggage selection isn't enormous, but what it lacks in variety it makes up for in style. Otte looks like it would be at home on Bleecker or Madison, but instead makes its home here on Greenwich Avenue; it sells fairly pricey women's clothing, but in a more subdued atmosphere than places like Scoop or Intermix. Most of the regular-priced merchandise is a splurge, but it does have good sales (there's a store in Williamsburg, too). In our opinion, MXYPLYZYK is one of the coolest stores in the city. It scores big points for being a fun home décor store with items that one can actually afford, housed in a space that New Yorkers can relate to (i.e., very cramped, with three tiny rooms); and it gets a bonus point for longevity (it's been there since 1992). The name comes from a character in Superman comics.

Flight 001, 96 Greenwich Avenue, at Jane Street, (212-691-1001) www.flight001.com

Intermix, 365 Bleecker Street, at Perry Street, (212-929-7180) www.intermixonline.com

Marc Jacobs, 298 and 301 West 4th Street, near Bank Street (212-206-6644); 382, 385,
and 403-405 Bleecker Street, between Perry and West 11th streets, (212-929-0304)
www.marcjacobs.com

mxyplyzyk, 125 Greenwich Avenue, by West 13th Street, (212-989-4300) www.mxyplyzyk.com

Olive & Bette's, 384 Bleecker Street, at Perry Street, (212-206-0036)
www.oliveandbettes.com

Otte, 121 Greenwich Avenue, between Horatio and Jane streets, (212-302-3007)
www.otteny.com

Ralph Lauren, 380, 381, and 390 Bleecker Street, all near Perry Street, (212-638-0684)
www.ralphlauren.com

READ THE WEST VILLAGE IN: While most of his poetry was written across the Atlantic, one of the great literary heroes of the West Village is Dylan Thomas, who famously spent his final night on earth drinking at the White Horse (he died at St. Vincent's Hospital). The West Village also makes an appearance in Michael Cunningham's *The Hours*, as the setting for the contemporary narrative.

BROOKLYN

BOERUM HILL, COBBLE HILL, CARROLL GARDENS

IN BRIEF: Is it three neighborhoods in one, or one neighborhood that can't decide on a name? Differences are impossible to distinguish with the naked eye, yet the despicable bastardization "Bococa" (Boerum Hill, Cobble Hill, Carroll Gardens) may have destroyed the possibility of a uniting hybrid name that everyone knows how to pronounce. To complicate matters further, while Cobble Hill and Carroll Gardens have long been known by those names, "Boerum Hill" is a more recent moniker, nudging this formerly undesirable part of the neighborhood away from the projects on its border, and closer conceptually to the other two. Today, the area as a whole looks less *Clockers* (which was set and shot in the nearby Gowanus projects) and more *The Squid and the Whale*.

Together, the three neighborhoods occupy about a twenty-block stretch south of Atlantic Avenue, between Fourth Avenue and the Brooklyn-Queens Expressway. Inside, the boundary lines between the three vary by who you ask, and although residents say there are definite differences in character between the three 'hoods, superficially they seem more similar than different: brownstones and townhouses on side streets, charming restaurants and quirky boutiques, a modest and useful amount of chain outlets, a couple of small pleasant parks, and a calm, safe-feeling—but not stuffy—atmosphere. If not for the green bulbs by the subway entrance, this could be a small town in New England, the Midwest, or anywhere else in the country.

The demographics, however, tell a different, more diverse, story. Carroll Gardens was primarily a working-class Italian neighborhood until a few decades ago (Al Capone was married there in 1918), and some of the old guard remains, as do some of its bakeries, restaurants, and social clubs. And the now highly desirable Boerum Hill was until recently a rough area, with the projects casting a long shadow over the rest of the neighborhood. More recently, Smith Street has tried to fashion itself as Brooklyn's French *quartier* (there's a great Bastille Day block party there), and there is some evidence of a small community of bona fide French-speaking ex-pats. Arabic writing can be seen on several storefronts on Atlantic Avenue, and there's a small artsy Scandinavian presence in Boerum Hill. And there's no homogeneity age-wise, either. While this is the close second (after Park Slope) for the title of Brooklyn's official family neighborhood, there are also plenty of young singles, as well as life-long veterans from the days before it went by Bococa. Despite the differences in the neighborhoods, everyone seems to get along; as one resident put it, the area's got "a great Cosby vibe."

LOCATION: Cobble Hill is the westernmost of the three neighborhoods, bordering Brooklyn Heights. Boerum Hill is east, adjacent to Park Slope, although the projects are in between them. Carroll Gardens is south of Cobble Hill, between Red Hook and the Gowanus Canal (an area that used to be as unattractive as it sounds but now is starting to be revitalized as well). The most convenient subway lines in the area are the F and G (which both make three stops on Smith Street). From Boerum Hill and Cobble Hill, it's possible to walk to the Hoyt-Schermerhorn (A, C) and the enormous Atlantic Avenue-Pacific Street hub (which has the 2, 3, 4, 5, B, D, M ,N, Q, and R, plus the LIRR), though Carroll Gardens is too far from Atlantic to call those stops "convenient." The F is the local lifeline to Manhattan; the G train would not likely be anyone's first choice in subway lines, but it's useful for getting around Brooklyn and into Queens.

LIVE THERE FOR: NICE NEIGHBORS. Though there is a bit of new construction here, much of the living takes place in townhouses that have been broken up into a few apartments, which seems to foster more neighborly inclinations than other settings. The friendliness extends outside buildings as well; "community" and "co-op" (as in food co-ops) are two more C's that get thrown in the Boerum Hill/Cobble Hill/Carroll Gardens talk, and people tend to be involved and interested in their neighborhood in a way that's not often found in Manhattan. **THE COBBLE HILL CINEMAS** has gone through several incarnations (it's been a kung fu theater, and part of the Clearview chain, among other things), but in its current form, it's hit a high note. Today it's an independently owned five-plex that shows a mix of mainstream first-runs, independent, and foreign films, intelligently curated to the specific tastes of the neighborhood (heavy on anything French, literary, quirky, or good for kids; light on horror, action, and blockbusters). **Cobble Hill Cinemas, 265 Court Street at Butler Street, (718-596-9113)**
www.cobblehilltheatre.com

KEEP LOOKING: IF YOU WORK ON THE EAST SIDE OF MANHATTAN, OR UPTOWN. It's hard to find anything really objectionable about this area, but one potential drawback is that there isn't a lot of choice for subways into Manhattan right in the neighborhood, and the F only connects with subways that go up the west side. While plenty of residents do use the trains at the Atlantic Avenue stop, the station is a considerable hike from a lot of the neighborhood, and quite unpleasant to navigate.

EAT: You won't starve; in fact, you may never need to cook at home again. The neighborhood is bursting at the seams with restaurants of all different kinds. Of the many good, casual Italian places Frankies 457 is our favorite, because it has a long menu of interesting crostini, salads, and antipasto, in addition to pasta and meat mains. Or you can sample the neighborhood's imported French cuisine at Bar Tabac, Robin des Bois (don't miss the garden!), Provence en Boite, and Patois (see page 217 for more on its brunch). There's also no shortage of places for cakes and sweets, with everything from old-time Italian bakeries and French patisseries to newer sweets shops like Sweet Melissa and One Girl Cookies.
Bar Tabac, 128 Smith Street, at Dean Street, (718-923-0918) www.bartabacny.com
Frankies 457, 457 Court Street, between 4th Place and Luquor Street, (718-403-0033)
www.frankiesspuntino.com
One Girl Cookies, 63 Dean Street, between Smith Street and Boerum Place, (212-675-4996)
www.onegirlcookies.com
Patois, 255 Smith Street, between Douglass and DeGraw streets, (718-855-1535)

Provence en Boite, 263 Smith Street, at DeGraw Street, (718-797-0707)
    www.provenceenboite.com
Robin des Bois, 195 Smith Street, between Warren and Baltic streets, (718-516-1609)
    www.sherwoodcafe.com
Sweet Melissa Patisserie, 276 Court Street, at Douglass Street, (718-855-3410)
    www.sweetmelissapatisserie.com

DRINK: Brooklyn Inn is a neighborhood bar that any neighborhood would love to have—but that would probably look out of place anywhere but the bucolic corner of Boerum Hill that it's on. The crowd is local—both true veteran and post-Giuliani transplants—but unlike many establishments with a heavy neighborhood clientele, newcomers are welcomed warmly. The drinks aren't fancy, but if you like beer, pool, and a jukebox, then you're set for life. (And even if you don't like any of those things, it's got a beautiful carved wooden bar that is lovely to sit at with any kind of drink.) If you mix up the names and accidentally end up at Brooklyn Social in Carroll Gardens instead, you'll still find a neighborhood crowd, but fewer old-timers and more transplants. Housed in a former Italian men's social club, it feels more venerable than many of the other bars on Smith Street. This is the place to go for cocktails and civilized conversation. On sweltering summer afternoons, head to a seasonal outdoor bar called the Gowanus Yacht Club. Try to get there early (and get over the annoyingly ironic name) so that you can enjoy your cheap beers and burgers in relative peace before the crowds descend.
Brooklyn Inn, 148 Hoyt Street, at Bergen Street, (718-625-9741)
Brooklyn Social, 335 Smith Street, at Carroll Street, (718-858-7758)
Gowanus Yacht Club, 323 Smith Street, at President Street, (718-246-1321)

SHOP: Shopping is a bit of a mixed bag in this 'hood. Most of the stores here are small boutiques, concentrated on Smith and Court streets, and many are independents and locally owned—which has its ups and downs. On Court Street, there's a bit of crunchy-looking fashion that looks like it came straight off a college campus (blousy dresses, woolly sweaters), while Smith has several boutiques whose merchandise looks a little too magazine-slick for this laidback 'hood. (One exception is Soula, an independent shoe store that clearly reflects the neighborhood's penchant for cool-but-not-too-flashy looks, with shoes for both men and women.) If you make the trip up to Atlantic Avenue, you'll be rewarded with two great finds. One is Opalia, a sweet little flower shop filled with antiques and glorious (but not extravagantly priced) arrangements. It also sells single stems, which make lovely no-reason gifts to a loved one (or to yourself). The other is Sir, which looks like it might be as snooty as those boutiques on Smith, but is every bit as warm as an indy store should be. (A recent visit found the shopkeeper sitting on the store's chaise longue mending her child's clothing.) The store carries the owner's own line, Sir, as well a small selection of pieces from other small labels, and some shoes and bags.

Opalia, 362 Atlantic Avenue, between Hoyt and Bond streets, (718-643-9160)
        www.opaliaflowers.com

Sir, 360 Atlantic Avenue, between Hoyt and Bond streets, (718-643-6877)
        www.sirbrooklyn.com

Soula, 185 Smith Street, between Wykoff and Warren streets, (718-834-8423)
        www.soulashoes.com

READ BOERUM HILL/COBBLE HILL/CARROLL GARDENS IN: If you can get through its 500-plus dense pages, *Fortress of Solitude* is an excellent fictional primer on this neighborhood. Written by native (and current) Brooklynite Jonathan Lethem, the novel is as much about the neighborhood as it is about the young protagonists growing up there, and illustrates the evolution of the area from the 1970s through the 1990s, including racial tensions and gentrification; it even proposes a scenario for how the name "Boerum Hill" came about.

BROOKLYN HEIGHTS

IN BRIEF: With a heritage stretching back to the early nineteenth century, Brooklyn Heights is one of Brooklyn's very oldest residential neighborhoods, and much of its charm today stems from its history. In the 1830s and 1840s, Brooklyn Heights was Manhattan's first commuter satellite town, an expensive and gentrified neighborhood whose imposing and austere brownstones were built to be occupied by wealthy city types who were ferried to and from Wall Street in a steamboat. A century or so later, the area became the first to be protected under the New York Landmarks Preservation laws, thanks to which the stunningly beautiful blocks in its historic district still exist in all their glory.

The neighborhood also has a venerable old character, the result of an older demographic and of the sense you have, inspired by the buildings and the peace of the surroundings, that Brooklyn Heights continues in the era and the mindset of its creation. Fewer of its grand old townhouses have been divided into apartments than in Carroll Gardens or Park Slope, and the neighborhood attracts a well-off family crowd with an eye for permanence. But there are still places here and there for the younger and less affluent, and if you enjoy peace and quiet and an idyllic, kids-selling-lemonade-on-the-sidewalk ambience, it can be a wonderful place to live. The neighborhood's star attraction is the Esplanade, the wooden walkway that rises above the docks along the Brooklyn shore and stretches out across the East River from downtown Manhattan, with extraordinary views of the city, the bridges, and the water around.

LOCATION: Brooklyn Heights occupies the space along the Brooklyn coast between Dumbo and Red Hook, beginning at the Brooklyn Bridge and stretching down toward the industrial end of Smith Street—Carroll Gardens and Boerum Hill are its neighbors to the east, and Jay Street is its northern boundary. Perfectly situated on the river across from Lower Manhattan, Brooklyn Heights enjoys what its residents would say are the most beautiful views in the borough, from the city skyline down to the Statue of Liberty and out across the water beyond. The neighborhood is pretty well served by the 2 and C trains (and the transit hub at Borough Hall is walkable), as well as the arterial B61 bus, and is near enough to Jay Street, the Brooklyn Bridge, and the Brooklyn-Queens Expressway to be easily accessible whatever time of day or night.

LIVE THERE FOR: THE MOST BEAUTIFUL STREETS IN THE CITY. In the pretty blocks of its historic district, Brooklyn Heights contains some of the warmest and most inviting tree-lined streets and the most gorgeous buildings imaginable, from majestic brownstone mansions to pastel-colored townhouses with overflowing front yards. Even the street names themselves are quaintly romantic—Pineapple, Willow, Cranberry, and Montague, to name a few—and the Esplanade is the icing on the cake.

KEEP LOOKING: IF YOU'RE NOT QUITE READY TO SETTLE DOWN YET. Brooklyn Heights isn't as frenetic a meeting ground of strollers and nannies as Park Slope or Carroll Gardens, but only because a lot of its little ones are all grown up and have moved to the city, leaving their parents to tend the yards. Brooklyn Heights is a quiet, family-oriented neighborhood, and has been since the nineteenth century. For fun and games the neighborhood's livelier residents head across the river or out into the busier scenes of Atlantic Avenue, Park Slope, and Williamsburg.

EAT: While Brooklyn Heights can't compete with Park Slope or Williamsburg as a destination for the borough's diners, there are a handful of favorites that are great enough to warrant a visit whether you live here or not. The Atlantic Avenue branch of Chip Shop, Brooklyn's homage to the deep-fried cuisine of the British Isles, has the best fish and chips and the juiciest battered sausage in the city (and deep-fried battered

Mars bars for after). The blintzes at Teresa's Restaurant are legendary, and the spot is especially interesting for being the best Polish café in Brooklyn without even being in Greenpoint. And the Brooklyn Ice Cream Factory, down by the water beneath the bridge, is as fun and romantic a taste of old-school Brooklyn as you can find.

Brooklyn Ice Cream Factory, 1 Water Street, at the East River, (718-246-3963)

Chip Shop, 129 Atlantic Avenue, between Clinton and Henry streets, (718-855-7774)
    www.chipshopnyc.com

Teresa's Restaurant, 80 Montague Street, at Hicks Street, (718-797-3996)

DRINK: Henry Street Ale House is one of the few decent bars in Brooklyn Heights proper; anybody looking for a livelier drink should head to Atlantic Avenue at the edgier edge of the neighborhood. All the action is on Atlantic, from the tastefully rowdy Pete's Waterfront Ale House to Last Exit and Floyd, the nicest of the few bars in the city to boast a bocce court where the pool table should be.

Floyd, 131 Atlantic Avenue, between Henry and Clinton streets, (718-858-5810) www.floydny.com

Henry Street Ale House, 62 Henry Street, near Orange Street, (718-522-5801)

Last Exit, 136 Atlantic Avenue, between Henry and Clinton streets, (718-222-9198)
    www.lastexitbar.com

Pete's Waterfront Ale House, 155 Atlantic Avenue, between Henry and Clinton streets,
    (718-522-3794) www.waterfrontalehouse.com

SHOP: Brooklyn Heights has a reputation as one of the best neighborhoods in the city for furniture scavengers: trawl the streets on weekends and recycling nights and you can find enough pieces of other people's old furniture to fill your own deplorably underfurnished pad. It makes sense, then, that the only Brooklyn outpost of the city's legendary Housing Works thrift store chain is in the Heights. As well as a fine selection of thrift furniture, Housing Works also carries everything from second-hand clothes to used books and records, and in a neighborhood like Brooklyn Heights the donations can be better than anything you'd pick up in Manhattan.

Housing Works, 122 Montague Street, near Henry Street, (718-237-0521)
    www.housingworksauctions.com

READ BROOKLYN HEIGHTS IN: *A House on the Heights*, Truman Capote's nostalgic mini-memoir of his "quiet" period on Willow Street. Things have changed a little in the near half-century since Capote lived there, but the neighborhood still has the feel of a bygone era, still functions as its own little world, and still bears many of the contradictions of character Capote observed back then.

DUMBO

IN BRIEF: An important commercial neighborhood around what were Brooklyn's busiest docks in the nineteenth century, Dumbo—an acronym for "Down Under the Manhattan Bridge Overpass"—enjoyed a renaissance in the 1990s when artists and architects transformed its beautiful industrial buildings into apartments, lofts, and studios. While traces of old Brooklyn remain in the warehouses by the East River, in the cobbled roads and long disused trolley tracks, and in the forgotten residential streets of Vinegar Hill by the Navy Yard, the artsy community has given way to inevitably escalating prices and a fairly yuppie-ish atmosphere. The neighborhood is still a stronghold of Brooklyn artists—the Dumbo Arts Center keeps that side of the community alive with yearlong programs that include workshops, open studios, and the Art Under the Bridge Festival, an annual event that reclaims the area's post-industrial landscape as a playground for public installations. Surprisingly, Dumbo retains a rare serenity—in spite of its morphing status and expanding population, it's less of a destination for drinkers and diners than its neighbors on the Brooklyn coast, Boerum Hill and Williamsburg. Happily, Dumbo remains a neighborhood more for locals than for visitors.

LOCATION: Dumbo boasts one of the best locations in Brooklyn: on the waterfront, within walking distance of all of Downtown Brooklyn, and a short train ride away from downtown Manhattan. The neighborhood's borders are defined by the Brooklyn Bridge on the south side, by Vinegar Hill's Hudson Avenue on the north edge, and by Sands and Tillary streets on the way east toward Jay Street and Downtown Brooklyn. But it's the vaults and arches of the city's most celebrated bridges that define the area, framing one of Brooklyn's finest green spaces as they cut into the borough, and standing as eternal monuments to the lights and life of Manhattan across the East River.

LIVE THERE FOR: EMPIRE-FULTON FERRY STATE PARK, the beautiful and underexploited sliver of green land on the waterfront between the Manhattan and Brooklyn bridges. More people stare down at the park from trains trundling across the bridges than actually take the time to go there, which means that in spite of its beauty and unrivaled views of the city, it's one of Brooklyn's most peaceful parks. Movies are screened here from July through September, and orchestras serenade the park from a boat moored in the East River during the summer's Bargemusic program. But all year-round the park is a stone-skipping, toddler-paddling, sunbathing, people-watching treat.

KEEP LOOKING: IF YOU NEED YOUR ACTION ON YOUR DOORSTEP. For a neighborhood with rents and prices as high as they are, Dumbo offers comparatively little in the way of indulgences and amenities for its residents. Its industrial buildings have invited more galleries and furniture warehouses into the area than delis, cafés, or smaller stores—at the time of writing there is only one bookstore, one gym, and a couple of places for coffee in Dumbo—and unless you're lucky enough to fall in love with the bars and restaurants that dot Water and Front streets, you're likely to spend most of your fun time in Dumbo's busier downtown neighbors or across the river in Manhattan.

EAT: Although Dumbo isn't entirely starved of restaurants—there's Bubby's for brunch by the river, the Water Street Restaurant and Lounge for lunch in rustic and old-fashioned surroundings, and Pete's Downtown for good Italian suppers—the Jacques Torres Chocolate shop on Water Street is a luxury among Dumbo's underfed streets. The first of "Mr. Chocolate"'s three New York locations (the others are in Tribeca and on the Upper West Side), the store adjoins the factory, so while sitting at one of the café's tables you can peer inside and see the magic at work. It's the perfect place to find a good dessert after dinner, a warming cup of hot chocolate in the colder months, or just a sweet snack on your way around the neighborhood.

Bubby's, 1 Main Street, at Empire-Fulton Ferry State Park, (718-222-0666) www.bubbys.com

Jacques Torres Chocolate, 66 Water Street, between Main and Dock streets,
   (718-875-9772) www.mrchocolate.com

Pete's Downtown, 2 Water Street, at Old Fulton Street, (718-858-3510)

Water Street Restaurant and Lounge, 66 Water Street, between Main and Dock streets,
   (718-625-9352) www.waterstreetrestaurant.com

DRINK: Superfine on Front Street remains Dumbo's most popular watering hole. A cavernous bar beneath the Manhattan Bridge, Superfine has a generous happy hour, a pool table, and a tasty Mediterranean-flavored bar menu, as well as sofas, stools, and a surprising range of eccentric four-leggers to suit every behind.

Superfine, 126 Front Street, at Pearl Street, (718-243-9005)

SHOP: The powerHouse Arena on Main Street is one of Brooklyn's treasures. Relocated from Tribeca in 2006 and housing the offices of powerHouse publishers, the vast gallery is a great bookstore by day and a trendy venue for photography exhibitions and book-launch parties by night.

powerHouse Arena, 37 Main Street, between Water and Front streets, (718-666-3049)
   www.powerhousearena.com

SEE DUMBO IN: Sergio Leone, master of the Western epic and creator of some of twentieth-century cinema's most iconoclastic films, shot parts of *Once Upon a Time in America* in the streets of Brooklyn. While much of the movie takes place in Williamsburg, young Dominic's tragic murder at the hands of Bugsy after a chase through Dumbo's cobblestone lanes is one of the film's most memorable sequences. The view from Washington Street of the Manhattan Bridge rising boldly between the red-brick buildings of Water Street hasn't changed much since the film's production in 1983 and remains an iconic glimpse of Prohibition-era New York.

FORT GREENE AND CLINTON HILL

IN BRIEF: Despite an embarrassment of beautiful landmarked buildings and a central near-Manhattan location, the Fort Greene/Clinton Hill area feels sleepier and a bit less put-upon than the other 'hoods of "Brownstone Brooklyn." Streets aren't crowded, restaurants don't look like they're trying as hard, and if you're into churches, you'll love it here—storefront parishes outnumber indie boutiques handily. (Not to mention the amazing-looking Brooklyn Masonic Temple on Lafayette and Clermont, which we recommend even devout atheists visit at least once—if only to catch one of its live music shows held regularly.)

One reason that this neighborhood hasn't been overrun by young professionals is its location adjacent to the famously dangerous neighborhood of Bedford-Stuyvesant, and the existence of housing projects interspersed with the historic townhouses. Neighborhood residents boast about the ethnic mix, but the socioeconomic diversity is way more stark, and the neighborhood definitely still feels a bit rough around the edges. This is literally true on Myrtle Avenue, the neighborhood's northern commercial strip. Here, the juxtaposition between the old guard and the new one is vivid, with a cheap supermarket, no-frills bodegas, laundries, and check-cashing places sharing the street with newish cafés with artsy décors, a yoga studio, and a swanky nail salon called the Polish Bar of Brooklyn. DeKalb Avenue, the other major commercial strip, is the fancy one, with a wine store and an organic juice bar alongside the cafés and yoga.

Aside from these storefronts and the occasional student housing or project building, the area looks like the setting for a Henry James novel. Because so many of the buildings here are landmarked, there's virtually no new residential development, and it's all brownstones, townhouses, and mansions as far as the eye can see, whose architectural diversity rivals the racial and ethnic mix. In terms of architecture and ambience, it's hard to think of a better place to be.

Fort Greene Park provides the requisite green space, as well as a weekly Greenmarket on Saturdays. There's also the Pratt campus, with its outdoor sculpture and a cool new architecture building designed by Steven Holl Architects. Dogs are popular here; babies not so much, at least compared to some other nearby neighborhoods. And lest a potential resident wonder if everyone is here because they couldn't get into name-brand hoods, it doesn't seem like this was anyone's second choice. Walking around, you get the distinct sense that everyone is very happy to be living here.

Brooklyn Masonic Temple, 37 Clermont Avenue at Lafayette Street, (718-857-3885) www.brooklynmasonictemple.com

LOCATION: Fort Greene and Clinton Hill are two adjacent neighborhoods that extend roughly south from the Brooklyn Navy Yard to Atlantic Avenue, with Fort Greene on the east side and Clinton Hill on the west. Located southeast of the Manhattan Bridge, the neighborhoods are sort of in "east-central Brooklyn," south of Williamsburg and the Brooklyn-Queens Expressway, and north of Prospect Park. It's much closer to Manhattan than neighborhoods like Park Slope and Carroll Gardens, though subway access isn't the best, which makes it feel farther away if you've got a regular commute. On the other hand, taking a cab or a car service into the city isn't cripplingly expensive. The Brooklyn Academy of Music, the Atlantic Avenue transit hub (for both the subway and the LIRR), and the Atlantic Terminal Mall (home of the famous Brooklyn Target) are within walking distance—a longish walk, but a pretty one, if you choose the right street. (Try South Elliott.)

LIVE THERE FOR: STOOP SALES. Fittingly, this stoop-filled neighborhood is also a thriving district for stoop sales. From early spring through late fall, they're all over, some advertised with chalk-written directions on the sidewalk or lamppost signs. (We once saw this sign posted on lampposts all over the neighborhood: "The divorce is final, the sale is on!" Admirably cathartic.) DINING AL FRESCO. Like most of the first-floor (garden-level) apartments here, just about every restaurant around this neighborhood has a backyard. The best of the bunch is the unusually uncramped garden at iCi. The food is also a step above the numerous other bistros-with-gardens in the neighborhood, with a focus on seasonal ingredients befitting a restaurant that showcases its outdoor space. But prices are still casual, and you don't need a reservation on a weekday night, making it a perfect garden at which to become a regular.

iCi, 246 DeKalb Avenue, at Vanderbilt Avenue, (718-789-2778) www.icirestaurant.com

KEEP LOOKING: IF YOU NEED YOUR SUBWAY TO RUN LIKE CLOCKWORK. Fort Greene and Clinton Hill feel more remote than they actually are because neighborhood subway transport depends on the erratic dwarf-size G train. When the G is being sluggish or running in sections, there's also the Clinton-Washington and Lafayette Avenue stops on the C. Atlantic Avenue is a hike, but you can get pretty much any train there, as well as the LIRR. There are car services, but if you can make it to Flatbush, cabs are easy to flag down, and you can get over the Manhattan Bridge to the Lower East Side, Nolita, or the East Village for about $10.

EAT: Charming little bistros are a dime a dozen in this neighborhood; some (like the previously mentioned iCi) are better than others. When you are craving something more exotic, check out Madiba, the only South African restaurant in the city. If "bunny chow" (a kind of curried bread) is not your thing, it also has excellent mojitos. Though it's technically a branch of a Manhattan joint (see page 56), Habana Outpost is still one-of-a-kind. It proudly proclaims itself to be the city's first "eco-eatery," but that hardly scratches the surface of this indoor-outdoor restaurant-flea-market-community gathering-space's quirkiness. A solar-paneled awning provides much of the 'post's juice, outdoor benches are made from recycled lumber, and it's got a bike-powered blender (customers get a dollar off if they blend their own drinks). Meanwhile, consumption of everything else besides energy abounds: Latin food and drinks served out of a stationary food truck outside, on biodegradable plates made from cornstarch. Movies, clothing sales, and art shows all take place there as well.

Habana Outpost, 757 Fulton Street, at South Portland Avenue, (718-858-9500)
    www.ecoeatery.com
Madiba,195 DeKalb Avenue, between Carlton Avenue and Adelphi Street, (718-855-9190)
    www.madibarestaurant.com

DRINK: Alibi is a true dive bar and local hangout, not for the faint of heart; an easier initiation to the neighborhood might be found at Moe's (guess who it's named for). The Stonehome Wine Bar is great for a drink before or after BAM, when Moe's is too packed, or you need to stop your spending at Stuart & Wright (see page 88) next door. When you are drinking at home, Thirst and The Greene Grape are two sweet neighborhood wine shops. (The Greene Grape also delivers.)

Alibi, 242 DeKalb Avenue, at Vanderbilt Avenue, (718-783-8519)
**The Greene Grape, 765 Fulton Street, between South Portland Avenue and South Oxford
    Street, (718-797-9463) www.greenegrape.com**
Moe's, 80 Lafayette Avenue, at South Portland Avenue, (718-797-9536)

The Stonehome Wine Bar, 87 Lafayette Avenue, between South Elliott Place and

South Portland Avenue, (718-624-9443) www.stonehomewinebar.com

Thirst, 187 DeKalb Avenue, at Carlton Avenue, (718-596-7643) www.thirstwinemerchants.com

SHOP: Since stoop sales are the neighborhood's favorite way to shop, and it's hard to plug a local boutique when dresses and lamps are going for $2 on the street. On the other hand, for those used to shopping in Manhattan, a boutique that looks like it belongs in Soho save for the attitude straight out of Kansas should not be overlooked. The clothes at Stuart & Wright are not cheap (*NYLON* magazine called it "the Barneys of Fort Greene"), but they're not boring either, and the friendly owners are an added perk to purchasing (as one of your authors can attest to, having been unable to resist buying a bag there. Research!). For the home, RePop is a kooky store near the Brooklyn Navy Yard that sells vintage furniture, home décor, and collectibles to give your brownstone apartment that perfect flair of kitsch. (It sells clothes, too.)

RePop, 68 Washington Avenue, between Flushing and Park avenues, (718-260-8032)

www.repopny.com

Stuart & Wright, 85 Lafayette Avenue, between South Elliott Place and South Portland

Avenue, (718-797-0011) www.stuartandwright.com

SEE FORT GREENE IN: *She's Gotta Have It.* This is Spike Lee's home turf, so it's fitting that the neighborhood played a part in the film that launched his career.

GREENPOINT

IN BRIEF: Greenpoint is the dark horse of residential Brooklyn. A little over twenty years ago, the warehouses and townhouses of this historic shipbuilding neighborhood were the first on Brooklyn's west coast to feel the gentrification that would later spread down to Red Hook. Its beautiful historic brownstone blocks began to draw families from the city, and its former industrial buildings became havens for artists and designers before the warehouses of Dumbo had opened their doors. Having risen early to the call of yuppiedom, however, the neighborhood's relative seclusion proved to be its savior—or its downfall, depending on how you look at it. While Williamsburg and the more accessible parts of Downtown Brooklyn soon took over as the borough's most sought-after locations, Greenpoint's transformation was arrested and the area has retained much of its former character as a lively and inclusive residential neighborhood.

With a heritage that includes large numbers of Irish, Italian, Puerto Rican, and predominantly Polish immigrants since the middle of the nineteenth century, Greenpoint is also among the most ethnically mixed areas in western Brooklyn. Still referred to as "Little Poland," Greenpoint is thought to be the second-largest Polish enclave in the United States after Chicago, and everything in the neighborhood—from its delis and restaurants to the number of blue eyes you'll pass in the streets—reminds you of that. Along with unusually diverse architecture, Greenpoint's cultural heritage remains one of its most charming aspects.

While some point to Greenpoint's resistance to gentrification as a strength in community, others are stymied by the area's limited cultural and commercial development relative to its hipper neighbors farther south. Manhattan Avenue, the area's main drag, can seem like a down-market strip of discount stores and markets to anyone more attuned to the hipster bars and cute boutiques of the borough's trendier neighborhoods. But after the highly publicized rezoning of much of the area in 2005 from manufacturing to residential, Greenpoint is once again on the rise among the younger contingent, and with plans under way to develop a park along the waterfront it will soon be more widely known as one of Brooklyn's most attractive neighborhoods.

LOCATION: Bordering Williamsburg at McCarren Park to the southeast and otherwise defined by the East River and Newtown Creek, Greenpoint is waterfront Brooklyn's last stand before Long Island City and the expanse of Queens to the north. Situated directly across the water from Murray Hill and lower Midtown East, the neighborhood enjoys some of Brooklyn's finest views of the Manhattan skyline and the city's most beautiful sunsets. But like Red Hook down the coast, Greenpoint is notoriously poorly served by the MTA, with only a handful of buses making it to the tip of the borough and the untrustworthy little G train its only link to the subway. Sandwiched between Williamsburg and Long Island City, however, the neighborhood is just accessible enough to make it among Brooklyn's more affordable residential areas—and when you finally do get yourself to a train, Greenpoint's cooler neighbors are only minutes away.

LIVE THERE FOR: PEACE AND PIEROGI. The tree-lined blocks that run between Manhattan Avenue and the East River are just as beautiful as any in Brooklyn Heights or Park Slope, the waterfront is wonderful for strolls on lazy Sunday afternoons, and the area boasts some of the most interesting old buildings in Brooklyn—look out for the Polish and Russian churches, the McCarren Pool, and the old Merchants and Traders Bank among others. While the neighborhood is already soaking up hipster excess from Williamsburg, it's still a little off the beaten trendy track. And if you have a taste for Eastern European food, there are enough markets, delis, and Polish cafeterias to keep you in kielbasa for years.

KEEP LOOKING: IF WALKING ISN'T YOUR FORTE. You have to be brave to rely on the sporadic G train and the B61 bus, and even then Greenpoint is a walker's neighborhood with the prettier residential blocks a fair distance from either. Getting into Manhattan can be a lot of effort, particularly on weekends when MTA services are most likely to be disrupted and more crowded. Some of the perks of the neighborhood lie in its seclusion, and a lot of the best nearby action from shopping to movies, venues, and non-Polish restaurants is to be found in neighboring areas. So if the thought of a long walk down into Williamsburg or up into Long Island City doesn't appeal to you, maybe Greenpoint isn't the place.

EAT: When in Little Poland, do as the Polish do . . . . Another phrase to remember about eating out in Greenpoint is that you can't judge a book by its cover. A lot of the Polish restaurants in the neighborhood look like cafeterias, with little decoration and a fondness for plastic chairs and tabletops, and it's not uncommon to line up for counter service from a matronly woman in a hair net. But you shouldn't let this put you off: the standard of food is pretty high across the board, and it's reassuring to see that the locals give the neighborhood joints their seal of approval. Menus don't change much from one place to another, with simple Polish staples such as pierogi, kielbasa, pork cutlets, mashed potatoes, beets, Greek-style salads, and sauerkraut always available for very reasonable prices. Surround yourself with Polish locals at the intensely nationalistic Antek; share a table at the lively Christina's for lunch; and try Lomzynianka for just about the most upscale Polish supper in the neighborhood.

Antek, 105 Norman Avenue, at Leonard Street, (718-389-6859)

Christina's Polish Restaurant, 853 Manhattan Avenue, between Milton and Noble streets, (718-389-1516)

Lomzynianka, 846 Manhattan Avenue, between Milton and Noble streets, (718-389-9439)
www.lomzynianka.com

DRINK: Beware the Eurotrash Polish dance clubs . . . . Instead, Mark, Matchless, Lyric Lounge, and Enid's are all good bars in the comfortable Brooklyn mold, with cozy wood interiors, cozy indie jukeboxes, and a dependable mix of new-hipster and old-man clientele. But The Pencil Factory is the neighborhood's best, a reformed social club that catered to dockworkers back when shipping was the focus of Greenpoint and which is now home to the more discretionary artsy crowd. The look and feel of the place is unquestionably Greenpoint: brick walls, dusty hardwood floors, a spacious post-industrial vibe, and a whiskey collection to rival any bar in the city.

Barmatchless, 557 Manhattan Avenue, at Driggs Avenue, (718-383-5333)

    www.barmatchless.com

Enid's, 560 Manhattan Avenue, at Driggs Avenue, (718-349-3859)

Lyric Lounge, 278 Nassau Street, at Morgan Avenue, (718-349-7017)

The Mark Bar, 1025 Manhattan Avenue, between Freeman and Green streets,

    (718-349-2340) www.themarkbar.com

The Pencil Factory, 142 Franklin Street, at Greenpoint Avenue, (718-609-5858)

SHOP: Secondhand. While the recent arrival of Greenpoint's first Starbucks on Manhattan Avenue might signal a shift toward a more mainstream future, the neighborhood's best shopping still exists in a handful of vintage clothing boutiques, independent bookstores, and record shops tucked away between the avenues. Word is a handsome and cozy bookshop with a selection that caters to the indie-minded and can save you a trip to Williamsburg or the city. Alter is a clever boutique with a fluid range of hipster-ish menswear and womenswear, much of which is reconstructed from vintage clothing and fabrics. Permanent Records and Eat Records keep vinyl alive with concise but varying archives of rock, indie, punk, and reggae records—and you can also grab a bite in Eat while you browse. And The Thing, a diamond in the rough of Manhattan Avenue's 99-cent stores, has a basement full of more records than you're likely to see in a lifetime. While prices are absurdly low for everything from rare 7-inch singles to Jimmy Buffet albums, the records are completely unorganized in stacks and crates, so shopping there is something of a treasure hunt. And it's seriously dusty—people have been known to strap on a surgical mask before heading downstairs.

Alter, 109 Franklin Street, between Greenpoint Avenue and Milton Street, (718-784-8818)

Eat Records, 124 Meserole Avenue, at Leonard Street, (718-389-8083)

Permanent Records, 181 Franklin Street, between Green and Huron streets, (718-383-4083)

The Thing, 1001 Manhattan Avenue, between Green and Huron streets, (718-349-8234)

Word Books, 126 Franklin Street, at Milton Street, (718-383-0096) www.wordbrooklyn.com

SEE GREENPOINT IN: *Third Watch* and *Rescue Me* on the small screen. Scenes from gangster classics *Donnie Brasco* and *The Departed* were also filmed on the green streets of Brooklyn's quietest waterfront 'hood.

PARK SLOPE

IN BRIEF: Park Slope's checkered history is something of a riches-to-rags-and-back-to-riches story. First developed into a residential community in the mid-nineteenth century, its spectacular brownstone mansions and proximity to Prospect Park meant that by the turn of the century, it had become one of America's richest neighborhoods. As residential Brooklyn grew and became more affordable, its exclusivity diminished and its richer residents moved out to Long Island and other suburbs, and by the 1950s Park Slope was left an underdeveloped working-class neighborhood. Today, its oldest brownstone blocks protected among New York's historic landmarks, Park Slope thrives as one of Brooklyn's busiest and most community-minded neighborhoods.

Its regeneration over the last two decades has also attracted a diverse and intelligent crowd. As well as being home to a large gay and lesbian community and a popular place for new parents, Park Slope is celebrated for being home to many of Brooklyn's best-known actors and authors, from John Turturro and Steve Buscemi to Kathryn Harrison and Jonathan Safran Foer. The prevalent attitude in the neighborhood is liberal and active. Park Slope is full of organic produce shops and boasts the city's largest cooperative organic grocery store on Union Street—as well as a successful Greenmarket at Grand Army Plaza. You'll often come across book groups in the neighborhood's many good coffee shops (the Tea Lounge on Union Street deserves a special mention here), and there's no shortage of community activity, from artists trying to control redevelopment of the Gowanus Canal to block parties, the ubiquitous stoop sales, and local participation in events in Prospect Park.

Tea Lounge, 837 Union Street, between 6th and 7th Avenues, (718-789-2762)

LOCATION: Park Slope borders Prospect Park for roughly twenty-five blocks along Prospect Park West (or Ninth Avenue, as longtime residents still sometimes call it), and extends westward as far as Fourth Avenue and the Gowanus Canal, which divides the neighborhood from Red Hook, Boerum Hill, and Carroll Gardens. Flatbush Avenue to the north separates Park Slope from Jay Street and Downtown Brooklyn, while 15th Street and Prospect Park Southwest define the end of the neighborhood and the beginning of Windsor Terrace. Sandwiched between the park and the canal, the neighborhood has an organic identity to match its eclectic and discriminating population. Well connected to the city with trains and bus routes and easily accessible from the Brooklyn-Queens Expressway, Park Slope is both practical and peaceful and is without a doubt among the most pleasant neighborhoods in New York.

LIVE THERE FOR: THE PARK. For many, Prospect Park is New York's most beautiful and enjoyable green space. Its designers, Frederick Law Olmsted and Calvin Vaux, also created Central Park, but felt that they had succeeded better in Brooklyn. Bordering several distinct neighborhoods, the park itself has come to reflect the diversity of the population, and has everything from playgrounds and sports fields to spectacular waterways, an ice rink in the winter, a wildlife conservation area in the ravine, and a dog pond. Even if your daily routine doesn't include a walk around Long Meadow with a Labrador straining at the leash, as it seems to for most Park Slopers, the air is noticeably fresher, you're able to enjoy even the briefest of New York springs and falls, and the whole feel of the neighborhood benefits from its presence.

KEEP LOOKING: IF THE SIGHT OF STROLLERS IN THE MORNING PUTS YOU OFF. With beautiful houses, the park and its many playgrounds, myriad amenities, and several good schools in the area, Park Slope has become Brooklyn's most popular place to raise a family. The neighborhood's sidewalks are frequently jammed with strollers and crisscrossed with leashes, and this, combined with steadily escalating rents, means that Park Slope is losing favor among Brooklyn's bachelor contingent, who might find more like-minded neighbors in Dumbo, Red Hook, or Williamsburg.

EAT: Park Slope is a major destination for eating and drinking in Brooklyn—Fifth and Seventh avenues, Park Slope's two main strips, are full of bars, cafés, and restaurants ranging from diners to sushi bars. Applewood on 11th Street is the best of the brunch bunch, a charming rustic restaurant with innovative takes on classic American breakfasts. A whole host of French restaurants on Fifth Avenue are great places for lunch, Moutarde being one of the best. And Convivium Osteria, the Portuguese-and-Italian restaurant at the Flatbush end of Fifth Avenue, is simply one of the best in the city—it's especially romantic downstairs, and meat lovers need to try the porterhouse steak.

Applewood, 501 11th Street, between Seventh and Eighth avenues, (718-768-2044)
   www.applewoodny.com
Convivium Osteria, 68 Fifth Avenue, between Bergen Street and St. Mark's Place,
   (718-857-1833) www.convivium-osteria.com
Moutarde, 239 Fifth Avenue, at Carroll Street, (718-623-3600)

DRINK: The nicest thing about drinking in Park Slope is the number of gardens and patios there are. The Gate and Bar Reis are Fifth Avenue staples, each with its own private garden and each with a great range of beers and Brooklyn ales. Total Wine Bar, also on Fifth, is something of a hidden treasure, a quiet wine bar with an amazing cellar and close seating that makes for a uniquely cozy atmosphere. Barbès on Ninth Street is a tiny, lively bar with a back room for surprising events from film screenings to music recitals. And at the neighborhood's southernmost edge, Buttermilk is one of the most fun bars in Park Slope. The jukebox is brilliant, it has board games behind the bar, there's a photo booth in the back, it hosts the best pub quiz in Brooklyn, and it orders in free pizza on Sunday evenings. What could be better than that?

Barbès, 376 9th Street, at Sixth Avenue, (718-965-9177) www.barbes-brooklyn.com

Bar Reis, 375 Fifth Avenue, between 5th and 6th streets, (718-832-5716)

Buttermilk, 577 Fifth Avenue, at 16th Street, (718-788-6297)

The Gate, 321 Fifth Avenue, at 3rd Street, (718-768-4329)

Total Wine Bar, 75 Fifth Avenue, at St. Marks Place, (718-783-5166) www.totalwinebar.com

SHOP: Since the arrival of Barnes and Noble on Seventh Avenue and the development of the Atlantic Center Mall at the corner of Atlantic and Fourth avenues, some of the smaller neighborhood stores have disappeared—but Park Slope still has a few gems for shoppers. Bird on Seventh Avenue is a cute designer boutique, and there's an outpost of Williamsburg's biggest vintage clothing store Beacon's Closet on Fifth Avenue. On weekends the playground of P.S. 321 is transformed into a charming flea market, with everything from second-hand furniture to clothes, books, records, and rugs. The Community Bookstore remains one of the very best independent bookshops in Brooklyn.

Beacon's Closet, 220 Fifth Avenue, between President and Union streets, (718-230-1630)
   www.beaconscloset.com

Bird, 430 Seventh Avenue, between 14th and 15th streets, (718-768-4940)
   www.shopbird.com

Community Bookstore, 143 Seventh Avenue, between Carroll and Garfield streets,
   (718-783-3075) www.cbjupiterbooks.com

PS 321, 180 Seventh Avenue at 2nd Street, (718-499-2412) www.ps321.org

READ PARK SLOPE IN: As part and parcel of being home to many of Brooklyn's most celebrated authors, Park Slope finds its way into a lot of books based in the borough. Pete Hamill's wonderful *A Drinking Life* paints a stark picture of Park Slope half a century ago, while you'll come across impressions of a more contemporary Slope in novels by local authors Jennie Fields, Paul Auster, and Nicole Krauss, to name but a few.

RED HOOK

IN BRIEF: Had we written this book ten or fifteen years ago, Red Hook might not have made the cut as a neighborhood worth considering as a place to live. One of the least accessible places in Brooklyn, Red Hook was also for a long time thought of as one of the roughest, with high crime rates and block after block of derelict and abandoned buildings leading up to largely unused docks at the waterfront. Today, with a Fairway supermarket, an Ikea store, and a growing number of shops, bars, and restaurants, the neighborhood is on the cusp of reaching the kind of yuppification that has transformed Williamsburg, Dumbo, and Greenpoint. Until it reaches that point, however, Red Hook is a surprisingly fun neighborhood, with a strong enough character from its formative years to temper the gentrifying tendencies of its increasingly hipster-ish inhabitants. The many bars, shops, restaurants, cafés and music venues dotted around the avenues toward the waterfront are independent and quirky, and reflect the young and creative crowd that is attracted to the area. Compared to its neighbors from Downtown Brooklyn up to Greenpoint, Red Hook is remarkably underdeveloped, with wide streets and spacious blocks of old warehouse buildings interspersed with yards, markets, and empty lots. The whole area has a loose and relaxed feel, and this combined with the fresh sea air and the sights and sounds of the water so close by make you feel like you're somewhere altogether removed from the city—even though you can see it towering in the background from the waterfront.

LOCATION: Red Hook is the point on the map that juts out from the Brooklyn coast into the water south of Manhattan. It's the southernmost point in the chain of hip and livable neighborhoods that runs from Long Island City in Queens down the Brooklyn shore from Greenpoint through Dumbo and Williamsburg to Brooklyn Heights, Red Hook's closest neighbor. Go north from Red Hook and you find yourself moving through the quiet residential beauty of the Heights to Jay Street and the bridges into Manhattan. Head East from Red Hook and you pass quickly through Brooklyn Heights to Carroll Gardens, over the Gowanus Canal and into Brooklyn's busiest young neighborhood, Park Slope. The catch? Red Hook is notoriously difficult to get to, with only the B61 and B77 buses traveling deep into the neighborhood and the sparse F and G trains stopping at the Smith/9th Street stop, which is a fifteen-minute walk away, across the entrance to the Brooklyn-Battery Tunnel and through a dark and unpleasant stretch at the end of the Gowanus.

LIVE THERE FOR: THE WATER AND THE SENSE THAT YOU'RE NOT IN THE CITY. As long as you're quick on your feet, steady on a bicycle, or patient at a bus stop, Red Hook can be a great place to live simply because it is unlike any other neighborhood in New York. If the eccentric buildings, the dockside warehouses, the local markets, and the surreal spectacle of the Statue of Liberty and the occasional passenger liner docking nearby aren't enough to give you that sense, there's always the long hike back to brownstone civilization to remind you where you are.

KEEP LOOKING: IF ISOLATION ISN'T YOUR THING. As energetically as Red Hook is growing and as lively as it can be, it's still a long way off the beaten track, even for most Brooklynites. On the plus side, this encourages a real community spirit—the people you find in Red Hook are there because they really want to be, not because they happened to be in the neighborhood. On the other hand, it's a long way out if you work or play in other parts of Brooklyn or in the city, and you may find that not all your friends are as happy as you are to make the trek out there every time you have a party . . .

EAT: Once a relative culinary desert, Red Hook dining has exploded in recent years into a vibrant and varied scene that marries hipster chic with the neighborhood's down-home Hispanic heritage. DeFonte's sandwiches, pretty much the best in the borough, are giant heroes stuffed with eccentric combinations of spicy meats, grilled vegetables, and cheeses, and put together with authentic old-school devotion. Baked is about as far in the other direction as you can get: a bakery and café decked out in brass and white tiles like a 1950s brasserie with a fanciful selection of pastries and cupcakes, that's heaven for hipsters with a sweet tooth. But Red Hook's real culinary forte is the local farmer's market, a weekly market of fresh locally grown vegetables lovingly maintained by local kids and green thumbs who appreciate the quality of leaves born out of the sweet Brooklyn soil.

Baked, 359 Van Brunt Street, between Dikeman and Wolcott streets, (718-222-0345)
   www.bakednyc.com

DeFonte's Sandwich Shop, 379 Columbia Street, between Coles and Luquer streets,
   (718-625-8052)

Farmer's Market: Two locations: 6 Wolcott (intersection of Wolcott and Dwight) Wednesdays,
   10 a.m.–2 p.m.; The Red Hook Farm, Columbia and Beard streets Saturdays, 9 a.m.–3 p.m.

DRINK: Sunny's on Conover Street was for a long time the most popular reason for outsiders to make the trek down to the waterfront: a timeless bar with a relaxed feel that hosts such quietly fabulous events as live music and story nights, all presided over by Sunny himself, the friendliest barkeep you'll ever have the good fortune to meet. Rocky Sullivan's is worth getting to know, if only for the locally brewed Sixpoint Craft Ale, whose brewery is right around the corner.

Rocky Sullivan's, 34 Van Dyke Street, at Dwight Street, (718-246-8050)

Sunny's, 253 Conover Street, near Reed Street, (718-625-8211) www.sunnysredhook.com

SHOP: The Brooklyn Collective embodies the prevalent mood among the younger residents of Red Hook—that this is the city's last bastion of independent creativity, free from the mainstream capitalism of chain stores and prescribed cool. The store stocks a changing and eclectic mix of clothes, books, accessories, and any other fruits of the artesian labors of its many young designers that month. Less radical but equally good is Atlantis, a used furniture store with an unusual selection that ranges from modern designer chairs and lamps to books, records, nautical antiques, and other odds and ends that reflect Red Hook's speckled past.

Atlantis, 351 Van Brunt Street, at Wolcott Street, (718-858-8816) www.atlantisredhook.com

Brooklyn Collective, 198 Columbia Street, between Sackett and Degraw streets,

**   (718-596-6231) www.brooklyncollective.com**

READ RED HOOK IN: *The Horror of Red Hook*, H. P. Lovecraft's uncomfortably suspenseful tale of fear and loathing on the Brooklyn waterfront. Lovecraft, not exactly the most positive or philanthropic of chaps, may have done the neighborhood a serious disservice by helping to construct its reputation as one of New York's darkest and nastiest corners. That reputation has, thankfully, largely been forgotten today—though whether or not that has anything to do with the city's decision to recast the neighborhood as "Columbia Heights" is another question.

WILLIAMSBURG

IN BRIEF: Williamsburg's reputation as the hipster capital of the East Coast is at once both completely true and misleading. The truth is in the people around the L stop on Bedford Avenue, and the shops, bars, and restaurants that cater to their well-styled, design-savvy, high-mindedly edgy ways. This scene is visible, and for those to whom it appeals, it still exerts a strong pull, even as the rents that initially attracted the artists and musicians on the fringe have risen. To those for whom it doesn't, the neighborhood can seem weirdly insular, and even provincial—wearing Gap chinos here would be rebellious, and might get you some stares from the locals. But Williamsburg is a big place—you don't have to walk very far at all to find signs in Spanish or Polish— and there's more to every neighborhood than its most stereotypical residents. Here, there's convenience to Manhattan, a thriving art and music scene, and some of the most excellent food, drink, and shopping in the borough, if not in the entire city.

In terms of living, make no mistake—this is not brownstone Brooklyn. Compared to other neighborhoods in the borough, Williamsburg looks markedly industrial and unresidential. There are no grand townhouses, no picturesque tree-lined blocks, and few parks and grassy expanses. This is probably what makes it less appealing to all the numerous young Brooklyn families, and in turn reinforces its younger, less-settled feel. Though you can find a hip baby store or two, you won't be tripping over strollers here.

LOCATION: Located due east of 14th Street, Williamsburg spans the first three to four stops into Brooklyn on the L train. It's a huge and rather amorphous neighborhood; many residents specify their sub-neighborhoods by train stop or major thoroughfare. At its edges, Williamsburg also blurs into Greenpoint, East Williamsburg, and Bushwick.

The L is pretty much it in terms of subways, though the G transfer at the Lorimer-Metropolitan stop opens up other parts of Brooklyn and Queens. (The J, M, and Z do also run through the southern part of the neighborhood, but they won't get you to many places besides Chinatown and JFK Airport.) This isn't as bad as it sounds, however; from Bedford Avenue, it's less than fifteen minutes to Union Square, and all the subway options it affords; the west side trains are only one or two stops from there. Plus, the L is a "nice" line, with brand-new cars and on-track estimated time of arrival boards (ETAs). On the other hand, those ETAs don't make the train move any faster or more regularly; L service can be mercilessly spotty sometimes, and when it is, Williamsburg residents are left completely stranded.

LIVE THERE FOR: AMENITIES. Those who find some other Brooklyn neighborhoods lagging behind Manhattan in terms of recreation options might be more satisfied here. In the hubs around Bedford and Graham avenues are enough interesting shops, bars, restaurants, and cafés to rival a downtown street in that borough not-to-be-named across the river. There's also a Greenmarket, a bunch of Italian bakeries along Metropolitan Avenue, and an unaccountably large number of laundries. **THE MUSIC SCENE.** Williamsburg has pretty much replaced Manhattan as the capital for up-and-coming musicians in the post-CBGB era. Check out venues like Luna Lounge (a Manhattan transplant), Galapagos, the Music Hall of Williamsburg (formerly North-six), and the summer concerts at the McCarren Park Pool.

Galapagos, 70 North 6th Street, between Kent and Wythe avenues, (718-782-5188)
www.galapagosartspace.com

Luna Lounge, 361 Metropolitan Avenue, at Havemeyer Street, (718-384-7112)
www.lunalounge.com

McCarren Park Pool, Lorimer Street at Bedford Avenue, www.mccarrenpark.com

Music Hall of Williamsburg, 66 North 6th Street, between Kent and Wythe avenues,
(718-486-5400) www.musichallofwilliamsburg.com

KEEP LOOKING: IF YOU WANT PRETTY. Williamsburg's charm is not in its aesthetics. It's an ugly neighborhood, and construction, uneven development, and the fact that the Brooklyn-Queens Expressway rips right through it don't help. The one green patch in the area, McCarren Park, looks the way many city parks did in the 1980s, with the notable exception of the tennis courts, which don't see the traffic of those in the better known parks, and are comparatively uncrowded and well-maintained.

EAT: Williamsburg has a bunch of great restaurants, and the best combine tasty well-prepared food with a kind of fun atmosphere that isn't duplicated anywhere else in the borough, or the city. Our favorites are the adjacent Diner and Marlow and Sons; these sibling spots are Williamsburg at its best—quirky, cool, and completely delicious. For Diner, which opened first, the owners revamped a 1920s diner into a diner for the twenty-first century, interpreting comfort food for an audience that's into nostalgia, seasonal, and locally grown. At Marlow, the sidewalk café gets the edgy-in-the-shadow-of-the-bridge thing just right, while the dining room in the back is the most perfect place to hunker down for a hearty meal on an inclement winter evening. The regular menu at both restaurants is deceptively limited; these are places where you should always listen to the specials. Farther afield, by the Graham Avenue subway station, are some eateries that are lesser known to visiting Manhattanites. Fanny is a good French bistro that would always be mobbed if it were closer to Bedford Avenue, but since it's not, it has more of a true, cozy, neighborhood feel.

Diner, 85 Broadway at Berry Street, (718-486-3077) www.dinernyc.com

Fanny, 425 Graham Avenue between Frost and Withers streets, (718-389-2060)
www.fannyfood.com.

Marlow and Sons, 81 Broadway, between Berry and Wythe streets, (718-384-1441)
www.marlowandsons.com

DRINK: The Roebling Tea Room is located just far enough away from the Brooklyn-Queens Expressway and Bedford Avenue to provide the requisite serenity, with an ambience that's part tearoom, part tropical ex-pat hangout out of a Graham Greene novel. Whether you're drinking, tea, whiskey, or wine, it's easy to be inspired. In addition to drinks, Pete's Candy Store also offers a few sandwiches, plus live music, readings, and a slew of organized pub games on different nights of the week. The adult spelling bee is the signature example of the hipster humor the neighborhood is known for. The best latte in the neighborhood—if not in all of Brooklyn—is at Gimme Coffee. From the name, it may sound like it's serving sludgy swill from a premade pot, but that's just upstate understatement (it started in Ithaca). It's actually the kind of place where baristas serve each latte and cappuccino with a perfect milk-foam leaf on top.

Gimme Coffee, 495 Lorimer Street between Powers and Grand streets, (718-388-7771)
www.gimmecoffee.com

Pete's Candy Store, 709 Lorimer Street between Frost and Richardson streets,
(718-302-3770) www.petescandystore.com

Roebling Tea Room, 143 Roebling Street, at Metropolitan Avenue, (718-963-0760)
www.roeblingtearoom.com

SHOP: The Future Perfect is like Manhattan design store Moss with more of a sense of humor, though many people who get the joke won't be able to afford the design. A & G Merch is Perfect's kid brother, with plenty of pieces that are both aesthetically and financially accessible. After you've got the décor for the rest of your apartment figured out, you can get everything you need for your bedroom across the street at Sleep, a darling and aptly named boutique that carries bedding, lingerie, and some bedroom furniture and accessories. (Though this being Williamsburg, you should not expect to see any of the brands that you would at Macy's, and vice versa.) The indie record store Sound Fix also sells CDs—new, used, and on consignment—in addition to vinyl. It hosts free concerts and events in the café, including a monthly mix-tape party. Though not as demure as some of the neighborhood's vintage stores, Beacon's Closet is a second-hand superstore with over five thousand square feet of bargains. On the other end of the spectrum is Jumelle, a sweet, upscale women's boutique on Bedford. The clothing is pricey, but there are nice accessories and jewelry, much by local designers.

A & G Merch, 111 North 6th Street, at Berry Street, (718-388-1779) www.aandgmerch.com

Beacon's Closet, 88 North 11th Street, between Berry and Wythe streets, (718-486-0816)
www.beaconscloset.com

The Future Perfect, 115 North 6th Street, at Berry Street, (718-599-6278)
www.thefutureperfect.com

Jumelle, 148 Bedford Street, at North 9th Street, (718-388-9525) www.shopjumelle.com

Sleep, 110 North 6th Street, at Berry Street, (718-384-3211) www.sleepbrooklyn.com

Sound Fix, 110 Bedford Avenue, at North 11th Street, (718-388-8090)
www.soundfixrecords.com

HEAR WILLIAMSBURG IN: The music of its beloved homegrown bands like TV on the Radio and the Yeah Yeah Yeahs.

QUEENS

ASTORIA

IN BRIEF: Astoria is the home of Steinway Pianos; the birthplace of Christopher Walken, Tony Bennett, and David Schwimmer; the place where George Costanza's parents were supposed to have lived on *Seinfeld*; where much of *Goodfellas* was filmed; and the setting for the sitcom *All in the Family*. This is a more prestigious pedigree than many other high-profile NYC neighborhoods, but Astoria doesn't flaunt its ties to notoriety. This is a modest neighborhood, with affordable apartments and houses, all the basic amenities you need to get along, and little attitude about who should live here and who should not.

Astoria itself did have some brief moments in vogue a couple of years back. When the established and convenient residential neighborhoods of Brooklyn (Park Slope, Brooklyn Heights) became too pricey for the kind of Manhattanites who traditionally fled to them, attention turned to Astoria, an established and convenient residential neighborhood in Queens. But interestingly, while grittier neighborhoods in Manhattan, Brooklyn, and Queens got cleaned up and developed to take advantage of the exodus, Astoria remained the same. Thus, unlike Long Island City—where ten years ago few would have chosen to live—there are still no high-rise waterfront condos, cute boutiques, or wine bars in Astoria. The residential parts of Astoria look a lot more like the half-suburban neighborhoods people think of when they think of Queens, except that they happen to be fifteen minutes from Manhattan.

Step out to the main roads, though, and you'll know that you're in the city. Queens is well-known for its diversity, and the streets of Astoria illustrate its impressive intermingling of cultures and nationalities. Yet interestingly, the enclaves of Astoria resist the temptation to segregate. On commercial strips like Broadway, Steinway Street, and

31st Street, Greek, Indian, and Asian restaurants mingle with Irish pubs and Italian bakeries and meat markets. We even saw a restaurant on Broadway called Neuvo Jardin de Chinois.

It is likely that if you are considering living in Astoria, it will be because of the price (or because your money gets you more space or a nicer place than it would across the river), and not because it's where you have long had your heart set on living. And even so, Astoria doesn't have the charm of a Fort Greene or even a Red Hook. But there are pluses besides the affordability—a park with good, free amenities; great food; enough subway stations; the easy access to many neighborhoods in Manhattan—and you will see a different part of New York City by living in Astoria than you would by living in a more fashionable area.

LOCATION: Astoria is in northwest Queens, on the East River; it is about parallel to the East 90s and 100s in Manhattan, and with Long Island City, is the closest Queens neighborhood to Manhattan. East of Astoria are the Jackson Heights, Woodside, and Elmhurst neighborhoods, and LaGuardia Airport. Long Island City is to the south, which is remarkably more developed, particularly around the waterfront.

The streets can get pretty confusing in Astoria, particularly around the Triborough Bridge (the East River is a good way to orient oneself). Like Manhattan, streets and avenues are numbered for the most part. Unlike Manhattan, however, streets run north-south (the numbers get higher as you go east) and the avenues run east-west (the numbers get higher as you go south). Like the rest of Queens, Astoria also uses a hyphenated numbering system for street addresses. The first set of numbers in any address refers to the cross street, and the second set to the actual building number. So 36-12 30th Avenue is number 12 on the block of 30th Avenue that intersects with 36th Street. Still with us?

The N and the W are the two main trains in Astoria; they run on an elevated platform above 31st Street, stopping every three or four blocks. There is also the G, R, and V at the Steinway Street stop.

LIVE THERE FOR: THE LACK OF GENTRIFICATION. Considering Astoria's proximity to Manhattan, it is remarkably (if not quite beautifully) free of the marks of gentrification that you see in so many other up-and-coming neighborhoods in the city. There are no glass condos, buildings with silly names, or construction sites covered in sumptuous posters advertising upscale loft living. Cute boutiques and designer water have not arrived, and it doesn't look like they will anytime soon. The diversity on the streets is real, and includes not only every shade of skin color, but also the occasional Converse-and-leather-jacket-wearing hipster. If you really want to get away from the homogeneity that defines most other NYC 'hoods and still have an easy commute into Manhattan, then Astoria is definitely for you. **THE TENNIS COURTS, POOL, AND TRACK AT ASTORIA PARK.** Once you get over the fact that it looks over a particularly dismal stretch of the East River, you should be able to appreciate how much Astoria Park has going for it. That may seem like a lot to overlook, but the best things about Astoria Park aren't the green space but the amenities. The most famous is the Olympic-size outdoor swimming pool, the largest pool in the city. There are also ample tennis courts (fourteen), and a track that looks like it's a lot newer than many other things in the park. If you like swimming, tennis, or running, this is a perk to consider, as it's something that relatively few NYC neighborhoods offer as well as Astoria does.

Astoria Park, between 19th Street and the East River, and Astoria Park South and Ditmars Boulevard, www.nycgovparks.org/parks/AstoriaPark

KEEP LOOKING: IF YOU GET LOST EASILY. Even once you get the hang of Queens's anomalous hyphenated-street-number conventions, Astoria can be tricky to navigate. Streets and avenues disappear, change names, and pop out of the grid frequently. In addition to streets and avenues, there are also numbered roads and drives, which can appear out of nowhere, with no obvious pattern. If you are walking on 23rd Street, for instance, after 31st Avenue you'll hit 30th Road and 30th Drive before you come to 30th Avenue. **IF YOU DON'T LIKE UGLY.** The landscape in Astoria is blemished by a couple of unmovable eyesores: the Triborough Bridge and the elevated subway on 31st Street. Around the neighborhood, there isn't any architecture to speak of, nor are there any attractive streets that would make nice places to stroll around on weekend afternoons. The neighborhood's got everything one could need, but you get what you pay for in terms of ambience.

EAT: If you think Manhattan is packed with restaurants, then you probably haven't spent too much time in Astoria. The commercial strips are crammed with eateries of all types—restaurants, cafés, diners, coffee shops, food markets, take-out places, bakeries, butchers—and barely anything else. Much of the food is good, too, though restaurant décor here typically ranges from palatably nondescript to seriously cheesy. Astoria is most famous for its Greek food; of the many options to choose from, we suggest S'Agapo (which means "I love you" in Greek)—not only is the food outstanding, but we also have it on good authority that it's as authentic as what you'd get coming out of a grandma's kitchen in Greece. The best way to experience the restaurant is to get together a big group and order a ton of mezze to share. Astoria is also known for its diners, and in this category, the Neptune gets our nod for having exactly what a diner should—a crazy long menu, good but slightly sleazy food, and booths you could spend all day in—and not trying to be anything more. Speaking of authentic and no frills, the Spanish restaurant El Olivo is as nondescript as they come, but the traditional tapas and paella are better than many of the fancier iterations found at stylish joints across the river. Patrons are also given a complimentary glass of port after the meal.

Neptune Diner, 31-05 Astoria Boulevard, at 31st Street, (718-278-4853)

El Olivo, 21-15 31st Street, at 21st Avenue, (718-932-4040)

S'Agapo, 34-21 34th Avenue, at 34th Street, (718-626-0303)

DRINK: Want to get your Manhattan and Brooklyn friends out to Queens? Invite them to the Bohemian Beer Hall & Garden. This authentic European beer garden has been a gathering place for Czechs and Slovaks since the early 1900s, but today it's a supremely fun place to hang out on a summer afternoon, no matter what your nationality is. (The bar is open year-round, but the garden is the real attraction.)

Bohemian Beer Hall & Garden, 29-19 24th Avenue, between 29th and 31st streets,
(718-274-4925) www.bohemianhall.com

SHOP: Astoria does not have a lot of clothing stores; even chain retailers aren't plentiful, though there is an Express, a Gap, a Victoria's Secret, and a Modell's Sporting Goods on Steinway Street. Aside from that, unless you are into Euro club clothes (which you can find in a few small shops on Broadway), you'll probably want to do most of your clothing shopping in Manhattan and Brooklyn. The best shopping here is definitely for edibles. Bakeries, butchers, and fish markets abound, but our favorites were the larger international grocery stores like Euro Market, which was full of unfamiliar but tempting treats, like German breakfast cereals, Russian sodas, and beers from every country in and around the E.U. Particularly impressive was the international selection of chocolate-hazelnut spreads, of which Nutella was only one of about a dozen offerings.

Euro Market, 30-42 31st Street, between 30th Avenue and 30th Drive, (718-545-5569)

SEE ASTORIA IN: Astoria's been the setting or shooting location for many movies and TV shows. But it is also home to Kaufman Astoria Studios, one of the largest film and television production studios east of LA. TV shows and films shot there include *The Cosby Show, Sesame Street, Angels in America*, the *Pink Panther* remake.

Kaufman-Astoria Studios, 34-12 36th Street, between 34th and 35th avenues, (718-392-5600)
www.kaufmanastoria.com

LONG ISLAND CITY

IN BRIEF: Probably the coolest neighborhood in Queens, Long Island City is compara- ble to Greenpoint, Williamsburg, and Dumbo in that it's an area with a long industrial heritage that evolved first into a liberal and creative artistic community and later into a more gentrified haven for young commuters. Long Island City boasts the most dramatic of the East River's post-industrial landscapes: clearly visible from the city, its shoreline of old warehouses and factory buildings is marked by the distinctive red neon lights of the Long Island sign at the Gantry Plaza State Park and the Pepsi-Cola sign at the site of the old bottling plant. Beyond the coast, the area's mix of building styles—from great factories to red-brick tenements and brand-new condos—complements the neighbor- hood's mixed and eclectic character. With a demographic that includes Midtown commuters, young artists, and old-time Queens residents who keep the neighborhood from the sterility of complete gentrification, Long Island City is more difficult to label than its cool cousins across the creek in Brooklyn.

Formerly a hub of Queens industry—and, amusingly, the capital of the city's bak- ing industry—a change in the zoning laws in 2001 brought a rush of residential rede- velopment to the neighborhood, and a slew of Midtown commuters has been flooding in ever since, occupying the more attractive old houses and the shiny new apartment blocks along the waterfront. Even with this influx of money, the neighborhood suf- fers from a lack of urban amenities, such as coffee shops, supermarkets, and the friv- olous stores that make some neighborhoods so much fun. But for now, particularly with grander plans for development on the horizon and a sure future as another gen- trified Midtowner's neighborhood, it's this divided character that gives Long Island City its considerable charm.

LOCATION: Long Island City occupies the very southwestern corner of Queens, bor- dered on the north and the west by the East River, separated from Greenpoint and Brooklyn to the south by the Newton Creek, and bleeding into Astoria, Hunter's Point, Dutch Kills, and the expanse of Queens to the east beyond the New Calvary Cemetery. The neighborhood runs parallel to Roosevelt Island, and covers an area along the East River that roughly equates to the area between Murray Hill and upper Midtown Man- hattan. Its proximity to the livelier areas of Brooklyn and the hub of Midtown Man- hattan makes Long Island City the "first" neighborhood in Queens to anybody from outside the borough.

Isamu Noguchi famously made his way on foot from his home in the city to his studio at the northern end of Long Island City, the celebrated cable car from Manhattan to Roosevelt Island being his sole and stylish concession to public transportation. This is still as valid a route to and from the neighborhood as any, but the G, E, V, N, and 7 trains also serve the area decently, providing direct links to Brooklyn and across to Midtown. In addition, the area is easily reached by cab from the city across the 59th Street Bridge, and is adequately served by buses, including the B62 that travels down the coast to Downtown Brooklyn and the myriad transport options there.

LIVE THERE FOR: THE BEACH AND THE ARTS. The art scene of Long Island City holds a particular place between the indie and the mainstream, its more venerable artistic institutions such as P.S.1 and the Noguchi Museum and Garden sharing primacy with younger independent creative ventures such as the Socrates Sculpture Park and 5Pointz, the city's most successful interactive graffiti gallery. Even with the redevelopment along the waterfront, the neighborhood has retained an eccentric and youthful feel in the galleries and sculpture gardens dotted around, and still draws an artsy crowd alongside the city commuters. And during the summer, the stretch of park along the river becomes one of the city's best night spots: sand is brought in for a makeshift beach and people sit and drink and play music beneath the neon glow of the Pepsi-Cola sign.

5Pointz, Crane Street Studios, 46-23 Crane Street at Jackson Avenue,
   www.myspace.com/meresone
Noguchi Museum, 9-01 33rd Road at Vernon Boulevard, (718-204-7088) www.noguchi.org
P.S.1 MOMA, 22-25 Jackson Avenue at 46th Avenue, (718-784-2084) www.ps1.org
Socrates Sculpture Park, Broadway at Vernon Boulevard, (718-956-1819)
   www.socratessculpturepark.org

KEEP LOOKING: IF YOU DON'T LIKE TO TRAVEL. Getting to Long Island City from anywhere other than Midtown Manhattan can be a hassle, and for many people, dealing with the commuter crowds of Grand Central and the Midtown trains is stressful enough. So much of Queens is heavily residential that for exciting shopping and lively nights out, you have to make the journey across the river into the city or down into Williamsburg. While there are some great amenities within walking or cycling distance of the neighborhood—from the museums and galleries to the colorful Indian and Hispanic atmosphere of Jackson Heights—it's nowhere near as convenient or as spoiled for choice as its busier neighbors in Brooklyn or Manhattan. Also, if you happen to work in Brooklyn or have friends there that you visit regularly, you might want to steer clear. Relying on only one train to Brooklyn makes traveling to and from Long Island City relatively risky, especially when that train is the underwhelming G line.

EAT: Despite its proximity to the densest Indian, South American, and Greek enclaves in the whole of New York, Long Island City's best places to eat are an Italian and a Turkish restaurant. Manducatis is regarded by many who go there as the greatest Italian restaurant in the city, disguising the sophistication of its authentic Neapolitan cuisine behind almost crassly tasteless décor. Hemsin is a lively and homey Turkish restaurant with amazingly succulent kebabs, grilled meats and vegetables, and a mint yogurt that can counter and cool even the spiciest marinade.

Hemsin, 39-17 Queens Boulevard at 39th Street, (718-937-1715)

Manducatis, 13-27 Jackson Avenue at 47th Avenue, (718-729-4602)

DRINK: LIC Bar on Vernon Boulevard is not only the nicest place to get a drink in the neighborhood, it's also the most loyally emblematic of the area's character. A beautifully restored saloon replete with all the hallmarks of an old-school watering hole—tin ceiling, wood floors, and a sweet little backyard—the bar is now home to a young and mixed crowd of savvy city kids and artsy locals, and strikes the perfect balance between lively and cozy. Communal tables and a long wood bar make it easy to spend a night chatting away with new friends, and the malt liquor selection is second to none.

Long Island City Bar, 45-58 Vernon Boulevard, at 45th Road, Queens, (718-786-5400)

www.longislandcitybar.com

SEE LONG ISLAND CITY IN: Grand Theft Auto IV, the best-selling video game of all time. The game is set in the fictitious "Liberty City," modeled on New York, and anyone familiar with the buildings and landscapes of Long Island City will recognize familiar signs, storefronts, and corners in the game's waterfront district, "East Island City." Just try to remember that car-jacking is much less enjoyable in real-life Queens.

ARRIVING (REDUX)

←——→

Moving to live somewhere new can be a life-changing experience. The great thing about New York is that with care and knowledge you can live however you want to. Those of us like Caitlin who have lived here all their lives absorb the intricacies and the eccentricities of the city the way children pick up languages, so organically and unquestioningly that it takes a little distance even to recognize how complex they are. But for those of us like Jacob who arrive here from somewhere else, those details and those differences can mean everything, and can be both daunting to get your head around and thrilling to at last comprehend.

While there are elements to moving to New York that are true of moving any-where, some parts of the process are as unique to the city as the Statue of Liberty or the smell of the subway in Chinatown. In a city of such scope and such contrasts, knowing where you want to be and how to get there is of the utmost importance. The hassle of tracking down an apartment, scoping out a neighborhood, wrestling with brokers, cross-examining roommates, and deciphering legal jargon is a small price to pay for anywhere from a month to a lifetime of happiness. Whether you're buying a brownstone in Brooklyn, sharing an apartment with strangers in Astoria, or hopping from alcove to studio in Manhattan, it's worth taking the time and making the effort to learn all that you can about the places you're moving to—and not to forget about the places you're not.

If there is a note of caution in our words, it is there not because we feel that with-out it our readers would be lost, doomed in blind optimism to fall afoul of some terri-ble urban treachery. It's simply because in New York, so much is possible that it seems a shame for anyone to move here and not be able to find the niche that's waiting for him or her. Like jobs, shoes, or relationships, having a home that fits just right is worth more than almost anything in the world. And with patience, forethought, and a book like this, anyone should be able to find the right place in what remains, in our eyes at least, the greatest city in the world.

SETTING UP HOUSE

$\longleftrightarrow$

Maybe you've taken a closet-sized studio so you can walk to work; maybe you're subsidizing your dream house by taking on multiple roommates. Perhaps you even moved to a remote, supposedly up-and-coming neighborhood for more space . . . and still wound up feeling cramped. Regardless of where you live, your NYC place is likely to be smaller than any you could have gotten in another city, or even just a few miles outside of this one. New York City apartments are infamously, maddeningly small—a fact that can be accentuated by awkward layouts and quirky chop jobs that have turned one apartment into two. And storage space, not the sexiest thing to think about while imagining yourself in your new digs, is either barely there or nonexistent.

The specific conditions of NYC living—the small spaces, the trendsetting atmosphere, the access to so many different kinds of stores and services—defy the strategies and offerings of mainstream shelter magazines and mail-order kingpins, making New Yorkers fringe consumers by default, even though, ironically, we're crammed into the same few square miles as millions of others in some of the most desirable real estate in the country. Our advice: Make the most of it! What New York lacks in big-box retailers, and expansive yards, basements, and garages, it more than makes up for in aesthetic inspiration. Decorate your apartment with treasures from flea markets and stoop sales. Put some patio furniture on the tiny patch of grass that comes with your ground-level apartment and have parties all summer. Get rid of every ugly sweater, useless kitchen gadget, and space-sucking knick-knack you own, and use the money you would have spent on storage to buy one amazing piece of furniture. You can set up a stylish little living room with secondhand finds, cheap, practical furniture, and even things you've found on the street. You can grow herbs in a windowbox, keep a grill on your fire escape—or give up cooking altogether, turn your kitchen into a guest alcove, and get by on takeout. In this section, you'll find everything you need to make your apartment your home—and a pretty great looking one at that.

Welcome to the neighborhood.

FURNISHING, FIXING, AND DECORATING

Setting up an apartment anywhere can be overwhelming, but given the wealth of options for home improvement and décor at reasonable prices available here, there's even more reason to resist the temptation to decorate on autopilot with an exclusively Crate and Barrel aesthetic. Here are some of our favorite (and a few not-so-favorite) places to get your place furnished, polished, and equipped.

ABC Carpet & Home Warehouse Outlet

WHAT IT IS: Luxurious rugs, exquisite furniture, eclectic knick-knacks, and other colorful and well-made pieces at up to 70 percent off what they would be in ABC's regular store in Manhattan.

WHAT'S GOOD: Besides top-notch merchandise at great prices? The store will send someone over to measure your door before a piece of furniture is delivered to make sure that it will fit through, for no additional charge.

WHAT'S NOT: Getting there. Using public transportation, it's either a very sketchy walk from the nearest train station, or a bus ride from the 2 or the 5. Best to save this one for a trip with a friend who has a car.

1055 Bronx River Avenue, near Bruckner Boulevard (Bronx), (718-842-8772) www.abchome.com

Bed Bath & Beyond

WHAT IT IS: Bed Bath & Beyond is an anomaly here: a superstore in the city, everything stuffed into awkward multilevel layouts, with merchandise stacked unreachably high. The normally unpleasant shopping experience becomes downright frightening during August and September when college freshmen flock to these stores to buy their twin extra-long sheets and dry-erase boards. During these months, the store should be avoided at all costs.

WHAT'S GOOD: These stores have a lot of stuff. This is good if, say, you aren't sure what kind of pillow you want, because they have about thirty dozen different kinds.

WHAT'S NOT: They have too much stuff. Bed Bath & Beyond specializes in one-stop shopping, but if you are looking for one specific item, you will probably have a more pleasant time getting it somewhere else. Remember: Bed Bath & Beyond has a lot of things, but nothing that you wouldn't be able to get at another store.

Multiple locations; see www.bedbathandbeyond.com

Housing Works

WHAT IT IS: When is a thrift store better than a thrift store? When the merchandise comes from design-savvy New Yorkers, or in the best cases, straight from a designer's showroom. You can find clothes, books, shoes—really, just about anything— at Housing Works Thrift Shops, but furniture is the big score. Dishes, ceramics, lighting, and knick-knacks can also be good—this is the place to come to if you want a perfect offbeat accent for a boring end table.

WHAT'S GOOD: Knowing that the proceeds from your snazzy new dining set are going to a good cause (helping New Yorkers who are homeless and have HIV or AIDS).

WHAT'S NOT: Stuff goes fast — if you come after noon on a weekend, any furniture on the floor is likely to be marked with a "SOLD" tag. You can still score lamps, kitchen gadgets, and other items, but go early for the best of the day's offerings.

Multiple locations, see www.housingworksauctions.com

N.B.: Housing Works is just one of many thrift stores around the city that sell used furniture. We single it out here because it's the best known and has several locations. But it's worth checking other stores in your area as well—competition for merchandise can be less intense elsewhere.

Lighting & Beyond

WHAT IT IS: There used to be a bunch of lighting stores along the Bowery, back in the day when the area was a bit rougher and the rent was cheaper. Nowadays, a good lighting store is hard to find, which can be a real problem when you need a replacement for an unusual bulb, a specific kind of dimmer, or a floor lamp. Lighting & Beyond, a comparatively centrally located lighting emporium on 14th Street, is that store, a holdover from the era of excellent one-off specialty stores. It sells nothing but lighting, and lots of it, and is staffed by people who are experts on the subject.

WHAT'S GOOD: The wealth of offerings; good prices; helpful and knowledgeable staff.

WHAT'S NOT: The aesthetic of anything not strictly functional. The table lamps range from discreetly unglamorous to ridiculously kitschy (a shade with a revolving fish hologram, for example).

35 West 14th Street, between Fifth and Sixth avenues, (212-929-2738)
www.lightingandbeyond.com

Tiny Living

WHAT IT IS: The antithesis of a big-box chain retailer. Going way beyond under-the-bed storage and over-the-door shoe holders, Tiny Living caters exclusively to the typical NYC apartment dweller who lives in smaller quarters than the buyers at places like Bed Bath & Beyond could even imagine. The small-scale living aids sold here range from the mundane (over-the-tank toilet-roll holders; extra narrow dish racks) to the imaginative (a stovetop cappuccino maker)—all either stylish or subtle enough that you won't be embarrassed to have them in your place. There are miniature versions of essentials like fire extinguishers, tea kettles, and ironing boards; ingenious two-in-one appliances (a blender that doubles as a travel mug, for instance); and storage and organization implements that are slimmed down to apartment-size proportions.

WHAT'S GOOD: Anything that goes on a counter, in a cabinet or closet, or is shoved in a corner—you'll gain some valuable space by replacing whatever you've got with the Tiny Living version. Also don't miss the extensive selection of magnetized accoutrements. You can get magnetic towel racks, magnetic measuring spoons, magnetic spice containers, magnetic magazine holders, even cookbooks with magnetized back covers. Magnets, you'll soon learn, are a great friend to the cramped apartment dweller.

WHAT'S NOT: You can shop online on the store's web site, but the web design isn't great for browsing offerings and comparing similar gadgets, and it's hard to appreciate the genius of some of the cleverest items without seeing them in person. Best to make a trip to the actual store.

125 East 7th Street, between First Avenue and Avenue A, (212-228-2748) www.tinyliving.com

Two Jakes Used Office Furniture

WHAT IT IS: A vast and thoroughly delightful secondhand furniture store whose concept is more brilliant than it sounds. If the name makes you think Staples-brand furniture, don't be put off. The selection changes regularly, but nothing looks like the furniture from any office we've ever worked in—and that's a good thing. Two Jakes specializes in modern furniture from real designers and manufacturers, like Knoll and Herman Miller. But you don't have to be a design aficionado to appreciate the look and feel of the pieces they have, and it's a great place to shop if you want something with style, but are new to (or wary of) used furniture shopping.

WHAT'S GOOD: Perhaps because it specializes in furniture that was used in offices rather than in homes, items look less worn and, well, less "used" than you might expect. Prices are extremely reasonable, and service is beyond helpful, particularly once you've made your purchase. Rather than coldly tacking on an enormous delivery charge, you're offered a variety of different delivery options, including calling a car service to pick you up at the store (if you've ever bought a bulky item in NYC and then had to drag it from the store to a place where you could hail a cab yourself, you'll know what a big perk this is), letting you leave it there until you can come back with a car, or holding it in the store until they need to make another delivery in your area, and letting you split the cost.

WHAT'S NOT: Two Jakes gets large shipments from businesses and corporations, so the selection is vaster than most used furniture stores—you'll have a greater chance of finding pairs or multiples of a certain item. But even so, the inventory can be a little uneven, which can make it hard to buy matching sets. Caitlin's got three chairs from there that almost match . . . but not quite.

320 Wythe Avenue, between South 1st and South 2nd streets (Brooklyn), (718-782-7780)

www.twojakes.com

West Elm

WHAT IT IS: Depending on whom you are talking to, West Elm is either a revelation in chain home and furniture retail, or a despicable purveyor of big-box design dressed up with cheesy contemporary touches. Our feeling is this: Used smartly (tables, chairs, and desks) and sparingly (display pieces should be chosen with care), West Elm is a good tool to have in your local home-décor arsenal.

WHAT'S GOOD: Prices, lots of sales and discounts, furniture that's ridiculously easy to assemble, and convenient locations in Chelsea and Dumbo. It's always helpful to see (and measure!) a piece in person, even if you've seen it in the catalog or online, and if you take it home with you, you'll save on shipping.

WHAT'S NOT: If you can't bring your item home with you, delivery is often *more* expensive than what the shipping cost would be if you'd ordered online. And you get what you pay for in terms of manufacturing: this is not the place to invest in a dining room table you plan to keep for the next generation.

112 West 18th Street, between Sixth and Seventh avenues (Manhattan), (212-929-4464)

75 Front Street, between Main and Washington streets (Brooklyn), (718-875-7757)

www.westelm.com

White on White

WHAT IT IS: A small but successful chain of stores whose mission is to "bring design to the masses," by creating affordable (and authorized) versions of interior design classics from Herman Miller, Charles and Ray Eames, and other modern furniture standards.

WHAT'S GOOD: The showrooms are informal, navigable, and unpretentious, and the prices are great. Unless you absolutely need to pay top dollar for an original designer chair, you can pick up an expertly made imitation model here at a fraction of the price. And if anything ever goes wrong, they can order parts or repair the pieces themselves for a very reasonable rate.

WHAT'S NOT: The stock of the stores can fluctuate unpredictably, which means they're better for browsing than shopping for a specific item. And one of their strongest points is also their Achilles's heel: the banter of their immeasurably knowledgeable staff can be overwhelming at times; for example, when a simple question about a Jacobsen footstool is answered by a forty-minute lecture on the notion of opacity in Danish architecture.

Multiple locations; see www.whiteonwhite.com

Crate and Barrel

WHAT IT IS: If Crate and Barrel were a building, it would be on the corner of Ikea and West Elm. Seeking to cover every inch of domestic ground, but reaching with their designs to a more sophisticated yuppie crowd, the Manhattan branches of this national giant are undeniably—though slightly shamefully—useful resources.

WHAT'S GOOD: The little things—you find yourself picking up trivial things you didn't know you needed here, like candle snuffers, garlic crushers, or napkin rings. And the kitchen and bathroom departments are the best parts of Crate and Barrel. While a lot of the furniture seems too expensive for what it is, the stores stock a huge range of good crockery, cutlery, and cookware, as well as surprisingly tasteful towels, bath mats, and laundry baskets.

WHAT'S NOT: Although it lacks any kind of serious designer heritage, much of Crate and Barrel's furniture is prohibitively expensive to anyone except the kind of person who would do better shopping at West Elm, Pottery Barn, or Design Within Reach.

611 Broadway, at Houston Street, (212-780-0004)

350 Madison Avenue, between 59th and 60th streets, (212-308-0011)

www.crateandbarrel.com

HOMEWORK

Anyone arriving in New York from somewhere less crowded—and that's pretty much everybody, since only residents of Tokyo or São Paolo can claim to live more compactly than New Yorkers—will have to adapt to the city's unique brand of apartment living. If you live in Manhattan or in one of the more popular residential areas of Brooklyn, you're likely to move into a place that's smaller than you would have thought possible for the money and find that it bears the marks of a checkered history of inhabitants. Downtown tenements built to house four families per floor have been converted into apartments for one or two, while uptown townhouses built for one rich family are divided and divided again until they accommodate twelve, so a lot of people end up with a similar space in the end.

In some cases, the eccentricities of New York apartments past can profoundly influence the lives of their present inhabitants. As Winston Churchill put it, possibly after one of his trips to the Bronx, "We shape our buildings; thereafter they shape us." We have known grown men who have built themselves cribs, women in their sixties who climb ladders into lofts, hairdressers who have knocked holes through brick walls, even Englishmen who have installed fridges in fireplaces—all in the name of optimizing the spaces they have. What's surprising is that while New York may appear to be too cool and cosmopolitan a city to have the time or the energy for such things, there is a thriving home-improvement culture here that will rival that of almost any city in the world.

However, with every avenue a vista of easy options for the mass-market decorator, it takes a trained eye to find the right tools for original home improvements, and a creative mind to make the most of them. The city's dozen or so Home Depot and Lowe's superstores are undeniably useful resources for all your more common household work, supplying everything from spirit levels to power tools, fiberboard, and shelving brackets. With thousands spread across the city, you're never far from a neighborhood hardware store either. But, whether your motivation comes from a need to save money or simply the desire to do something out of the ordinary, there are many more interesting ways to fix up your place, and many more interesting places to find what you need to do it.

Take doors, for example. Around 30 percent of downtown Manhattan's tenement-building apartments now have no interior doors, as a result of a slow gentrification that has seen certain neighborhoods evolve from ethnic ghettos into yuppie havens. For anyone living alone this is a boon: it makes the apartment look larger and lighter, and less effort is required to move from one tiny room to the next. But if you have a roommate, you may need the privacy a door can provide. Likewise, anyone renting a loft space, however big and beautiful it may be, might find that dividing a space is key to achieving harmony at home. For roommates who prefer privacy, the time and cost involved in buying and installing doors, handles, hinges, or dividers is a high one to pay for what seems like a basic domestic right. But there are stores dotted around the city that can provide fun and economical solutions. Canal Plastics, a treasure trove of raw materials, sells sheets of plastic or Plexiglas in various colors, cut to whatever specifications you like, at a fraction of the price of a new wooden door—and these can serve just as well as room dividers, too.

When it comes to wood, taking your pick of types and cuts from a bona fide lumber yard is not only more fun than making do with what's on offer at Home Depot, but it's often a lot cheaper, too. With rudimentary instruction, Jacob was able to build a dining table, two benches, and walls of bookshelves from scratch for next to nothing compared to what they'd have cost either whole from ABC Carpet & Home or in pieces from Home Depot. As much as the city's more elite residents might like to think otherwise, New York is accessible enough to the wooded wilderness for there to be a wealth of lumber yards across the five boroughs carrying everything from cherry to pine. Places like Metropolitan Lumber, Tiffany Lumber in the Bronx, or Ace on the Upper West Side will cut pretty much any kind of wood into any size you need for reasonable rates—and, being familiar with the peculiar demands of New York residents, they are fully equipped to deal with the eccentric requirements of small spaces. Buying your wood from yards rather than hardware stores almost always guarantees a wider range; you can often strike deals depending on the quantity you're buying, and the cutters are much more likely to be able to carry out specific requests that Home Depot simply won't do.

The most common apartment complaints among New York residents tend to center around space: how to make the most of it, how to keep the most in it, and how to divide it happily between everybody who shares it. The key to all three is to be original. If you can't find a perfectly sized mirror at West Elm or Two Jakes, seek out Rosen- Paramount on the east side and have glass cut to the size you want. If the only storage space you have is in cupboards above your closets, find a beautiful wooden ladder in a used furniture store in Brooklyn and make yourself happier to use it. And if you want to make your kitchen feel bigger, head to Grassi Sheet Metal Works downtown, pick up some hinges and chains, and convert a boring countertop into a flexible breakfast bar that can fold away when you're not using it.

Ace (AJO Home and Lumber), 610 Columbus Avenue, at 90th Street, (212-749-3632)

www.acehardware.com

Canal Plastics Center, 345 Canal Street, between Greene and Wooster streets,
(212-925-1666) www.canalplasticscenter.com
Grassi Sheet Metal Works, 33 Cooper Square, between 4th and 5th streets, (212-475-2384)
Home Depot, multiple locations, www.homedepot.com
Lowe's, 118 Second Avenue, at 12th Street (Brooklyn), (718-249-1151); 2171 Forest Avenue,
near Grandview Avenue (Staten Island), (718-682-9027) www.lowes.com
Metropolitan Lumber, multiple locations, www.themetlumber.com
Rosen-Paramount Glass Company, 45 East 20th Street, between Broadway and Park Avenue
South, (212-532-0820) www.rosenparamountglass.com
Tiffany Lumber, 422 East 165th Street, near Melrose Avenue (Bronx), (718-993-5542)
www.tiffanylumber.com

EXCESS BAGGAGE

Moving, gaining a roommate, cohabiting with a significant other, and routine changes in taste can all necessitate the chucking of a perfectly good piece of furniture or home décor—especially in New York where one is considered really lucky if you've got a tiny storage locker in the basement for which you pay a monthly fee. It doesn't take much here for a few "just in case" items to take over an apartment and turn it into a full-on pack-rat lair, so a smart New Yorker will edit his or her possessions rigorously and regularly. Luckily, what NYC lacks in space it makes up for in creative options for how to purge. So think like a mountaineer, take only what you need to survive, and send the clutter to its reward.

OPTION 1: SELL

Unless your items are particularly valuable or you have a particular buyer in mind, Craigslist is the best place to sell furniture and other home items. Post your info in the "For Sale" category, with the price (pictures are good if the item is in good shape, but can work against you if the photograph makes the item or your apartment look scary). Posts expire within seven days, but you'll probably want to repost each day anyway, just to keep your item near the top of the strand. Having the buyer pick up the item will not only save you the hassle of removing it from your apartment yourself, but it will also ensure that you won't get scammed (so long as you have the person pay you on the spot).

PROS: Craigslist is a seller's market. Even a five-year-old futon with holes in the cover will sell . . . eventually. It's excellent for getting rid of things that no one else will take.

CONS: No matter how good the condition of your item is or how new, you rarely get as much money as you think you deserve. If you're not getting calls within the hour, your price is too high.

GOOD FOR: Large furniture items, particularly ones that you haven't gotten enough use of to take a complete loss on.

NOT SO GOOD FOR: Anything that's original value was under $100. What you'll get for it will probably not be worth the hassle of coordinating viewing and pickup times with a buyer.

OPTION 2: STOOP

Stoop sales are the NYC version of yard sales. They don't happen everywhere, but there are a couple of very residential 'hoods where they occur all the time, particularly in certain parts of Brooklyn (page 86). If you don't live in a place that has them, ask friends who live in stoop-sale districts if they'd like to go in on one with you. Pick a day, make some flyers, set up your table early, and bring a book.

PROS: An enjoyable day hanging out in the neighborhood.

CONS: You might not sell everything (or anything), and you do have to be willing to give up at least one full weekend day.

GOOD FOR: Anything that you aren't super desperate to sell.

NOT SO GOOD FOR: Anything that's heavy or hard to carry. If it's a pain for you drag outside, it'll be a pain for the buyer to take home.

OPTION 3: DONATE

New York's got tons of thrift stores—you've probably noticed at least one somewhere around your place already. Your neighborhood thrift store should be a vital part of your de-cluttering routine (Caitlin brings at least a thing or two to hers almost once a week), and unless you are partial to one charity, you'll probably frequent the one in closest drop-off distance to your place. A smart donater, however, will check the thrift shop's donation policy before dragging his or her stuff over, as some have designated donation hours, and/or only accept certain kinds of items. And while some thrift stores do take furniture donations, it's usually a hassle to schedule a pickup.

PROS: Charity, convenience, and the modest tax deduction.

CONS: Some thrift stores will accept anything you bring in, but the pickier ones—they may take clothing, but not books or furniture, or take specific items at certain times—can make donating a bit of a pain.

GOOD FOR: Books, clothes, and other items to be purged in bulk.

NOT SO GOOD FOR: Anything in poor condition.

OPTION 4: DISCARD

Like stoop sales, this option depends a bit on where you live, and is even more restricted to real residential side streets—this is not a maneuver you want to call too much attention to as it's technically illegal. But there are some neighborhoods where people leave unwanted goods on the street in front of their apartments for passersby to claim. Caitlin and her husband have left books, clothing, chairs, art supplies, a yoga mat, and more, and never have items lingered in front of their door for more than an afternoon. In exchange, they have scored an eight-foot easel in great condition and a beautiful wooden chest.

PROS: Convenience and instant gratification. Good-bye Excercycle, hello floor!

CONS: Can only be done along streets where you've seen people leave their stuff before, and when no one's super is looking.

GOOD FOR: Whenever you feel like selling or donating is too much trouble.

NOT SO GOOD FOR: Anything you'd be embarrassed to see when you walk outside your door.

BECOMING A CITIZEN OF THE CITY

←——→

What makes a real New Yorker? Unlike most others in the world, the very nature and history of the city make it difficult to identify a native from an adopted New Yorker. Ever since the dawn of New Amsterdam centuries ago, the city has become home to people from all over the world, people who bring with them their own cultures and ideas from foreign realms as far afield as Asia, Europe, and New Jersey. People still come and go, and the identity of every part of the city changes from generation to generation. With such a diverse range of inhabitants and such a rich and varied past, the idea of a real New Yorker becomes something beyond heritage alone.

Instead, being a true New Yorker essentially equates to wanting to live here. Caitlin is a true-blue city girl, born and raised in Manhattan, while Jacob is an Englishman who left London and made the city his new home. But both of us face the same challenges and opportunities, and both of us stay because living here and exploring everything the city has to offer is so much fun. Moving to New York means finding the parts of town that suit you, finding the right people to spend time with, and carving out a niche for yourself in whatever kind of life you want to lead here. And if you can do that, you have every bit as strong a claim to being a real New Yorker as anybody else does.

But there are still ways to mark your permanence in a city beyond having a place to hang your hat. The longer you're here and the more deeply you engage in New York life, the more you'll learn about how the city can help you to make the most of your time. To really make your presence felt, there are certain things you'll want to know: how and where to vote, how to influence life in your neighborhood, what to do when things go wrong, and which cards you should carry in your wallet to make things go right. Becoming a citizen of the city means getting to know it and feeling like you belong here; but knowing exactly how basic things work and what to look out for from the start can help transform an arriver into a survivor.

NOISE!

Noise you can't control is one of most annoying and most infuriating parts of urban life. There are so many forms it can take here: If your neighbors aren't rowdy, then there's some sort of renovation going on in or next to your building, and just as that stops, a garbage truck will change its route to go past your window every morning before dawn. So it may surprise you to learn that New York's two main noise-control laws are actually considered some of the strictest in the country. The New York City Noise Control Code, enforced by the Department of Environmental Protection, covers noise that occurs outside residential buildings. The other is a statute of the Department of Buildings (DOB) code; this covers noise that happens inside a building.

Would that these laws worked as well as they're supposedly written. Violations are rampant—you've probably encountered some today—and not only is the enforcement of these laws poor, but mounting a case against a violator is time-consuming and rarely successful. In the case of a DOB code violation, for instance, a tenant would have to hire an acoustical expert to measure the noise level in his or her apartment and testify in court that it was above the legal limit.

Fortunately, there is a less time-consuming way to take action. The web site for the Public Advocate's office has a rather reassuring page listing many common sources of menacing noise in NYC, and the most effective numbers to call for each. Having your complaint go to an authority that has control over that type of noise is a big step toward getting results, as it's not always obvious who's got control of what.

www.pubadvocate.nyc.gov/services/noise.html

NYPD 101

Probably—hopefully—the extent of your involvement with the NYPD will be at parades and concerts. Nevertheless, you should know where to go if you need the police. Here are the basics.

The NYPD has nearly 40,000 officers spread across seventy-six local precincts, plus special units like the Transit Police and the Housing Police, and all of the *Law & Order* divisions: SVU, Major Case Squad, and the Crime Scenes Unit. Speaking of *Law & Order*, there is also a special movie and television unit that works with the Mayor's Office of Film, Theater, and Broadcasting to manage the production of all of the movies and television shows shot on NYC streets.

Assuming that you haven't been arrested, the branch of the NYPD that you are most likely to need is your local police precinct. The NYPD web site has an embarrassingly primitive precinct finder application that can, after much tinkering, help you figure out where the nearest precinct is (it will take a few more clicks to get to the specific precinct web site to confirm that it's actually yours). Precincts are responsible for law enforcement and safety in the areas under their jurisdiction; they are also where officers will be dispatched from in an emergency. For this reason, it's probably not a bad idea to know which precinct you live in (having the precinct number in your phone would be super-prepared) in case you do need them. Equally important is knowing what you should call the precinct for. Here's a quick chart:

CALL 911
- If you see a crime being committed
- If you have been the victim of a crime
- If you're having a medical emergency

CALL YOUR PRECINCT
- If you have a noise complaint
- If your wallet is stolen
- If your apartment has been broken into
- If you suspect illegal (but nonemergency) activity is going on in your building

NYPD web site: www.nyc.gov/nypd

YOU AND YOUR COMMUNITY BOARD

It's easy to go an entire lifetime in New York City without having direct contact with your community board. Then why mention this, you might ask? Well, it has to do with a swimming pool. But we'll get to that in a second.

The city is divided into 59 smaller districts that are overseen by community boards. Each community board encompasses a few adjacent neighborhoods, so if you live in Cobble Hill, for instance, you share a community board with Red Hook, Park Slope, and Carroll Gardens. There are 12 community boards in Manhattan, numbered south to north (so Tribeca and Lower Manhattan are Community Board 1; Washington Heights and Inwood are 12); 18 in Brooklyn, 14 in Queens, 12 in the Bronx, and

3 on Staten Island. Community boards act as advocates of the neighborhood and its residents, and through their many subcommittees (comprised of board members), they oversee everything from street-fair applications to street cleaning, parks, and public spaces. While they can't actually make or change laws, community boards can bring up problems and issues in their neighborhoods to the correct city agencies, and get to weigh in on city decisions that affect their neighborhoods, like construction projects and liquor-license applications. Board members are appointed by the borough president, but each board holds a monthly meeting that is open to the public, and each sets aside a certain portion of these meetings to hear from community members (the public can also join some of the subcommittees, and then can attend their meetings as well). Although many of the public grievances (noise complaints, gripes about construction) are the same from community board to community board, each collection of neighborhoods is unique and diverse. Even if you never plan on making it to a meeting, knowing which community board you live in can give you interesting (and sometimes valuable) information about your neighborhood and the ones around you.

Which brings us back to the pool. Caitlin likes to swim, and a few years ago, NYU opened an enormous gym—with a pool—across the street from her apartment in the East Village. Knowing that there was a brand-new pool across the street from her was driving her crazy, and she racked her brain trying to figure out a way that she could join the gym without either enrolling at or going to work for NYU. A friend who lived on the other side of the campus told her that NYU's other gym offered a special membership for people who lived in Community Board 2, where the older gym is located, as a gesture to the community they share their campus with. So Caitlin figured out that she and the new gym were in Community Board 3, and contacted the gym about community memberships . . . only to find out that they weren't offering any such memberships at this new gym. However, now that she knows how community boards work, she knows how to make her complaint.

BLOCK PARTIES

Among the few genuine perks of the city's steely grid system, block parties are as much a feature of a New York summer as stoop sales, flea markets, and trips to Coney Island. Strolling through the city's residential neighborhoods on any given weekend from May to September, you might find block after block closed off to traffic and thronged with people eating, drinking, singing, dancing, and playing games up and down the street. While the innumerable summer street fairs that pop up along avenues across the city tend to be more commercially oriented, block parties are the preserve of community-minded locals and are essentially excuses for friends and neighbors to come out and play on one another's stoops for a day.

A block party's character is a perfect gauge of the nature of a neighborhood, and what goes on between the avenues can differ wildly from one part of town to another. Where in Brooklyn Heights you might find residents enjoying a sit-down dinner warmed by gas lamps and serenaded by a local string quartet, in West Harlem you might come across a feast of dishes laid out on long tables along the sidewalk, kids playing basketball at one end of the street, and DJs taking turns on a massive sound system at the other. Wherever you live, though, a block party can be a happy occasion for kids and grown-ups alike.

One important thing to know about block parties is that they don't just appear of their own accord. Residents have to apply for a permit through their community board, which in turn has to receive permission from the city, and the process can take a few months to complete. If you find yourself living in a community-minded neighborhood, chances are you'll have neighbors who will have made it a tradition to hold a block party at a certain time every summer, and who will take it upon themselves to fix things up long in advance. But getting involved can be a great way to get to know your neighborhood, whether you take it upon yourself to organize a party or just ask around to find out whom to pitch ideas to and how to help out on the day.

PAPERWORK

←→

New York City bureaucracy is the stuff of legend: incomprehensible documentation doled out with ruthless disregard and calling confused masses to nondescript offices around the five boroughs. Impatience and bewilderment are universal reactions among New Yorkers who are waiting in lines everywhere from the post office to the IRS offices and the DMV. But getting a handle on your paperwork is an essential part of living legit in the city, and sorting things out right in the first place can save a lot of time and complication in the long run.

PASSPORTS

Wherever you are, the centerpiece of anybody's ID collection is his or her passport. The easiest way to get or to renew a passport in New York is through the trusty post office. Turn up at almost any USPS outlet (it's wise to check online to be sure your local branch offers the service first) with two photos of yourself, a valid form of photo identification, and proof of American citizenship, and you can expect to receive a new passport in a matter of weeks. If time is a factor and you need your new passport in anything from a day or two to a week, there are a number of independent agencies around the city that can expedite your application for a fee, normally between $40 and $200. The best way to find these is through the Yellow Pages or by looking online.

For anything more complicated, such as a lost or stolen passport or an immediate (24-hour) renewal, you'll need to face the formidable New York Passport Agency. This one central office on Hudson Street in downtown Manhattan handles all serious passport issues for the city, from emergencies to traveling visas, and requires considerable patience and commitment to conquer. In the event of any such crisis, the best thing to do is to call ahead and establish where you need to go, what you need to bring, and whether or not you need to book an appointment. Even with the best planning, however, a trip to the agency to do something as simple as hand in an expired passport can take an entire afternoon: security is overwhelming, the lines are long, and the staff operate on a need-to-know basis that makes comprehending the procedures just about impossible any way other than through painstaking trial and error.

New York Passport Agency, www.travel.state.gov/passport/about/agencies/agencies_912.html

STATE ID AND DRIVERS' LICENSES

Like any other city in America, it's important to have valid photo ID in New York, and that means a driver's license or, for non-drivers, a state identification card (more on that later). Anyone arriving from outside the country will be amazed at the ruthlessness with which New York stores, bars, bouncers, and cops insist on proof-of-age identification, and—as Jacob can testify—carrying around a passport for three years is a fool's solution to being denied a beer everywhere you go. You need to be 16 years old to get a learner's permit, 18 to get a full license, and 21 to drink and get into bars and clubs. Whether you're itching to get your driver's license or looking to cement your pedestrian citizenship, a single trip to the DMV is all it takes to set you up with the all-important card.

The DMV is of course a ubiquitous force in every city in the country, and there are a dozen offices dotted around the five boroughs: four in Manhattan, three in Queens, two each in Brooklyn and the Bronx, and one solitary outpost on Staten Island. Once a scapegoat of civic unrest on a par with the Internal Revenue Service, the reputation of the DMV has improved considerably over the last few years with the help of the Internet. Time was you needed a trip to the office just to get the forms you'd need to fill out before you came back to the office a week later to schedule your next appointment at the office. These days, you can work out (and in most cases print out) exactly which forms you'll need, exactly which branch you'll need to go to, and which forms of identification you'll need to bring with you by visiting the DMV's web site.

That's not to say that the whole thing is easy. The DMV's responsibilities extend beyond licenses and identification cards to innumerable necessities of daily life, from administering vision tests for new drivers to officially changing people's names. The offices are always busy, lines move unforgivably slowly, and the paperwork required for anything can be extensive and baffling. The "points" system that classifies how much prior identification you need to bring with you is a science in its own right. Thankfully, though, for the most part, the procedures required to receive the bare minimum of identification as a citizen of the city aren't too complicated. If you have a passport and a social security number you'll always be all right. The biggest hurdle is establishing which office to go to for what you need, since not every branch offers the same services or operates on the same hours.

When you become a resident of New York, out-of-state or international drivers with existing licenses are required (rather ominously) to "surrender" their old licenses and apply for New York State ones within 30 days of their new lives as New Yorkers. This is not only essential in terms of anything practically relating to having a car in the city—from registering a vehicle to applying for parking spaces and arranging insurance—it's also helpful should you have any run-ins with traffic cops, who tend to react worse to out-of-state auto perps than locals. Whether you already drive or not, to get your license you'll need to turn up at the appropriate office armed with six points of identification (plus your old license if you have one) and get in line.

If you're a driver, your license also serves as a proof-of-age ID under any other circumstances too. But non-drivers—and there are a lot in New York, where public transport is always on your doorstep and parking spaces are few and far between—can apply for a state ID. This is essentially the same card, minus the stamp that entitles you to be behind the wheel of a car, and requires essentially the same application procedures. Make sure you have six points of identification, wait your turn at the office, and primp up for the photo—it's got to last you eight years.

The only other important thing to know is that once your name and address are confirmed for your ID, you are obliged to notify the DMV of a change of name or address within ten days of the change occurring. You can do this either in writing (by fax or by mail), over the telephone, or in person at any of the DMV branches around the city. Legally speaking, an ID card with a false or outdated address is not valid and can get you into trouble, so it's important to do. There's a space on the back of each card to write in your new address, which you should do as soon as that address becomes effective.

DMV, www.nydmv.state.ny.us

VOTING

There is no clearer symbol of citizenship than having the right to vote in New York elections. And there is no worse feeling than the realization on election day that you've passed it up—stumbled into the wrong polling station, failed completely to work the machine, or, most criminally of all, forgotten to vote altogether. Whether you've arrived in the city from upstate or from across the country, you'll want to make your political feelings known. With the help of the ultimate tool of democracy, eligible New Yorkers can cast their votes freely in mayoral, gubernatorial, primary, and general elections that can influence every aspect of life in the city and the country beyond it. And while we can't tell you who to vote for—however much we'd like to—we can help to make the voting process easier.

The first step on the path toward embracing a New Yorker's suffrage is registering to vote. The city's Board of Elections issues registration forms, which can be obtained online, ordered over the phone, or picked up at post offices, DMVs, libraries, and other government offices around the five boroughs. The Board itself has six offices in the city—one in each borough and an executive branch in Midtown Manhattan—as well as a multilingual telephone assistance line and a surprisingly lucid web site. Because your signature is important in verifying your identity, registration forms have to be filled in by hand and either mailed or delivered to the Board at least twenty-five days before an election. In registering to vote you also affirm your residence in New York and acknowledge affiliation to a political party—or your status as an independent—both of which are permanent records until you say otherwise, so if you don't notify the Board in time when either changes, you may not be able to vote.

Once you've registered, the next step is to work out where you're supposed to vote. The Board sets up polling stations across the city—usually in the kinds of public buildings you're never likely to set foot in again, ranging from senior centers to school gymnasiums—but you can only cast your vote at the one designated for you. The location of your polling station is determined according to the residence you give when you register, and you can find out where that is either by going to the Board's web site and entering your address in a helpful search that also maps the station's location, or by calling up and requesting its location by phone. When you move, you need to notify the Board of your change of address—otherwise, you'll have to continue to vote in the polling station of your former address until you do so. Polling stations stay open from six in the morning until nine at night, giving even the most frantic Gordon Gekkos and the laziest Ferris Buellers ample opportunity to sneak in a quick vote.

The third and final step is the ballot itself. Once you get to your polling station, you need to sign in, which will confirm that you're at the right place and earn you a voting card to carry to the booth. When you reach the booth at the front of the line (and there will be a line), you'll be confronted with a voting machine. At the time of writing, New York is one of the few states where lever voting machines are still in operation, their old-fashioned mechanics having been deemed more reliable than the current digital alternatives. It's a pretty straightforward manual system of pulling levers and flicking switches that actually lends a physical sense of catharsis to the act. But if you're from elsewhere and have never taken one on before, you can request assistance from any of the polling station officials (the Board provides a hilarious instructional video online that will guide you through the process from the parting of the polling curtains to the final pull of the red lever).

The New York Board of Elections web site is the most useful resource for any further information, from explanations of the city's absentee-voting procedures to the locations of the Board's offices, breakdowns of voting qualifications, and special advice for would-be voters in extenuating circumstances. All information is available in

English, Spanish, Chinese, and Korean, and it's easy to download registration forms and to locate your polling station online. So follow our advice, register and stay up to date with the Board, and enact the ultimate expression of your citizenship of the city. Just remember that timing is the most important thing: you can only register to vote after you've been a resident in New York for 30 days; you must register at least 25 days before an election; and, for the love of God, you have to make it to the polling station on time.

Board of Elections in the City of New York, vote.nyc.ny.us

MARRIAGE LICENSES AND DOMESTIC PARTNERSHIPS

Getting married in New York unfortunately requires spending a bit more time in the Byzantine webs of city government. The steps one must follow to successfully and legally be married are numerous, and sometimes have no obvious justification beyond perhaps trying to make people think twice before they go through with it. In this bizarre and idiosyncratic land, you must first apply for a license to get married and then receive a certificate to prove it's done, and money orders are the only form of payment accepted. On the bright side, you can change your name to anything you want, and there's no blood test in New York. Oh, and you're getting married, of course!

The first step on the road to matrimony in this state is to apply for a marriage license at the City Clerk's office. There are offices in each of the five boroughs (see page 133), and they are open on weekdays from 8 a.m. to 4 p.m. (3:45 p.m. in Manhattan). Don't confuse the license with the marriage certificate. The license is sort of like permission to get married at a later date (between 24 hours and 60 days after getting the license) and you must present it to the person who marries you (the officiant); the certificate is the proof of your marriage that you'll need to hang on to. Both members of the couple must appear in person to apply for the license. You will each need to bring valid (not expired!) photo IDs, and one $35 money order. When you arrive at the office, you'll see a bunch of lines, but you don't need to stand in one . . . yet. First you and your spouse-to-be need to fill out the application form. The application form is an affidavit where you list personal information, marriage history, and sign a statement that there are no impediments to you being married. (If you are over 18—or over 16 with parental permission—not trying to marry your sister or brother, and not currently married to someone else, you're in the clear.) After you fill it out, you go to the next window to get it processed. This only takes a few minutes (a little longer if there is a line), and then you take it with you. Before you leave, be sure to read everything over carefully, as there is a money-order-only fee for any changes.

This is also the time when you can change your name. In this state, whether you are male or female, your choices are: taking the name of either spouse; a former surname of either spouse (probably only applies to people who have been married previously); a name with both spouses' surnames hyphenated; or for the very creative, a new name that combines the names of the two spouses in some way. They strongly encourage you to "consider very carefully" your name change, because if you have second thoughts later and want to change it on the license, it'll cost you as much as any other change. On the other hand, there is no law that you have to use any name just because it's on the license (or isn't), so what you put down on your license doesn't have to be what you end up using the rest of your life. (You can legally go by any name you want as you long as your intent isn't to impersonate or defraud, so what's on the certificate doesn't have to be the same as what you go by at work, or what's on your driver's license, or anything else.) Our advice? If you've wanted to get rid of your last name all your life, this is your chance. Otherwise, don't let them scare you, and do whatever you feel comfortable with without fretting about the ramifications down the road.

After getting the marriage license, the next step is to have the marriage ceremony. A marriage ceremony must be performed by a judge or clergy member who is a registered marriage officiant in New York State. After the ceremony, the officiant must fill out the license, and mail it back to the City Clerk's office within five days of the ceremony. After that you will receive a marriage certificate in the mail, which is your actual proof of marriage.

If you have the marriage ceremony at City Hall (see page 162), you don't have to worry about accidentally not getting married. But if you are having your ceremony in another place, there are a few things you should keep in mind. First, the license is only good in New York State—you can't get your license here if you want to get married in the Caribbean. Second, the person you choose to perform your wedding ceremony must be a registered marriage officiant in the state. This means that if the person you want to perform your wedding is from out-of-state or if he or she is from the state but not registered, he or she will need to fill out the registration form, meet the eligibility requirements, and send a $15 money order. FYI, the only people who are eligible to perform marriages here are clergy people and judges.

You can register for domestic partnership at the City Clerk's office as well. Domestic partnership guarantees partners in unmarried couples similar rights and benefits to those of married couples. It applies to gay and lesbian relationships, as well as unmarried heterosexual couples. Registered domestic partners in New York

City have the right to receive the same treatment as spouses in matters such as hospital and prison visitation, insurance eligibility, and succession benefits in tenancy issues. To qualify, both people must live in New York City at the same residential address (they ask for mail as proof), be over 18, and cannot be married or a registered domestic partner to anyone else. To register, couples must pick up an affidavit at the clerk's office, have it signed and notarized, and send it back to the clerk's office with proof of valid ID and—guess what—a money order for $36.

Office of the City Clerk, 210 Joralemon Street, between Court and Boerum Place (Brooklyn); 851 Grand Concourse, between 158th and 161st streets (Bronx); 1 Centre Street, at Chambers Street (Manhattan); 120-55 Queens Boulevard, at Union Turnpike (Queens); 10 Richmond Terrace, at Bay Street (Staten Island), www.cityclerk.nyc.gov

JURY DUTY

No matter how infrequently it comes, jury duty is almost always inconvenient. But once you are there, it's actually not so bad. Like jury duty in most places, there's usually plenty of down time, the hours are great, and the people can be interesting. But in New York, you also get to take advantage of the many attractions of whatever neighborhood you are serving in. If you live in Manhattan, for instance, you can use your lunch break to explore Chinatown, Tribeca, and the Financial District; visit Battery Park; stock up on discount designer clothing at Century 21; have dumplings or dim sum in Chinatown; or splurge on a fancy meal at Bouley (see page 60) on a weekday afternoon. Not so bad, right?

Each borough has different courts, and you only serve in the borough in which you are currently living. Each court has several different jury assembly rooms where pools of juries are called each day, so be sure to check the address on your summons each time you are called. Each jury room is run by a small team of bureaucrats who give instructions, call the names for *voir dires*, and tell you when you can come and go. The atmosphere of the room depends a lot on the people running it: some are jolly, some have a bit of a dry wit, some are real sticklers, most have authentic Noo-Yawk accents, and all will thank you for your service when you are released.

There are some urban myths about how to avoid jury duty, but not registering to vote or avoiding getting a New York driver's license won't necessarily prevent you from being called. The city pulls names from tax returns and other official lists, so if you really do live here, you'll probably get a summons eventually.

Most courts give a phone number on the summons, and you call in the night before to confirm the room you are supposed to go to, and that you are actually needed; usually you are, but sometimes you'll get off the hook right then and there. The first day, jurors are usually asked to arrive by 8:45, and are shown some instructional videos before the day begins. If you are not picked for a trial by the time they let everyone go for the day, you'll be asked to come back at 10 the next day. Lunch is officially from 1 to 2, but if you are in the jury room around noon, they usually let you go a little early. After lunch, they keep you for a bit longer, then let you go by 5 p.m., or when they hear that there are no more cases coming down. If you are picked for a trial, then the judge sets the hours, which are usually normal business hours, 9 a.m. to 5 p.m. Trials in civil court (disputes between two parties) usually take only a few days; criminal cases (a case by the state against a defendant) are usually a bit longer.

Jurors must serve two consecutive days, but you don't have to serve on the days for which you are summoned. To encourage people to show up, the court system has become extremely flexible about scheduling, and people are encouraged to pick days when they know they'll be able to serve. Here's how it works: your summons will be for a specific date about a month or two in the future. After you get it, you can call anytime before the date you are supposed to serve and get it postponed. You can choose the date, though it has to be between two and six months from the date you were called for. (You can even postpone your service on the day you are called, but in that case, you have to show up at the courthouse at the time you are called anyway, so it's better to postpone before.) You can also reschedule your service to choose what day to start on. If you start on a Tuesday or Wednesday, there will be two crops of jurors in the pool each day: your pool, and the one that started the day before or after you. If you start on a Thursday, there will be no new jurors on your second day (Friday), so the pool is smaller, and your chances of getting picked for a *voir dire* are probably better. On the other hand, Fridays are generally the lightest days for starting trials, so you are more likely to be sent home early. Monday is probably the worst day to start on, as there will be only one pool in the jury room on your first day, and it's less likely that you'll be let go early at the beginning of the week.

At the end of the second day or when you complete your trial, you'll get a proof of service. Don't lose it. You legally can't be called for another two years, but New York's current policy is not to call you again for six. However, because names are drawn from so many lists, you might get another summons sooner than that, and you'll need your proof of service to get out of it. If you qualify for the stipend, you'll also get a check in the mail about six weeks later. (Currently, the stipend is $40 a day.) However, only jurors who are unemployed, self-employed, or work in companies with fewer than ten employees are eligible. Otherwise, your employer should be paying you for full day's work anyway.

One tip to avoid being called again too soon: Keep the same name on all of your identification. If you use your middle initial on your driver's license, for instance, use it when you file taxes or register to vote. Also, if you have officially changed your name for any reason, change it on all of your IDs, or at least make sure to fill out your juror card with the name on the summons. Making sure your name is the same everywhere will also help prevent mistakes that might hold up getting any payment you are due for your service.

The actual experience of being at jury duty has improved vastly in recent years— really! Many of the assembly rooms have Wi-Fi, and some have laptop stations as well. There are also TV rooms, vending machines, areas where you can talk on the phone, and plenty of breaks. And, of course, you can still take advantage of your time in the waiting room the old-fashioned way, by reading.

In addition to the physical amenities, there's definitely less of an "incarceration" atmosphere about jury service than there used to be. This might have to do with the fact that some categories of automatic exemptions (lawyers, for instance) have been eliminated so the pool is much bigger, and therefore the system is less strapped for potential jurors. Or it might just have to do with the same policy changes that got jury rooms those amenities. Whatever it is, you definitely get the sense that everything is being run efficiently, with the most respect to the juror's time. For example, if you show up on the first morning and decide you want to postpone after all, no problem. The clerk would rather have you there on a day that's convenient for you, so you won't try to get off every trial you are called for. And judges are strict about a lot of things, but if you're self-employed and aren't making millions of dollars or are a student, you have a good chance at getting a pass on a potentially long trial.

SMALL CLAIMS COURT: A HOW-TO GUIDE

Small claims courts may exist in other places, but in this city of great opportunity and hard knocks, they have an urban-mythical aura. People we know have used it to recoup money from crooked landlords, evil dry cleaners, sketchy bosses, and other unsavory local characters; others dream of getting even with a plumber who's done a shoddy job or a "man with a van" who stole some of their stuff; still others have worked in fly-by-night operations where they have been on the receiving end of phone calls from creditors threatening to use it to recoup the money they are due. Frequently invoked by the city's millions of freelancers, independent contractors, and mid-market rental tenants (anyone to whom $500 or $1,000 is more than a minor annoyance), small claims court is "where everyday people come to solve their everyday civil legal problems." Here, you can try to buy your justice with time, patience, and diligence.

Small claims court resolves disputes involving money in sums of up to $5,000. A landlord who doesn't return a security deposit, a store that has sold you damaged goods and won't give you a refund, or a client who refuses to pay an invoice are all examples of people one might consider taking to small claims court. You can't use small claims court to sue for discrimination, because you've been unfairly fired or evicted, or to compel goods or services—the court only hears suits for money. Small claims court is set up for the individual; you don't need to have a lawyer to make your case (whether you are suing or being sued), and court sessions are typically held in the evening rather than during the day.

The person who sues is called the claimant; the person or party being sued is the defendant. If you are the claimant, you first have to file a claim in the clerk's office at the court. There are three offices in Manhattan (Centre Street, Harlem, and Midtown), and one in each of the other boroughs. In the claim you'll describe the suit (the incident or situation that resulted in the defendant owing you the money), name the amount you are trying to recoup, and supply the names and addresses of the people you are suing. The clerk will assign you a court date and summon the defendant to appear on that date. There's a $15 filing fee for claims of up to $1,000; $20 if it's over $1,000.

At the hearing, the claimant and the defendant will each present his or her side, and present any evidence or witnesses. (If a witness refuses to appear voluntarily, he or she can be subpoenaed, unless the person is an expert witness or anyone else who wasn't actually a witness to the specific incident that the suit pertains to.) No matter what side you are on, any relevant evidence will be helpful—invoices, checks, contract, samples of the work completed (or not completed), photographs, letters, or e-mails. The person presiding over the hearing will either be a judge or an arbitrator. Most cases are heard by arbitrators, but either party can choose to have the hearing presided over by a judge. You'll probably have to wait longer for a hearing with a judge, but unlike an arbitrator's decision, a judge's can be appealed. (Not that you'd probably want to go through an appeal—appeals in small claims cases are extremely rare, hard to win, and would likely cost more to mount than the amount in question.) Like a regular trial, the burden of proof is on the claimant, who has to prove that the defendant owes him exactly what he claims he does. But unlike a regular trial, there's no jury, and the judge (or arbitrator) can question the claimant and defendant, and the claimant and defendant can directly question each other and each other's witnesses.

Sometimes defendants don't show up because they think the case won't be able to happen without them. They're wrong. The hearing can go on without them, and the judge or arbiter can award a judgment of default against them. If the claimant doesn't show up, though, the case is automatically thrown out.

If the claimant wins, the judgment is awarded as a sum of money, about which both parties will be officially notified. From there, the claimant must contact the defendant directly to get the money. If the defendant refuses to pay, the claimant can contact the clerk's office to get an enforcement officer to collect the payment.

If you are the defendant, you don't have a choice about going to court—if you've been summoned, you should go. But if you are considering making a claim, you might want to look into resolving your case in other ways (mediation, for instance) called "alternative dispute resolution." For more information on both small claims court and alternative dispute resolution, visit the civil court web site (www.nycourts.gov/courts/nyc/civil), and go to the small claims court page. If you're thinking of making a claim, we definitely recommend reading "A Guide to Small Claims Court," which you can download from the site. The guide explains the process step-by-step, in plain English, from who is eligible to file a claim through to enforcing a judgment, and it also has all of the addresses and phone numbers you'll need to do it, as well as some information on alternative dispute resolution.

JOIN THE CLUB

←→

MEMBERSHIPS

A museum membership is perhaps not the first thing that comes to mind when you are thinking about getting settled in New York; after all, it's not like there aren't museums and other institutions of the like in other places. But considering this city's wealth of cultural offerings in every discipline—and the respect they are given by its residents—associating yourself with one or more of them is arguably more useful here than, say, having an in-state driver's license, and visiting them is far more entertaining than going to the DMV. Becoming a member of one of the city's cultural institutions is an excellent way to put down some roots here, and, frankly, memberships are some of the best deals in town. For as little as fifty tax-deductible dollars a year, you'll get discounts, free gifts, invitations, subscriptions, special offers—as well as free entry and/or tickets to whatever institutions you choose to join.

The city is teeming with nonprofits and institutions that want your money, so it's a buyer's market. You can become a member of museums, theater companies, parks, libraries, movie theaters, and even some stores. Most offer individual and dual options, and indicate how much of the membership fee is tax deductible. Benefits range from discounts on tickets and entry fees, and food and merchandise at their own stores and cafés (some better than others); to advance notice and tickets for special events; the privilege to bypass ticket lines for general admission and/or special exhibitions (in some cases a big perk!); subscriptions to magazines and newsletters; discounts to neighborhood restaurants, stores, and even hotels and parking lots; and random but useful freebies like T-shirts, tote bags, and coffee mugs. While what kind of institutions you'd want to join depends on your own tastes and interests, benefits like a discount at some restaurant that you like can tip you in favor of one of two you're deciding between, and plenty of interesting member privileges come from places that you might not even think would offer memberships in the first place. Following are some options with notable membership perks, as well as a few places beyond museums and theaters that you might not consider otherwise.

N.B.: You can sign up for memberships online at all of the institutions listed, and we would strongly encourage you to do so rather than calling. Particularly with museums, what takes a few clicks online can take an hour on the phone.

Film Society of Lincoln Center

WHAT YOU GET: Discounted and advance tickets for film programs at the Walter Reade Theater and for the New Director/New Films Festival; opportunity for advance booking for the New York Film Festival; subscription to *Film Comment* magazine.

WHY IT'S GREAT: Early booking. Film festival tickets can be hard to get unless you are a member; many films sell out before tickets become available to the public. Though members still have to pay full price for tickets ($20 or less to most screenings), they get to order theirs two weeks before the public and can request up to two tickets for as many screenings as they want.

COST: Individual, $75 per year; dual, $95.

Walter Reade Theater, Lincoln Center, 65th Street between Broadway and Amsterdam Avenue, (212-875-5600) www.filmlinc.com

Housing Works Used Book Café

WHAT YOU GET: A 10 percent discount on everything in the store (including items at the café); an invitation to special members-only events; free T-shirt or tote bag.

WHY IT'S GREAT: If you like to buy books and music, the membership can start paying for itself pretty fast. Members at the $125 level also get three coupons for 30 percent discounts that can be used anytime during the year. And the complimentary "Text, Mugs, and Rock and Roll" T-shirt or tote bag is cute.

COST: $50 or $125 per year.

126 Crosby Street, between Houston and Prince streets, (212-334-3324) www.housingworks.org

Jazz at Lincoln Center (JALC)

WHAT YOU GET: JALC offers both membership and subscriptions; a membership gives you 50 percent off tickets on the day of performance; subscriptions are annual packages of tickets for a certain number of the season's shows. Both include discounts at area restaurants and shops, including some in the Time Warner Center where JALC is located, plus invitations to private events throughout the year.

WHY IT'S GREAT: Opportunity to see amazing live music performances in the amazing (and brand-new) JALC home at the Time Warner Center. The main venue, the Rose Theater, is a great place to see a concert in, but a single show in the Allen Room—the more intimate amphitheater with the window of walls overlooking Central Park—is worth the cost of a subscription alone. Of course, you could visit both without a subscription or membership, but members can get their tickets at a substantial discount, and subscribers get to go to whatever shows they want throughout the season. JALC subscriptions are unusually flexible; there are a ton of packages to choose from, with different themes and performers, at the different JALC venues. (Packages usually include four shows.) With subscriptions, you also get to order your tickets before they go on sale to the public, are guaranteed the same seats for each performance, and can keep seats from season to season if you continue your subscription.

COST: Individual membership, $50 per year. Contact JALC for subscription pricing.

Broadway at 60th Street, (212-258-9800) www.jalc.org

Brooklyn Academy of Music (BAM)

WHAT YOU GET: Becoming a "Friend of BAM" earns you discounted tickets, allows you to buy tickets before they go on sale to the general public, gets you discounts at BAM's restaurants as well as at various local Brooklyn eating establishments and watering holes (up to 20 percent), and gets you invited to all sorts of BAM events from dress rehearsals to parties, depending on the level of your membership.

WHY IT'S GREAT: BAM is one of the most highly regarded cultural centers in the city. Ranging from Mikhail Baryshnikov's ballets to intelligent seasons of new and classic movies, cutting-edge modern dance, and the world's best theater productions, BAM offers an eclectic selection of the arts all under one roof. The theaters themselves are beautiful, the atmosphere is fun and relaxed, and the programs tend to draw a relatively young crowd. All of it is just as fun for nonmembers as it is for "friends," but having the edge on the rest really helps when it comes to getting good seats; avoiding crowds before shows in the private Natman Room is also a luxury. And on top of it all, BAM is in a great and accessible part of Brooklyn, which means it's easy to get to and there are plenty of places to go after a show.

COST: The cheapest "Friendship" level is $75; gradations of benefits go up to the shockingly friendly $50,000 BAM Visionary.

30 Lafayette Avenue, between Ashland Place and St. Felix Street (Brooklyn), (718-636-4100) www.bam.org

Museum of Modern Art (MoMA)

WHAT YOU GET: Privilege to bypass entrance lines to the museum and special exhibitions, and special members-only exhibition previews; entrance to film programs and P.S. 1 Contemporary Art Center; discounted museum admission ($5) for up to five guests a year; 10 percent discount at the design store, bookstore, and museum cafés on the second and fifth floors; discounts on neighborhood stores, hotels, and parking lots; unlimited free admission to the museum all year.

WHY IT'S GREAT: MoMA membership leads the rest of the art museum pack by sheer number of perks. To highlight a few: The benefit of bypassing ticket lines should not be underestimated, as the major shows draw hoards of locals and tourists. Admission to the film programs and the P.S. 1 Contemporary Art Center as well as the museum itself means not only additional free events and venues, but also access to P.S.1's excellent outdoor summer art party/concert series, Warm Up. Discounts at the cool MoMA design store come in handy, especially during the holidays or if you are decorating a new apartment. (Watch for special member discount weekends around Christmas and Mother's and Father's Days, when the discount increases to 20 percent.) And even if you never took advantage of anything but the museum itself, with the regular admission price at $20, a membership pays for itself in only four visits.

COST: Individual, $75 per year; dual, $120. (A $55 membership is available for full-time students with valid ID.)

11 West 53rd Street, between Fifth and Sixth avenues, (212-708-9400) www.moma.org

The New Museum

WHAT YOU GET: Invitations to special events and exhibition previews, 10 percent discount at the museum store, 15 percent at the café, 20 percent on publications, discounts at other neighborhood restaurants and stores, and unlimited free museum admission for a year.

WHY IT'S GREAT: In addition to regular individual and dual/family memberships, the New Museum also offers special $35 memberships for students, artists, and New York City teachers.

COST: Individual, $60 per year; dual/family, $100.

235 Bowery at Prince Street, (212-219-1222) www.newmuseum.org

New York Society Library

WHAT YOU GET: Permission to browse the stacks and check out up to ten titles at a time from the library's nearly 300,000-volume collection, plus audiobooks, children's books, and periodicals; access (and borrowing privileges) to books not in the library collection through inter-library loan; ability to renew and reserve books; access to the library's rare book and material collection (for on-site use only); use of the library's members' reading rooms, study rooms, and writing rooms; option to rent day or long-term lockers.

WHY IT'S GREAT: All the perks of a public library—free books, great selection, enforced quiet—in the most un-librarylike setting of a 250-year old membership library housed in a majestic Upper East Side building. The public is limited to the reading room on the ground floor, so only members get to search the stacks at their leisure; read in the comfy chairs in the gorgeous (and laptop-free) member's reading room; and work in the light-filled writing rooms and the secret study carrels that are scattered around the stacks. (Caitlin felt very jealous that she wasn't writing this book here when she took her tour.) When members want breaks from the books, there are also paintings in the stairwells, a gallery with revolving exhibitions, and all the newspapers and magazines one could ask for. Many of the members are writers who come to work here every day; membership is a fraction of the price of a writing room or a shared office space, and the setting is infinitely more inspiring. Especially great if you live in the area, and if you have to do writing or research but aren't affiliated with a university or institution that has its own library.

COST: Individual, $150 per year, or $100 for six months; educational membership for full-time students or teachers available for $125 per year.

53 East 79th Street, between Madison and Park avenues, (212-288-6900)

www.nysoclib.org

New York Theater Workshop (NYTW)

WHAT YOU GET: Four passes to performances at the trendsetting NYTW; advance booking, discounts on guests tickets, ticket exchange privileges; discounts at neighborhood restaurants; free unlimited coffee and tea at NYTW shows, and one free baked good from the café per season.

WHY IT'S GREAT: Flexibility. NYTW's membership program offers what they call SmartPasses; the annual membership fee gets you a book of four passes. You can see four different shows, or go to one with three friends. Passes are good for 18 months, so you can spread them out over a few seasons; but once you use up your passes, you can renew immediately—you don't need to wait for the next season as with most theater memberships. Also, NYTW is near some excellent restaurants (Prune, La Palapa, Butter, and Nomad are a few good ones), so the neighborhood discounts are nice to have even when you're not seeing a show.

COST: Individual SmartPass packs are $180 to $200. Discounted student memberships are also available.

79 East 4th Street, between Second Avenue and the Bowery, (212-780-9037) www.nytw.org

Wildlife Conservation Society (WCS)

WHAT YOU GET: Sixteen free passes to special attractions (like the Congo Gorilla Forest and the Butterfly Garden at the Bronx Zoo) and a 50 percent discount on additional passes; parking passes for the Bronx Zoo and the New York Aquarium; discount on WCS educational courses; 10 percent discount at WCS gift shops and restaurants; invitations to members-only events; admission to WCS zoos.

WHY IT'S GREAT: It's like five memberships in one! A WCS membership gives you unlimited entrance to all of the WCS parks: the Bronx Zoo, the New York Aquarium, and the Central Park, Prospect Park, and Queens zoos. Even if you visit each park just once, it's a good deal. With the premium membership option, you also get unlimited free admission for a guest, and unlimited special attraction passes.

COST: Individual membership, $75; individual premium, $90.

For more information, addresses, and directions to each park, visit www.wcs.org

LIBRARIES

Every membership card in a New Yorker's wallet is another string in his cosmopolitan bow. Libraries, neighborhood pillars of the greater New York establishment, are no longer the preserve of reluctant schoolchildren and Grisham-hungry seniors. Go into any branch today and alongside the usual suspects you'll also find tech-savvy kids researching homework online, film buffs perusing the movie selection, and neighborhood locals reading magazines. In these days of e-diplomas, literary podcasts, and Project Gutenberg, it's good to know that New York's public libraries have kept up with the times and remain an indispensable resource for students, writers, researchers, and peace-seeking citizens across the city.

Public libraries in New York are divided into three systems: the New York Public Library, covering Manhattan, the Bronx, and Staten Island; the Brooklyn Public

Library; and the Queens Library. Taken together, the three library systems comprise more than 200 branches, host more than 35 million visitors a year, and stock a combined collection of more than 30 million books, making New York's the largest public library system in the world.

Joining one of the city's public library systems is easy—just walk into a branch with some ID and get yourself a card—so the only question is which one. If you live in Manhattan, Staten Island, or the Bronx, join the NYPL and you'll probably never need anything else. But heavy users in the other boroughs, for whom one supplier might not be enough, should consider joining the NYPL as well as either the Brooklyn or the Queens operation, giving themselves access not only to all their local lending libraries but also to the greater archives and specialized collections in Manhattan. Serious bibliophiles should also consider applying for an ACCESS card, which grants entry to online articles and the special collections held in the four central research libraries. A library card is not only a ticket for borrowing books: it's also a key to innumerable other materials, a password to vast online archives and directories, and, above all, a symbol of your belonging to New York.

Like delis (see page 176), libraries vary according to neighborhood, and the contents of their shelves can tell you a lot about an area. While the four main research libraries are in Manhattan—the Humanities and Social Sciences Library, the New York Public Library for the Performing Arts, the Schomburg Center for Research in Black Culture, and the Science, Industry, and Business Library—the regular branches spread across the five boroughs cater to local taste and demand and therefore reflect their neighborhoods in both atmosphere and content. The recently opened Mulberry Street branch is a peaceful duplex of red brick walls, hardwood floors, and brushed steel shelves on a quiet corner in Nolita, and its collection—heavy on graphic novels, independently published fiction, and hip journals—complements its location. Likewise, the understated Inwood branch has one of the city's strongest selections for children and one of the largest Spanish-language fiction collections.

Even as digital words come to replace printed matter—and in spite of the fact that the entire population of New York seems to do all its work ostentatiously on laptops in cafés—the city's libraries remain wonderful resources and invaluable refuges for anyone who wants to read or work. From audiobooks and works in Braille to CDs and DVDs, from obscure articles and ancient manuscripts to *New York Times* bestsellers, New York's public libraries have it all. Take the time to scope some out, work out which libraries suit your needs, and you'll be able to take advantage of one of the most amazing resources any city has to offer—and feel like more of a true New York citizen at the same time.

GETTING AROUND

⟵⟶

With as much as there is to do in this city, becoming fluent with the many transportation options is a necessity. The best method of transportation to a given place depends on a constellation of variables: where you are coming from and going to; time and day of trip; how much you are carrying; and how strict your time constraints are. The swiftest New Yorkers are not unflinchingly loyal to a single mode, but rather are informed and open to all, so they are able to make the right calls when faced with transportation dilemmas like how to get to a Broadway show, whether a cab is a good investment for a trip from Tribeca to the Upper West Side, or whether it's faster to walk across 14th Street or take the L. (Answers: Subway, always, because Times Square is terrible to drive through; yes, because you can avoid traffic by taking the West Side Highway; and trick question, because it depends on how far you are going.) Put on some comfortable shoes, invest in an unlimited MetroCard, forget about driving, and you'll be well on your way.

SUBWAYS

WHAT THEY ARE: Communal commuter vehicles, convenient transport to and from most areas in the city, and subterranean microcosms of urban life. The New York City subway is iconic, but it's not a relic, and its good reputation is entirely deserved. The subway is extremely efficient and easy to use—and it's a bargain. What about the bad? Most of the downsides of the subway come from how popular it is: packed cars at rush hour, litter in the stations, and the occasional long wait between trains off-hours. The subway is beloved (at least grudgingly) by most New Yorkers, and more than a few non-residents, though some from places with less weathered mass transmit systems criticize the grit and grime. But though its ambience and aesthetics may be debatable, the New York City subway unquestionably excels in its basic function as public transportation.

WHO TAKES THEM: Suits, strivers, artists, celebrities, babies, high school students with cleats hanging off their backpacks, musicians, break-dancers and more . . . At hubs like Union Square, Grand Central, Times Square, and Atlantic Avenue, the stations are as diverse as the streets above them. The farther you go toward the ends of the lines, the more the people on the platforms and entering the cars reflect the specific demographics of the neighborhood. On the L train, for example, kids with edgy hair-cuts and fashionable glasses pack the cars the first few stops into Brooklyn, but after Jefferson Street, they give way to a Polish-speaking ridership, and then the West Indian inhabitants of Canarsie.

WHAT'S GOOD: 24 hours a day, 7 days a weeks, 365 days a year—unlike those in many other cities, our subway never closes. It's also more democratic—a single ride is $2, whether you're going one stop from Penn Station to Times Square or riding the Q from Carnegie Hall to Coney Island. And the subway goes everywhere—with the exception of Staten Island—usually offering you more than one route to any destination. The icing on the cake: the trips that offer unexpected bonuses, like the views of the Brooklyn Bridge from the trains that cross the East River above ground (B, D, N, and Q).

WHAT'S NOT: The PA systems on the new lines are automated and very clear, but on older lines, it can be impossible to understand the conductor's announcements. This is most frustrating when what you've missed is that your train will unexpectedly be skip-ping your stop (which is rare, but does happen). And certain lines have annoying quirks: the G train is infrequent and short (it has fewer than the standard number of cars, so if you are standing at the end of the platform, you have to run up to get in); the transfer situation at the Broadway-Layfayette/Bleecker Street connection is absurd; and the J, M, Z line is super creepy. But the subway's greatest shortcoming is airport transport. There is no subway to LaGuardia, and while you can take the A, E, J, or Z to JFK, the trip is brutally long, a bit confusing, and you still have to take the AirTrain once you arrive at the last station. (See page 153 for better ideas on airport transport.)

BUSES

WHAT THEY ARE: A poor man's cab, a tourist's mistake, and a claustrophobic's sub-way, an MTA bus is the least-beloved mode of public transportation in the city. While there's something to be said for staying above ground—you can see where you're going, and daylight is pleasant—there is little beyond whim or necessity that could inspire most New Yorkers to board a bus. New York traffic is sticky to say the least, so rides are marked by screeches and jolts, and on busy routes, journeys of a few blocks can take longer than they would to walk. Still, buses manage to draw a loyal crowd of devotees—enough, at any rate, to make any rush hour trip a sweaty, lurching nightmare.

WHO TAKES THEM: The bus crowd is divided roughly into two camps: the rush hour set of subway-hating office workers, and the daytime crew of seniors and schoolchildren. People who don't have far to travel to and from work often opt for the bus because it seems like less hassle than the subway. And if you're not in a hurry, riding the bus around town on a quiet afternoon can be a lot more fun than watching the tunnel walls go by underground. The farther you go in the outer boroughs, where traffic is easier and crowds are lighter, the more the bus remains a local's choice—like the subway, the people you sit next to will vary from place to place and will clearly reflect the demographic of a neighborhood.

WHAT'S GOOD: Buses thrive most where subways don't. The east side of Manhattan is high bus country—at least until the mythic Second Avenue subway comes to fruition—and crosstown routes are the strongest weapons in the bus's arsenal, making shortcuts across boroughs where the subway simply can't. Almost all subway lines run up and down Manhattan, so to get from east to west a bus ride is sometimes the only option besides walking. And bus routes are quicker between Brooklyn and Queens, where the lowly G train is the only subway link between the boroughs that doesn't take you in toward Manhattan and back out again. Some bus lines offer both express and local options, and sometimes catching the express will be the fastest way to travel. And of course, once you have an unlimited MetroCard, it's useful from time to time to be able to hop on a bus that's going your way.

WHAT'S NOT: The waiting. In rush hour in a busy part of town, it's not uncommon to have to wait in line for ten minutes only for the bus to arrive too full to let you on, and if you do get on you'll probably have to stand. Late at night or on quieter routes, it's not uncommon to have to wait 45 minutes for a bus to show up, regardless of what it says on the schedule at the bus stop. And greenhorns beware: Familiarize yourself with the distinction between express and local routes, or endure the ultimate humiliation of waiting at the wrong stop and watching your bus roar by in the face of your wild protests.

N.B. While the MTA web site (www.mta.info) is useful for things like system maps and service advisories, www.HopStop.com is another excellent tool for subway or bus riders. HopStop is basically like MapQuest for mass transit: you plug in where you are starting from and where you want to go, and it gives you subway and/or bus directions to your destination, walking directions to and from the stops, and estimated travel times. You can also plug in an address and it will show all the subway stations nearby. While the estimated travel times are typically on the optimistic side, all other functions are reliable and detailed, and it's an invaluable resource for any New Yorker.

CABS

WHAT THEY ARE: Ubiquitous and irresistible, cabs are many New Yorkers' favorite way to travel. Whether it's a guilty pleasure, a last resort, or an everyday fact of life, a cab ride is almost always the quickest way to get where you're going—just look for the lit numbers above the windshield and hop in—and often the most fun. Widely regarded as the worst and most aggressive drivers on the city's streets, taxi men (and nearly all are men) are ruthless chauffeurs who can plough through traffic and swerve across lanes unlike any other. In some cities in the world, taxis carry a sense of luxury; in others, taxis are only really for ferrying people home from train stations and airports to leafy suburbs; but in New York, taxis manage to be both gritty and elitist, easy and indulgent, dirty and sophisticated—and therein lies their charm.

WHO TAKES THEM: Pretty much everybody in New York takes a cab once in a while. Some do so more than most: frantic businessmen jump in cabs from meeting to meeting; uptown ladies stroll elegantly to curbs and wait for their doormen to flag their rides to dinner; and a good percentage of anyone coming home late or drunk would rather spend money on a taxi than face the sobering ordeal of the subway. Of course, whoever you are, you're likely to be on your own—only when the MTA goes on strike or the city grinds to a snowy halt do people volunteer to share their cabs.

WHAT'S GOOD: They're everywhere, all the time. The streets are paved with yellow in Manhattan, and if you live in a busy part of Brooklyn or Queens you'll seldom have to wait long for one to come along. If you know where you're going, you can probably get there quicker in a taxi than you could any other way. And compared to most cities in the world, even with the recent fare increases, taxis in New York are relatively inexpensive, making them an indulgence you can afford more often than you think.

WHAT'S NOT: Yellow taxis aren't the comfiest cars in the world, and an especially reckless driver can leave you at your destination feeling violated and disoriented, as if you've been kidnapped and roughed up in the back seat, yet still had to pay ten dollars for it. There are still drivers who will refuse point blank to take you out of Manhattan, and the farther out in the outer boroughs you end up the harder it is to find one to take you back in. When shifts change—usually around 4 p.m.—it can be difficult to find one with his lights on anywhere in the city. And in busy parts of town, at limousine hotspots like Times Square and Lincoln Center, or even simply when it rains, you have to put up quite a fight to beat off the competition for the few cars with their lights still on.

CAR SERVICES

WHAT THEY ARE: While yellow cabs are readily available throughout Manhattan and the nearer neighborhoods of the outer boroughs, the farther off the island you are, the more likely it is that you won't be able to hail one on the street. In these regions, on-call car services are the alternative when you need a private ride. Car services fall into two basic categories: companies with huge fleets that do airport trips and the like and smaller operations that serve the needs of a neighborhood by ferrying people out and around the city. The former require advance notice and reservations; the latter typically can send a car to pick you up anywhere between five minutes and half an hour after your call—these are the guys you want when you need to get home from Red Hook at 2 a.m. The rates that these companies charge are comparable to cabs, but it's better to settle on a price when you call, and confirm it with the driver when you get in.

WHO TAKES THEM: People straggling home from a night out in the outer boroughs; misguided airport-bound travelers (see "What's Not").

WHAT'S GOOD: Not having to wait on the street for a cab. If you are at a friend's apartment in Queens or Brooklyn, he or she probably has the numbers of a couple of nearby car services. (If not, ask any bar, restaurant, or deli.) The car service will give you an ETA for the car, and then you can return to your evening until it arrives.

WHAT'S NOT: Airport trips. Car services are neither cheaper nor necessarily more comfortable than a cab, and they're not terribly punctual. Better to just hail a cab or use the AirTrain when you are trying to make a plane.

CARS

WHAT THEY ARE: New York is truly unique among U.S. cities in that nuisance almost always outweighs convenience when it comes to cars. Practical if not essential in the rest of the country, car ownership here is a considerable expense and a burden that must be considered carefully before being taken on. On top of the hassles of parking and driving in the city (Manhattan is the worst, but other boroughs are no picnic either), the alternative modes of transport (subways, buses, cabs, and walking) are cheaper and easier ways of getting around. Having a car isn't even necessary for getting out of the city. Between the commuter trains (to New Jersey, Westchester, the Hudson Valley, Long Island, and Connecticut), Amtrak, the Chinatown buses (and their many imitators), and the lovely Hampton Jitney, there is no shortage of places you can get to on local mass transit. (See page 249 for more on nearby getaways.)

WHO USES THEM: Reverse commuters (people who live in NYC but commute outside the city to places not easily accessible by bus or train); those with places to weekend; families; Calvin Trillin, who wrote the novel *Tepper Isn't Going Out*, a cult classic about parking in New York. (Excellent for keeping in the glove compartment for when you are waiting for a spot to open up.)

WHAT'S GOOD: Cars come in handy for DIY moves, road trips, and for shopping treks to places like the ABC Carpet & Home Warehouse Outlet (see page 112). But unless you're going to the outlets every weekend, you're probably better off renting cars when you need them.

WHAT'S NOT: Parking. NYC treats cars like the second-class citizens they are, putting the needs of every other resident before theirs. Cars parked on the street are subjected to cryptic and sometimes contradictory messages on parking signs; myriad forbidden parking zones (signaled by NO PARKING ANYTIME and the even more menacing DON'T EVEN THINK OF PARKING HERE signs); the nearly ubiquitous alternate-side-of-the-street street-cleaning laws that require a biweekly evacuation of comfortably parked vehicles at inconvenient hours; and the blood-sport of jockeying with hyper-vigilant veteran NYC car owners to reclaim their spots after each street cleaning is done. All for the privilege of parallel parking fender-to-fender outside, at the mercy of the weather, somewhere in the general area of where you live or are trying to go (if you're lucky). But there are few alternatives: Apartments that come with parking spaces are as rare as free hundred dollar bills, and keeping a car in a garage is like putting a kid through private school.

WALKING

WHAT IT IS: In many other cities, even those with good public transportation, it is rare to see people walking on the street outside certain proscribed business districts and promenades. New York, obviously, is completely different. Here, walking doesn't take place in specific designated areas or along multi-lane roads at your peril. Pedestrians truly have the right of way, and cars have no choice but to bow to our multitudes, crossing in the middle of the street and weaving through cars stopped at lights. And how much walking will you do? A mile is roughly 20 blocks or 7 avenues, which can be conquered on a typical day; throw in a few extra stops, and it's easily two miles or more.

WHO DOES IT: Everyone! People run errands, stroll leisurely, catch up with friends, cross bridges, and get to dinner, lunch, brunch, parties, dates, and work, all on foot. In fact, a longish walk to the office on a pleasant morning is a great treat before a long day's work.

WHAT'S GOOD: Walking (or a combination of walking and public transport) can get you anywhere; there are few uncrossable intersections or insurmountable neighborhoods in this city. With a basic sense of direction and a bit of common sense, you can conquer the city with your feet alone. New Yorkers are infamous for being harried, and it's true that we often do walk fast, but we also get to take in way more of the world around us on a daily basis than those trapped in their cars. Instead of traffic jams, road rage, and soulless highways, we get fresh air, historic sites, and the occasional movie shoot or celebrity sighting.

WHAT'S NOT: New York is safer than it's ever been, but we still wouldn't recommend walking through parks or unfamiliar neighborhoods late at night. If do you find yourself walking around a less-than-bustling locale after dark, veer toward commercial strips with bars and all-night delis, where you might be able to call a car service if you need one.

STATEN ISLAND FERRY

WHAT IT IS: The ferry is Staten Island's celebrated link to mainland New York, carrying more than 60,000 passengers every day to and from Manhattan's South Street. Traveling on the ferry is a bona fide tourist attraction, and the only other way to travel between the island and Manhattan is by car via the Verrazano Bridge in Brooklyn.

WHO RIDES IT: The ferry exists almost entirely for the sake of Staten Island's commuter population—which is larger than you would think—and for the tourist crowd. Providing a direct link from the island to the Financial District in Manhattan and subway hubs to Midtown, the ferry brings crowds of suits back and forth during the rush hours and spends its daytimes giving tourists fantastic views of the city from its deck.

WHAT'S GOOD: It's free, the views are great, and how often do you get to ride in a boat anyway?

WHAT'S NOT: If the weather's bad or the water's choppy, riding the ferry can be an unpleasant few minutes. And who wants to ride in a boat anyway?

ALL THE REST OF THOSE TRAINS . . .

There are a bunch of trains that connect the city to other nearby areas and suburbs, but they are not only for commuters. These trains can be useful for things like day and weekend trips and getting to and from the airport. And who knows, you might have a friend living in Hoboken.

The PATH is a subwaylike train that runs from the west side of Manhattan to several New Jersey towns across the river. The PATH stops in Manhattan are on Sixth Avenue, from 33rd Street down to Christopher Street and at the World Trade Center. (The 33rd, 23rd, 14th Street, and World Trade Center PATH stations are connected to subway stations.) PATH trains officially run on a schedule, but you can generally count on their running about as regularly as subways, with frequent service on weekdays and longer lulls between trains on the weekends. You can also pay for the pleasantly low $1.50 ride with a MetroCard. The PATH is particularly useful in the event of an MTA strike, as its trains will still run when our subways don't.

NJ Transit, Metro-North, and the LIRR are the real commuter trains. These trains run on timetables, and are crammed at peak hours with workers going to and from the suburbs of New Jersey, New York, and Connecticut. However, these trains also stop at some destinations of interest to carless New Yorkers. For instance, you can take NJ Transit to Atlantic City, Metro-North to the Hudson Valley, and the LIRR to the Hamptons.

Newish additions in the local public transport arsenal are the AirTrains at Newark and JFK airports. The AirTrains are monorails that are connected to a nearby train station, which go around each airport and make stops at each terminal. AirTrain is swift (leaving every two to twelve minutes), economical, and very easy to use, though the protocol differs slightly between the two airports. For Newark, take NJ Transit to the Newark Airport stop (you can also take Amtrak, but the ticket is much more expensive), and use the same ticket on both trains (the AirTrain cost is built into the $15 NJ Transit ticket). The trip from Penn Station to the Newark Airport stop takes 20 minutes, and it's a quick walk from the platform to the AirTrain. For JFK, you can take the LIRR from Penn station, or take the subway. Unless you live in Queens, we strongly encourage you to splurge on the LIRR. It's more comfortable, much quicker (exactly 20 minutes, as opposed to an hour or more), and the transfer to the AirTrain at the Jamaica LIRR station is much easier than at the Howard Beach or Sutphin Boulevard/Archer Avenue subway stations. (A one-way peak fare to Jamaica on the LIRR is $7.25; off-peak is $5.25.) One nifty thing about taking the AirTrain to JFK is that you can pay for it with a MetroCard; it's $5 if you have a pay-per-ride card, but less if you have an unlimited weekly or monthly card. FYI: you can also ride AirTrain for free within the airports if you need to make a connection at a different terminal.

For information and schedules for PATH Trains and AirTrain, visit the Port Authority of New York and New Jersey web site, www.panynj.gov

For information and schedules for Metro-North and the LIRR, visit the MTA web site, www.mta.info

For information and schedules for NJ Transit, visit www.njtransit.com

→ Subway Etiquette ←

Whether it's your dad screaming at you to take your feet off the seat in the car, or an irate customer wincing in the back of a cab at the incessant chatter of his negligent driver, every mode of transport has its own established guidelines for good and bad behavior. The New York subway system is the busiest and most crowded way to get around the city, and only years of agonizing experience can teach you all the nuances of subway etiquette. So we've digested them for you here, in a short guide to the unwritten rules of riding the subway.

- WHAT YOU LOOKIN' AT? We're not saying you should rule out social interaction altogether, but unchecked subway staring gets a bad rap in the city.

- BEWARE THE EMPTY CAR. If a crowded train pulls into a station with one conspicuously empty car, it's probably empty because there's a smell in there you wouldn't believe.

- KNOW YOUR STOPS. While this isn't Mexico City or Tokyo, and there are no baton-wielding transit cops to persuade you into a crowded train, it can still be difficult to wade through rush hour jams to get to the train doors in time. If you know which side of the train the doors open on at your stop, get up and stand closer to the doors before you get there and save yourself a wrestle and a dozen excuse me's. (And this is more a matter of convenience than etiquette, but if you know where the exits are at the stop you are going to, you can avoid the bottle-neck at the bottom of the stairs when you get off by walking to the correct car and door when you get on the train.)

- KEEP IT TO YOURSELF. Make sure your efforts to keep yourself comfortable and entertained do not encroach on your fellow riders. If you are listening to your iPod, keep the volume at a level that will not be audible to those around you. If you want to read in a crowded car, choose books or magazines rather than newspapers, so that you don't have to reach into the personal space of the person sitting next to you whenever you try to turn a page.

- A FINAL NEW YORK COURTESY. If you have the choice, don't sit right next to someone; sit at least one seat over. We don't want to be over-friendly now, do we?

EMERGENCY!

←→

We don't want to scare you, but life being what it is, there's a good possibility that at some point during your time in New York, something will go awry: you'll leave your wallet in a cab, perhaps, or the boiler in your apartment building will break in February. There's nothing specific about living here that will make an emergency more likely, but there are specific things that you should know if or when they occur. Following are some unfortunate scenarios and the ways you can navigate them as swiftly and painlessly as possible.

IF YOU'RE LOCKED OUT

If you're locked out of your apartment and this book is inside, we can't help you too much. So the best thing to do is take steps to ensure that this doesn't happen in the first place. (If you live in a building with a full-time doorman, you can skip this part, as you will most likely be able to leave a copy of the keys with him.) Keeping a copy of your keys with a neighbor in your building is an obvious defense, but not always a straightforward one, if you don't live in a particularly social building, or don't have neighbors you feel you can trust (or that you can trust to be at home when you need them). Leaving them with a friend in the neighborhood only works as well as you can trust that friend not to lose the set of keys, and leaving them under a doormat or flower pot is just asking for trouble.

One nifty option for the hyper vigilant would be a membership to NewYourKey. This genius service stores sets of keys for members and will speedily deliver them to you on-call, at any time of day or night. Keys are stored anonymously, so there's no way to trace them to your address (or license plate number, in the case of car keys), and you choose a password so that no one will be able to access your keys but you. The basic membership ($30 per year) includes storage of two sets (a set is all the keys needed to enter your home or car); the premium membership allows you to designate another person to whom the keys can be given (e.g. spouse or roommate). There is a $20 fee for each key retrieval—much less than the price of a locksmith, especially when you factor in the aggravation of having your locks changed. (Of course, if you're locked out because your keys and wallet have been stolen, you should change the locks no matter what.)

If you find yourself locked out with no recourse, a locksmith is never hard to find. Locksmiths around the city regularly pummel apartment buildings with fistfuls of business cards, so many that not even the most dedicated of supers would be able to keep up. If there isn't one by your door, there's probably one somewhere on your block. **NewYourKey, 646-322-3857, www.newyourkey.com**

IF YOUR WALLET IS STOLEN OR YOUR APARTMENT IS BROKEN INTO

Call your local precinct and file a police report as soon as possible. (Also see page 124.)

IF YOUR TOILET/REFRIGERATOR/ STOVE BREAKS (RENTERS)

There's good news and bad news. The good news is that your landlord must make the repairs at his or her cost. The bad news is that depending on your building and landlord, getting it to happen in a timely fashion may not be so easy, and you're at the mercy of whatever plumber, electrician, or other workman they send over. In any case, the first step is to call your landlord or management company. If it's a weekend and the office is closed or the landlord is not around, there should be an emergency contact or some sort of call-in system—although if there isn't, and something's already broken, there's a chance that it will have to wait until Monday.

IF YOUR TOILET/REFRIGERATOR/ STOVE BREAKS (OWNERS)

You're free to hire anyone you like, but it's up to you to find and hire the person. For electricians and plumbers (probably the two most common types of repairmen), you can go either with licensed or unlicensed. Contractors in New York that are licensed by the Department of Buildings will have taken classes and passed exams specific to their fields (electrical, plumbing, etc.) and undergone background checks. In general, licensed workmen can do more extensive work and are more likely to have insurance, but they are more expensive, and as their work is regulated by the licensing board, they may refuse to do work in your apartment without permission from your building's board. Those who are unlicensed can work anywhere, in theory can take care of simple, cosmetic repairs, and are less expensive, but the downside is that because they are less accountable than licensed workers, they are often less reliable. Caitlin's husband recently had to hire a second plumber to fix the mess that an unlicensed plumber made of their shower, but plenty of people we know have had fine experiences using them. That's the thing, though—they're hit or miss. Your best chance of assuring that the job will be done properly without messing up anything else in the apartment (a major concern if you're an owner) or inconveniencing you farther is to splurge for the guy with the license.

Unfortunately, it can take a little legwork as an individual to get a licensed repairman to agree to the job. Some will not take "simple" repair jobs: replacing track lighting, or fixing a leaky faucet or shower; others require a large minimum of hours; and some won't even take on jobs from owners of apartments unless they have permission from or relationships with the board or condo management. A good trick is to get a referral from staffpeople at your local hardware store—they often can refer good candidates based on your problem, type of building, and location.

IF THE HEAT GOES OFF SUDDENLY IN FEBRUARY

Oh boy. The loss of heat during winter is pretty far up there on the list of most uncomfortable things that can happen in your apartment, but it is, sadly, rather common here, particularly in older buildings. It's happened to Caitlin twice, in two different buildings, once as a renter and once as an owner. There are a bunch of possible causes, so depending on what it is, the repair time can take anywhere from a few hours to several days. If the boiler needs to be replaced entirely it can even take a week or more. That's what happened in the first building Caitlin lived in; Caitlin was out of her apartment for a week. The second time, however, the boiler just needed a simple repair job, and was completed in a few hours. The loss of heat is usually building-wide, and almost always affects the hot water as well.

Whether you are a renter or an owner, the first thing to do is call the landlord or managing agent—who hopefully has heard about the problem already and is on the case. If or how you'll be notified when it's fixed depends on whom you are dealing with. For instance, some management companies send e-mails to tenants to update them on the progress or when the problem has been fixed; with others, you'll have to keep calling to see if you can expect a shower when you get home that night. (Here's a tip about management companies, though: many keep traditional business hours, so make sure to call a bit before 5 p.m.)

If you are renting, you can try negotiating with your landlord about getting a break from the rent, and if your rent happens to be due during that time, you can try withholding it. Caitlin was able to deduct the full week that she was out of her apartment from the month's rent.

Incidentally, the two times this happened to Caitlin was over weekends, and both times she found she wasn't able to get in touch with her management companies until Monday morning. Learn from her mistakes and make sure your management company has an emergency call-in number for weekends and holidays.

IF YOUR CAR IS NOT WHERE YOU LEFT IT

Understandably cause for some alarm. Here, your first step should be to call the police (or 311 to get the police precinct for the area where you left your car). Since they enforce parking laws, they should be able to tell you whether your car has been towed, stolen, or "relocated," which means that it was moved for construction, a street fair or parade, or some other reason. If it's been relocated, the police should also be able to tell you where it is. If it hasn't been relocated or towed, it's probably been stolen, and you will already be on the phone with the police, who will help you with the next steps.

Not being car owners (or even drivers!) ourselves, we were surprised to learn that nearly everyone we know who has a car here has had theirs towed at some point. Why? Most said it happened because they were tricked by contradictory signs on the block they parked on (i.e., the sign you parked in front of states that there is no parking during certain hours, but another one farther down the block says no parking anytime), or that the police were not actually as informed about parking and towing as the city claims they are. Consider this story from a friend of ours:

"That night I parked on 17th Street in Chelsea, between 8th and 9th avenues, and dutifully noted that I would have to move my car by 9 the following morning. But at

8:45, my car was nowhere to be found. I don't know why I didn't notice that the entire block was devoid of cars, but all I could think was that my car—my 1999 manual Jetta, a peerless driving machine—had been stolen. So I got a croissant and called the police. They acknowledged that cars get stolen all the time, but further suggested that I search for my car within a 10-block radius, as construction crews have the license and ability to move cars that get in their way. Luckily, before I embarked on that stupid quest, I wondered if someone else might have towed my car. Turns out all cars actually must be moved from 17th Street by 8 a.m., not 9 as the sign indicated. The rest was an expensive blur: I had to pay a cab to drive me to an impound lot on the West Side Highway, where I pushed a couple hundred dollars in cash through a cubbyhole and subsequently saw my car miraculously reappear. And all was again well."

It seems to us that the moral of this story is that a towing can befall even the most vigilant of parkers, so best to know how to get your car back first and fight the system later. (Though taking pictures of the posted signs is a good idea if you believe that you weren't really parked illegally.)

You can find out if your car has in fact been towed by calling 311, or online on the city's towed vehicle locator, which, ironically, is not so easy to find. (The best way to get to it is by going to the Department of Finance web site's home page and under "Parking & Vehicles" click on "Locate Towed Vehicle.") If your car has been towed, you actually don't need to call the towing companies, as our friend did. Towed cars are deposited in the city's Tow Pounds (their caps, not ours), and you can retrieve them there. There is one Tow Pound in each of the five boroughs except Staten Island, and cars are usually deposited in the borough in which they were towed. The Pound in Manhattan is indeed by the West Side Highway, at Pier 76, by West 38th Street; it is open 24 hours a day Monday through Saturday (it's closed from 5 a.m. Sunday through 7 a.m. Monday).

To retrieve your car, you'll need to bring your driver's license, car insurance card, and registration (if it's in the glove department, they'll let you retrieve it, along with any personal items, as long as your license matches the registration), and pay the fee. Don't send someone else to pick up your car for you: cars are only released to registered vehicle owners or their spouses; if you send someone in you place, he or she will need a notarized letter from you. Towing fees vary according to the reason for which your vehicle was towed.

Sounds too easy, right? Right. You can't retrieve your car if you have any outstanding parking tickets, and parking tickets cannot be paid at the impound lot. So if you do have outstanding tickets, you'll have to pay the tickets first and then pick up your car. Waiting for your car to reappear is the icing on the ordeal—try to minimize your time hanging around the Pound by going at off-peak hours (lunchtime through the late afternoon are the busiest times). Also, you'll probably want your car back as soon as possible anyway, but you'll also have to pay a storage fee for each additional day your car is left in the Pound after it is towed.

For more information, click on "Parking & Vehicles" on the home page of the New York City Department of Finance, www.nyc.gov/dof, or visit the NYPD web site, www.nyc.gov/nypd

IF THE DRY CLEANER RUINS OR LOSES AN ITEM OF CLOTHING

Though dry cleaning horror stories are memorable and regrettable, given the number of people and cleaners in this city, and the frequency with which many use them, the chances of your clothes getting ruined or lost by a cleaner probably aren't that high. Still, if it does happen to you, you should have a defense prepared if you want to recoup some of the damages.

If the cleaner has lost an item, then obviously you should address the problem when you try to pick it up. But if it's ruined somehow in the cleaning process, you should also make your complaint when the item is returned to you—it'll be a much harder battle to get any kind of compensation once the evidence has left the premises.

So what exactly are you battling for? Beyond not paying for the cleaning, what kind of compensation you'll get depends a little on your persistence and negotiating skills, and a lot on the particular dry cleaner. A friend of ours whose shirt was recently damaged at his regular dry cleaner was told that the "industry standard" was to give store credit of 50 percent of the piece's original cost. We couldn't find any official policy to back that up, but we say feel free to use that line, as it is a fair compromise. The one piece of leverage you do have is the stiff competition in the dry cleaning market. If you are having trouble getting your dry cleaner to agree to compensating you in some way, tell the proprietor that you will take your business elsewhere, and will tell people you know to stop going there. The threat of lost business may yield some additional concessions. Of course, you may want to stop going to that cleaner after one incident anyway. Luckily, the other bright side of having so many cleaners here is that you should be able to find another one without any trouble.

Still fuming? You can try taking the cleaner to small claims court (see page 135), where dry cleaning disputes are some of the most common. Be warned, though, that you risk investing more time and effort by doing that than the item is worth. You'll also need real hard evidence: a picture or some evidence of what the garment looked like before it was damaged, and a receipt or some other proof of how much the item cost.

IF YOU'RE OUT IN THE CITY AND YOU NEED A BATHROOM

An emergency of a different type, and a kind of logical side effect of the walking-heavy New York City lifestyle. If you're out for a couple of hours wandering or shopping, it's not unlikely that you'll need a restroom at some point, but not know where to find one, especially in a neighborhood you don't know that well. Unlike malls or shopping centers, you won't find large public restrooms conveniently placed in our shopping districts. New York City has been graced with some futuristic public pay toilets, but we wouldn't blame you for being a bit wary of those, and as they use fourteen gallons of water and tons of toxic disinfectants for each use, our environmental conscience prevents us from endorsing them.

So where to go? Chain restaurants, coffee bars, and cavernous stores like Barnes & Noble are an obvious fallback. But this is New York! There is as much diversity and idiosyncrasy in this category as any other, and the savvy citizen will set the bar higher. For instance, hotels always have a public restroom somewhere near the ground floor, and New York's got plenty of them, many of which are very pleasant places to visit. No one will know that you aren't staying at the Maritime or Gramercy Park Hotel when you walk through the lobby to use the bathroom. Department stores—another thing the city's got a bunch of—are also a sure bet, and the fancier the store, the fancier the bathrooms. If you belong to a gym with multiple locations, you can get access to the bathroom, and see what another branch looks like. A personal favorite is the Time Warner Center, which really is a fancy mall, because it has a ton of restrooms and there's never a wait. In a pinch, many restaurants and cafés will let you use their bathrooms even if you are not buying anything.

IF YOU NEED TO GET MARRIED—FAST

There are many reasons to get married at City Hall—many of them good. We've heard of couples who've done it for insurance, to co-sign a mortgage, because they couldn't wait until their actual wedding day, and because they thought why not? Of course, some couples end up at City Hall unintentionally, and in a hurry. The status of marriage can help couples get through certain legal, financial, and immigration issues that can pop up suddenly and unexpectedly, and require immediate attention. Unlike when you get married by a clergy member or another public official off-site, when you get married at City Hall, you get your marriage certificate immediately. You can also get official copies at the same time, which may be necessary for couples whose reason for getting married is time-sensitive, like some of those just described.

Regardless of how the couple ends up there, though, presuming that the union is one that is being celebrated, City Hall is as good a place to do it as any. You can invite guests (just remind them that they'll need to bring photo ID to get into the building), dress up as much (or as little) as you like, take pictures, bring flowers, have bridesmaids and groomsmen—pretty much everything you would have anywhere else, except an actual walk down the aisle. And while you won't have the venue to yourself, sharing the ceremony with a bunch of other happy couples from all over the city (and the world) makes for an experience just as special, and potentially more memorable.

If you're part of the couple, the first thing to remember is that New York State has a mandatory 24-hour waiting period between when you get the license and when you can get married. So you need to plan at least a day ahead. Once you get the license, call the office of the City Clerk for an appointment. (You can call immediately for an appointment, but can not take one until after the waiting period is over. There isn't usually a long wait for an available appointment, so if you are in a hurry, you can usually get one within a day or two after the waiting period ends.) You can get married in any of the five boroughs; ceremonies are held in the City Clerk's offices in each borough (see office addresses on page 133), Monday through Friday from 8:30 a.m. to 4 p.m. (3:45 p.m. in Manhattan). In Manhattan, ceremonies take place just across the hall from the marriage license office, in a room with an electric sign marked "Chapel." Make sure to bring the marriage license, another money order for $25, ID, and one witness (not related to either member of the couple) who is over 18 and who also has ID. After the ceremony, make sure to check the marriage certificate before you leave. Making corrections is time-consuming, and after the first 24 hours, you will be charged a $40 fee (of course, payable by money order only).

Both guests and the couple should arrive at City Hall about 15 minutes before the ceremony appointment, to allow time to get through security in the lobby. It's unlikely that the ceremony will actually start on time, though, so you will probably have to wait around for a while until you are called into the chapel. (They don't actually give couples numbers, but unless your name is John or Mary, don't count on anyone getting it right.) The ceremony itself will be brief—the one that Caitlin attended took less than two minutes. All told, the experience is a bit bureaucratic and not especially romantic, but if you bring a sense of humor and a bit of time, it can be pretty fun.

There are plenty of places within walking distance to go to celebrate, and because it will be in the middle of a weekday, getting a last-minute reservation probably won't be a problem. Caitlin's group got a table for ten at Bouley with less than 24 hours' notice. For something a little less extravagant and appropriately family-style, there are plenty of excellent Chinese restaurants in the area. If you are in a pinch, try to think of where you went to lunch the last time you had jury duty.

For more information, click on "Marriage Bureau" on the home page of the Office of the City Clerk: www.cityclerk.nyc.gov

⟶ Eviction: Can It Happen to You? ⟵

Last year, Bianca Jagger was successfully evicted from a rent-controlled apartment on Park Avenue that she had occupied for more than twenty years after an appeals court ruled in favor of her landlord. If the most famous rock divorcée in the world was sent packing, could it happen to you?

Fear not. It is extremely difficult to actually be evicted from an apartment in New York, even under the worst circumstances. Of the relatively few tenants who are actually served eviction notices each year (in the low thousands), only a fraction of those actually end up having to leave their apartments—most either resolve the dispute or prevail over their landlords in court. Assuming you are paying your rent and haven't engaged in any illicit interior renovation projects, the likelihood of its happening to you is probably about the same as stumbling on a rent-controlled apartment on Park Avenue (which, incidentally, there will be one fewer of, now that Jagger's will turn market-rate).

Of course, it's still preferable to keep eviction off the table altogether. Withholding rent when a service like heat or hot water is not working properly probably won't get you evicted, but to be safe, you should notify your landlord first, and be prepared to pay as soon as the service is returned. Besides paying rent, not doing anything illegal in or to the apartment will also keep you safe. There are situations where a landlord would like an apartment or a number of apartments to be vacated, so he or she may be looking for things that will provide justification for an eviction—tenants in rent-controlled and rent-stabilized apartments are most susceptible to this, because the landlord can sometimes rent an apartment at market rate once the current tenant leaves. In Jagger's case, the eviction occurred on the grounds that because of Jagger's visa status (she's a British citizen and is in the U.S. on a tourist visa), the apartment couldn't have been her primary residence, which is one of the conditions of keeping a rent-stabilized apartment. But given the desirability of the real estate in this situation, the landlord likely wasn't too broken up about being able to start charging a market-rate rent.

If an eviction notice does end up on your door for any reason, here's what you need to know:

- If you've received a notice to evict, it means that your landlord has been to housing court and a judgment was passed to evict. Assuming that you'll want to contest the eviction, you should go immediately to the clerk of the Housing Court office (officially known as the Housing Part of Civil Court) to ask for an order to "Show Cause." This will delay the eviction, and start a court proceeding with your landlord.

- Notices to evict guarantee the tenant seventy-two hours to vacate the apartment from the time of posting. Eviction can take place anytime after that, but you can find out when your eviction is scheduled by calling the City Marshall.

- No matter how much rent you owe or what you've done to the place, it is always illegal for a landlord to evict a tenant by changing the locks or padlocking the door. In the exceedingly unlikely event that either of those things happen, call the police.

For more information on landlord-tenant disputes, visit the Housing Part of the Civil Court web site: www.courts.state.ny.us/courts/nyc/housing/index.shtml

SERVICE GUIDE

$\longleftrightarrow$

Food shopping, filling prescriptions, having a computer repaired, getting dressed in the morning. All things that people do everywhere, every day. In New York, however, there are so many more ways to get these things done; knowing the best way to accomplish each task can minimize time wasted and money spent, and maximize quality of life and storage space.

Getting your sundries in this city boils down to one familiar, maddening irony: there is more choice and variety of things to buy here than anywhere else, but you'll probably have less room to keep what you get. Cheap multipacks of paper towels are only as good as the amount of rolls you can store. The same goes for clothes and shoes—mindless accumulation in this city never ends well. So this section is as much about what you really need as it is about where to go. As for repairs—if you've got something broken in your apartment, whether it's a watch or an armchair, it would be a much better use of space if it worked, right? So keep reading.

Besides making the most of your space and the offerings available here, this service guide is meant to outline the landscape in a couple of key areas, share a few of our personal favorites and tips, and get you prepared (and excited!) to face the day.

SUPERMARKETS

For any other city in the world, a guide to supermarket shopping might seem completely unnecessary: we all know our favorite chains, we all know where we go for one thing or another. But in New York, choosing the right place and the right time to shop can transform a mundane weekly stroll around the aisles into a joyful reminder of what makes the city such a unique place to live. Here you will find yourself faced with a dazzling array of options for food shopping, from small markets packed with fancy and unusual items to miniaturized versions of the monster markets that serve the rest of the country and old-fashioned bodegas and delis. Whether you get your kicks fighting for carts with sweatsuit-clad celebrities, chatting up the other boys and girls you bump into at the deli counter, or hunting gourmet bargains, New York's grocery aisles have it all. With that in mind, no self-respecting service guide would be complete without a rundown of the city's finest and most popular places to pick up the groceries—and some cautionary notes about the ones to avoid.

This is a particularly exciting time to be food shopping in New York. (Really!) The grocery landscape is in the middle of a transformation. Traditional supermarkets have been disappearing, with some longtime regional chains having recently vanished for good. Gourmet and specialty food stores, once the trademark of the Upper West Side, are now found all over the city. Fashionable national chains like Whole Foods and Trader Joe's have been embraced by the urban masses, and New Yorkers who wouldn't be caught dead in a Costco or Sam's Club will wait in line for thirty minutes or longer to pay for frozen canapés at Trader Joe's. At the same time, some of the more charming long-standing elements of city marketing are—for now—managing to hold on. The city's still got a strong deli culture, and though one can be found on just about every block in many places, each offers its own idiosyncratic selection. Trusty as ever for the day's newspaper and coffee, a stop in any deli can also turn up a cornucopia of unexpected delectables.

Each market has its own personality, but individual branches also often reflect their neighborhoods in subtle ways as well. Kosher-food sections are prominent on the Upper West Side, while ramen holds a pride of place in stores by NYU. The offerings at independently owned markets and delis also vary according to the tastes and whims of the owners. Exploring the markets in a neighborhood will tell you a lot about its demographics, but can also introduce you to things you'd never have thought to put in your cupboard. Dig in!

⟶ Shopping Tips ⟵

- **DON'T BE TEMPTED TO STOCK UP.** Do you really want to keep sixteen rolls of toilet paper piled up on your bathroom floor?

- **DON'T OVERESTIMATE HOW MUCH YOU CAN CARRY BACK TO YOUR APARTMENT.** Many grocery stores will deliver, but if you are planning on carrying everything back yourself, make sure you'll be able to handle it all. A good way to do this is to use a handbasket, rather than a shopping cart.

- **TO TRULY REAP THE BENEFITS OF THE CITY'S OFFERINGS, THINK LIKE A VILLAGER.** Instead of trying to get everything you need at one market, consider every market in an area, and explore and experiment with the options at each. Keep your eyes peeled for independent butcher shops, bakeries, cheese shops, wine stores, and the like, often found on side streets or a little off the beaten path. New York is one of the few places in the country where it's just as easy to get your cuts of meat from an experienced old-time butcher as it is from a generic supermarket deli counter.

- CONSIDER CARRYING REUSABLE BAGS WITH YOU. You'll be making more frequent trips to the store for smaller loads, and those plastic bags can accumulate very rapidly. A few stores, such as Whole Foods, give a small discount for bringing your own bag.

C-Town

WHAT IT IS: C-Town supermarkets are quiet contenders on the New York shopping circuit, particularly in the outer boroughs where they face softer competition than in Manhattan. And unlike other chains, their locations don't seem to influence their stock—the same range and quality of produce can be found in any of the dozens of branches from Brooklyn to the Bronx. Like Gristedes and Key Food, C-Town is essentially a second-tier supermarket without much strength in its prepared food departments, leading stores to rely on the value of fresh produce and brand-name goods to draw in a loyal crowd. But unlike the others, C-Town somehow manages to be both inexpensive and good at the same time. Why some branch names are preceded with the name "Steve" is a mystery.

WHO'S THERE: Unassuming shoppers with an eye for a discount. It's by no means a bargain bin of knock-off ham and twenty-nine-cent chicken wings, but it attracts a wide demographic, from students to seniors whose common priority is an affordable weekly shop. C-Town is one of the few supermarkets where it really pays to read the pamphlet featuring what's cheap that week—the only downside of which is that its aisles are the slowest-moving in the city, with shoppers pausing every few paces to see what else is on the list. Pineapples. Check. Coconuts. No? On we go . . . .

WHAT'S GOOD: The fresh fruit and vegetables are almost always outstanding, and the stores pay attention to the seasons—when it's mango time, you'll really know it.

WHAT'S NOT: The prepared foods counter is C-Town's Achilles' heel. Buy your "fresh" lasagna elsewhere and you can enjoy this pleasant, affordable market without reproach.

Multiple locations; see www.ctownsupermarkets.com

D'Agostino

WHAT IT IS: It's difficult to know whether D'Agostino should be seen as a chain of underwhelming supermarkets or a franchise of glorified delis. With so many locations across the city, including several in Brooklyn and Queens, it's often the biggest grocery in a neighborhood by default. Undeniably better stocked with the requisite sundries than bodegas and reliable as a source for culinary necessities, the stores' prices are higher than they should be, and in the absence of the kind of distinguishing specialties available in other supermarkets, shoppers tend to view a trip to D'Agostino more as a last resort than a proactive choice.

WHO'S THERE: With so many locations all over the city, D'Agostino is truly, for better or worse, a locals' market. Unlike Fairway, there's no particular feature of D'Ag that would prompt someone to make a longer trip than a walk around the block; and unlike a Trader Joe's, there isn't the sense of getting great value for money that would send someone out of his or her way to go there. D'Agostino instead is a regular destination for lazier locals who don't feel like trekking up—or down—town to the larger stores.

WHAT'S GOOD: Anything sealed. About the best thing that can be said about D'Agostino is it carries all the tinned, canned, jarred, and bottled brands that make a kitchen a kitchen, from good dried pastas and sauces to tuna fish, cereals, and olive oil. It's pretty standard stuff, but the stores stock a good range of the big-brand items that you might miss in the more exclusive or ethical aisles of a genuinely upscale supermarket.

WHAT'S NOT: Anything fresh. Often the only difference between the cold cuts, cheeses, or prepared foods at D'Agostino and its Boar's Head counterparts at the local deli will be D'Agostino's inflated prices. You'll need to allow yourself extra time to sort through the produce for the decent fruit and vegetables, and salad leaves and breads in particular are likely to be older than you might like them to be.

Multiple locations; see www.dagnyc.com

Dean & DeLuca

WHAT IT IS: To some, Dean & DeLuca is the prince of supermarkets, the jewel in Manhattan's grocery crown. To others, it's an overpriced tourist trap that won't stock hens' eggs when quails' eggs will do. There is truth in both ways of thinking. There's no doubt that Dean & DeLuca stocks only the very best of whatever it sells, from cookware to chocolate, peanut butter, and foie gras. But its dedication to the upper crust means it's more a luxury than a local market, a perfect mistress to roving gourmets but an unforgiving wife to regular shoppers.

WHO'S THERE: Eschewing the outer boroughs for the dependably glamorous custom of Manhattanites, Dean & DeLuca has outlets in only the pricier parts of the city, and therefore attracts a steady stream of hungry European tourists and spendthrift sophisticates. The company's flagship stores are in the busiest parts of Soho and the Upper East Side, so shopping there at peak times means rubbing shoulders with an unusually chic and frantic crowd. Its cafés, dotted around town from Greenwich Village to Murray Hill, are quieter and more accessible, and are popular with locals looking for good coffee and fancy sandwiches.

WHAT'S GOOD: Cost and company aside, it's hard to go wrong at Dean & DeLuca. The produce is fresh, the selection of cold meats and cheeses is the best you can get without going to a specialty store, and the meat, poultry, and fish counters are stocked with everything from exotic game to seasonal shellfish and fine examples of the humble sausage. Ordering from the cooked-food counter is the closest you can come in a supermarket to bringing a restaurant into your kitchen. But the stars of the show, surprisingly, are the baked goods: turn up early and you could walk away with warm crusty loaves sliced to your liking and the tastiest doughnuts in the city.

WHAT'S NOT: It's not that anything at Dean & DeLuca is bad—it's just difficult to justify paying double what you would at the deli down the block for eggs, ice cream, butter, and the daily sundries.

560 Broadway at Prince Street, (212-226-6800); 1150 Madison Avenue, at 85th Street, (212-717-0800) www.deananddeluca.com

Fairway

WHAT IT IS: A dark horse of the New York epicurean scene, Fairway has quietly remained a staple of good fresh food and reasonable prices for many years. With just three relatively out-of-the-way locations—in Harlem, on the Upper West Side, and in Red Hook—Fairway can nevertheless boast the city's largest supermarkets, vast and cavernous halls with more of everything than anywhere else. Unpretentious to the extent that it can feel colder and less user-friendly than its shinier and more expensive competitors, Fairway maintains incredibly high standards of fresh produce, meats, and cheeses, and stocks pretty much everything you could ever wish to find in a grocery store.

WHO'S THERE: People can live in New York for years and never go to a Fairway. On the other hand, there are people who drive across boroughs and state lines to shop there. A treasure for locals of the three New York locations and a mecca for foodies in the know, Fairway attracts a completely mixed and eclectic crowd. The down-to-earth atmosphere of the stores combined with the quality of the food make it as appealing to a chore shopper in sweatpants as it is to a gourmand the afternoon before a dinner party.

WHAT'S GOOD: Simply put, the fruit, meat, and fish. The sweet smell of the most resplendent fresh fruit department in the city reaches your nostrils blocks away from the Red Hook branch, and it's well known that meat and fish lovers will travel many miles to stroll around choosing cuts at the legendary cold room in the Harlem branch.

WHAT'S NOT: The physical experience of shopping at Fairway isn't always a pleasurable one. Unless you're there when they open the doors, you're likely to find yourself at the back of a very long line at the checkout. And with so much food in such huge spaces, Fairway has a distinctly unglamorous wholesale feel to it that can put off the city's more urbane shoppers, who prefer a quick in-out with a basket to a morning-long ordeal with an unwieldy cart.

Multiple locations; see www.fairwaymarket.com

Food Emporium

WHAT IT IS: A regular supermarket for the urban professional. While Food Emporium isn't really a fancy store, it obviously caters to a more upscale clientele than some of the other basic grocery chains here. Its 16 NYC locations are mostly in neighborhoods whose residents are known for working long hours, enjoy their sushi and gelato, and are willing to pay a premium for convenience and quality. While the prices are a bit higher than a Key Food or a Gristedes, the stores tend to be pretty clean, and better stocked and staffed. If this is your neighborhood supermarket, you're in good hands.

WHO'S THERE: Not all New Yorkers order in every night. Here you'll find residents of all ages shopping like they do everywhere else in the country, filling up regular-size shopping carts with Kellogg's, Tide, and Lean Cuisine. The only difference is that instead of loading everything in the trunk of their cars, they either cart their purchases home in their own shopping carts or have them delivered.

WHAT'S GOOD: Generous hours, with all stores staying open until midnight most nights of the week and a few open 24 hours. Home delivery is easy and speedy, and you can also order online. Specialty offerings are above average for a chain grocery store. There's no shortage of Kosher foods, seasonal items, and choices for vegetarians, sugar-avoiders, or cholesterol-watchers—this is the place to go for a box of menorah candles on the last day of Hanukkah. And many locations sell Carvel ice-cream cakes, the ultimate last-minute crowd-pleaser.

WHAT'S NOT: Bakery items are the giveaway that you're still in the supermarket.

Multiple locations; see www.thefoodemporium.com

Garden of Eden

WHAT IT IS: If Dean & DeLuca and the Food Emporium were to have a love child, it might come out like a Garden of Eden. G of E has a gourmet pedigree—with its selection of coffees, cheeses, and specialty condiments, it might have even been considered a real gourmet market a decade ago—but the stores themselves are modest, and many of the grocery offerings are the same as what you'll find at a regular supermarket, with a bigger markup. There's something a little mismatched about the merch at Garden of Eden—you get the sense that it has not done its market research the way Whole Foods has—but that can actually work to your benefit. There are lots of high-quality foods and ingredients, as well as almost any basic staple you'd need. If you're throwing a party or having a dinner and only want to visit one market, this is a good place to shop.

WHO'S THERE: On weekends, locals doing the grocery rounds (the Chelsea and Union Square branches are near a Whole Foods); singles and young professionals picking up ready-to-heat dinner during the week.

WHAT'S GOOD: Fresh pasta, the olive bars, and the cheese. The people working the cheese counter are usually friendly and more knowledgeable than they look, so don't hesitate to ask for recommendations. There are plenty of French, Italian, and American cheeses, but Greek cheeses (feta and others) also seem to be a specialty. Also, since most people shop with a handbasket rather than a shopping cart here, and because of the high ratio of cash registers per square foot, the checkout line moves quickly, even when it's crowded.

WHAT'S NOT: The produce is neither reliably fresh nor well-priced, and you'll save some pennies buying your Saran Wrap and cat food at a regular supermarket. Catering orders are hit or miss—while the prepared food is fine, composing platters for a party is not one of the staff's strengths.

Multiple locations; see www.edengourmet.com

Gristedes

WHAT IT IS: These apostropheless eyesores are the bottom of the supermarket barrel: uneven offerings, dirty stores, abysmal service, and no great values. Gristedes stores weren't always bad; we can only speculate on the reasons for the decline, but perhaps it has something to do with the rent increases that drove some of the other long-standing chains out of the city. Rumor has it that the chain's billionaire owner is considering a run for mayor; let's say that he won't be getting our vote.

WHO'S THERE: On our last visit, the single operating cash register had a young boy bagging the groceries.

WHAT'S GOOD: Products from brands you've never heard of (or didn't know were still around) can be interesting to try on a whim if you're seduced by the retro packaging, though you should try to find a sell-by date on the package before consuming, especially the dustier ones.

WHAT'S NOT: Ancient grocery items, dirty aisles, the conveyor belts that look like they haven't been wiped down since the Reagan years . . .

Multiple locations; see www.gristedes.com

Key Food

WHAT IT IS: Ubiquitous in Brooklyn, Queens, and the Bronx, but with only five locations shared across Manhattan and Staten Island, Key Food is a bane of the busier residential outer boroughs. Unhappily caught between a large deli and a small supermarket, a Key Food store is likely to have an incomplete and erratic selection of goods at irregular prices, cramped aisles, and unhelpful staff at the registers. The prices are low, but the exchange seems fair, as the quality of food is mediocre at best once you stray beyond Hellmann's, Heinz, or Bumble Bee.

WHO'S THERE: Few people would shop at Key Food out of preference alone: the many stores attract outer-borough locals who appreciate having a cheap store nearby.

WHAT'S GOOD: Residents of southeast Brooklyn can shop at Key Food online, which saves them the depressing chore of stalking the aisles.

WHAT'S NOT: The fresh meat, fish, and poultry counters are best avoided entirely.

Multiple locations; see www.keyfood.com

Morton Williams

WHAT IT IS: Characterless and charm-free, Morton Williams is a small chain with about ten locations in Manhattan and two in the Bronx. We'd love to throw our support behind a family-owned local business like this one, but though their web site claims that it's been in the NYC area since 1946, the stores feel like they're managed by a corporate office in New Jersey. It's not that these markets are bad, exactly, it's more that the atmosphere is totally nondescript, which makes shopping at them kind of soul-sucking. Though the offerings are fine and can even get downright exciting (the 57th Street location has a particularly impressive imported beer selection), that the stores are well lit is about the nicest compliment we can muster up for them.

WHO'S THERE: Locals. Morton Williams is fine, but not worth seeking out.

WHAT'S GOOD: Imported and international food offerings are notable. There is no lack of choice in the pesto aisle.

WHAT'S NOT: Anything that doesn't come in a box, jar, or can. Though several locations have eat-in areas, pass on the prepared foods, sushi, salads bars, and bakery items.

Multiple locations; see www.mortonwilliams.com

Trader Joe's

WHAT IT IS: Trader Joe's arrived in Manhattan to much fanfare in the spring of 2006. The single Union Square store has been mobbed since the morning it opened, drawing crowds from all corners of the borough that are willing to wait on Soviet-era lines to pay for their well-priced groceries and frozen foods.

WHO'S THERE: As of this writing, everyone, from every borough, all the time. A second location in Rego Park, Queens, has recently opened, but it hasn't made a noticeable dent in the crowds. Relief may come with the opening of a branch on Atlantic Avenue in Brooklyn.

WHAT'S GOOD: If you are into organic home products, you can save quite a bit of money by buying them here. Recycled paper towels and toilet paper, chemical-free soaps and detergents, and other cleaning products are dollars cheaper than at health food stores or Whole Foods. Free samples and coffee at the cooking station in the back are something to look forward to as the checkout line creeps through the store toward registers. Scrambled Egg Beaters with onion and cheddar? Yes, please!

WHAT'S NOT: Besides the crowds? Despite its fame in other parts of the country, the Trader Joe's wine store will probably seem a little bit lame to anyone with wine-buying experience in this city. Dirt-cheap offerings with cutesy but not particularly knowledgeable-sounding descriptions don't seem very appealing when you know you can get a perfectly respectable bottle for only a dollar or two more a block away at Union Square Wines, or one of the city's many other excellent wine stores.

Multiple locations; see www.traderjoes.com

Westside Market

WHAT IT IS: Though it only has three locations in the city (all in Manhattan), we want to single out this terrific mini-chain for excellence in neighborhood service. Westside Market is comparable to Garden of Eden, but its stores seem to have a better handle on what New Yorkers want in a grocery store. In addition to the requisite olive bar, cheese counter, and prepared food offerings, they also stock a smart selection of basic grocery items, including things like cleaning and paper products. So when you need to pick up groceries and dinner after work, you don't have to choose between a supermarket with so-so prepared food and a smaller market with fewer staple items.

WHO'S THERE: Because there are so few of them and they don't work to make their presence known, it's a strictly neighborhood crowd: local workers on quick lunch runs during the day, people grabbing a to-go dinner and some sundries on their way home from work at night, and a decent number of little old ladies stocking up on cat food.

WHAT'S GOOD: It's fitting that the best NYC market also features one the best of the city's favorite take-out meals: the tossed salad bar. It's priced by weight rather than ingredient, which is a great perk if you have trouble limiting yourself to the usual three or four included add-ins. Hearts of palm and artichokes? Why not?

WHAT'S NOT: During peak hours, the lines to check out. This is sort of the opposite of Garden of Eden: Because the store's offerings are so good, shoppers tend to go in for bigger orders than the number of registers can support.

Multiple locations; see www.wmarketnyc.com

Whole Foods

WHAT IT IS: For the uninitiated—if any still exist—Whole Foods is the giant of natural American food shopping that has grown from a small-town market in Texas to an international grocery phenomenon. For the most part, Whole Foods sells only natural and organic foods, drawing mainly from local and artisanal farms and supporting sustainable food sources. In many ways, it's the thinking man's supermarket—the produce is of a consistently high quality but is neither fancy nor overly expensive, so you can trust what you're getting and never feel pretentious about it. Its relative affordability and commitment to ecological causes have endeared it to New York's growing population of socially conscious young professionals, who shop there for everything from sushi to paper towels. And with the exception of the continual rush of the Union Square branch, the atmosphere of the stores themselves is more relaxed, clean, and enjoyable than any other supermarket's in the city.

WHO'S THERE: The first major grocery to make chores chic, Whole Foods is a sexy supermarket—so much so that *New York Press* even referred to the Bowery branch as having a "stealth meat market dynamic." Of the four locations in Manhattan, three are downtown—in Chelsea, Union Square, and on the Lower East Side—and pull in a crowd of unusually well dressed, slim yuppie and hipster shoppers. Part of the appeal lies in a commitment to the causes célèbres du jour of sustainable agriculture and the environment; and part of it lies in irresistible promotions like "free chocolate Thursdays" and the fact that you're more likely to hear hip-hop than Muzak while you're strolling down the aisles.

WHAT'S GOOD: For a middle-of-the-range supermarket, the Whole Foods cheese counters are especially good, with a surprising wealth of cheeses from the mildest and most innocuous Dutch breakfast slice to the runniest and stinkiest French after-dinner fright. The stores have a great selection of organic coffee beans, which you can grind yourself on site to your own particular coarseness (but which will probably leak coffee grinds all over your grocery bag on the way home). And they have the biggest and most appetizing fresh fruit and produce sections of any market.

WHAT'S NOT: Even the most environmentally conscious consumer might find Whole Foods' baffling range of agricultural-grade cereals and eco-friendly alternatives to mayonnaise difficult to stomach. With the exception of the soups, the prepared-food bars and salad counters are only a small step up from the cafeteria-style buffet pans that sit uncovered all afternoon in most big delis. And anyone with a weakness for junk food should look elsewhere—the healthier versions of American cheese and potato chips just don't cut it.

Multiple locations; see www.wholefoodsmarket.com

→ Meals on Wheels ←

In New York, it's not only the very rich and the very old that have their shopping done for them. In a city where so many people have so much to do and so few cars to do it in, home delivery companies that will bring high-quality fresh food to your door have transformed the grocery market. The rise of Fresh Direct and a host of smaller organic delivery ventures that have risen up around the flourishing Greenmarkets across the five boroughs are testament to an entirely unique approach to shopping that takes all the stress—but maybe some of the fun—out of shopping.

Fresh Direct was created for New York. It's simple enough: you browse its online aisles just as you would cruise a Whole Foods, click your way to a full cart, and then await the delivery truck. Convenient as it is, though, shopping that way can feel strangely inhuman, and you lose that sense of knowing where food comes from that is more tangible even in supermarkets. Much more worthwhile are companies like Urban Organic and Door to Door Organics, which bulk-buy certified organic produce from independent farms in the tristate area and deliver it to your door once every week. All you have to do is pick how big a box you want, and it will be filled with whatever's seasonal and fresh that week. You still sign up online, but receiving a big box full of earth-clod vegetables is a hearty reminder of the natural world beyond the city.

www.freshdirect.com

www.urbanorganic.com

www.doortodoororganics.com

DELIS

On a city as packed with megastores, Greenmarkets, Starbucks, gourmet specialty stores, and supermarkets as New York, it's amazing that the humble deli remains such a feature of the urban landscape and so indispensable a part of daily life across the five boroughs. Delis, bodegas, and corner stores of every description dot the streets of the city and become lynchpins of neighborhoods in ways that not even parks or laundromats can claim to rival. Newsagents to millions every morning, suppliers of bagels to truckers at dawn, florists for date-bound romantics at night, casual pharmacists and midnight hardware stores, delis are many things to many different people in New York, and it's worth taking the time to understand exactly how to make the most of them.

With so many thousands of delis around New York, it would be an impossible task to pick out favorites or caution you against the questionable ones. Instead, we've put together a shortlist of the things to look for in the world of New York deli shopping. Just like New Yorkers, delis have a lot in common, but it's the little things that make all the difference.

LITMUS TEST: It's often been said that you can judge a neighborhood by its delis. Certainly the atmosphere and the management of a local store can tell you a lot about an area's demographic, whether it's in the Bavarian charm of an Astoria deli or the hectic confusion of a Chinatown bodega. Get to know your deli and you get to know your neighborhood; scan the shelves and see what the products tell you. A deli stocked with exotic Goya juices and samosas means you're in a cheaper part of town with an ethnic bent, while Tate's cookies, Voss water, and overpriced bananas mean you're probably in a fancier neck of the woods.

FLOWERS: With hundreds of florists all over the city, Interflora in every Yellow Pages, and the flower market right in the middle of the city, it's worth remembering that delis will often sell perfectly respectable flowers at the most respectable prices. Through years of New York courtship, Jacob learned the hard way that throwing hundreds of dollars at expensive "floral decorators" didn't mean more than picking up a dozen tulips for $5 at a bodega on the way home.

COFFEE: Over the last two decades, New Yorkers have become more finicky about their daily caffeine than any other people in the world. All the clichés about high-strung businessmen yelling incomprehensibly complicated orders at sweating baristas are true—at least as far as the city's swankier coffee houses are concerned. But not so in a deli, where customers pour their own from a humble filter pot, cream and sugar to their hearts' content, and all for less than a dollar. Certainly, the standard is low and nine times out of ten it'll taste more like cardboard than coffee. But find a deli whose cheap stuff you like, and you're made for life.

LATE-NIGHT ERRANDS: A great proportion of the city's delis operate on a 24-hour basis, which makes them reliable ports of call for nocturnal New Yorkers from late-night revelers to wired students and hungry cops. Depending on your local's specialties, you can conceivably find anything you might ever need at one deli or another in the middle of the night, from light bulbs and candles to beer, toothpaste, and bizarre home décor. And there's something curiously entertaining about being able to take care of grocery shopping in the middle of the night.

MIDNIGHT SNACKS: Though the city does not lack for 24-hour eateries, delis can also offer interesting and heartburn-free alternatives to pizza for a late-night bite. In addition to chips and cereal, most delis have a section of goodies of ambiguous origin at the front. A Saran-wrapped fig bar that might have looked sketchy during the day can seem positively seductive in a deli's cold fluorescent light in the wee hours of the morning—Caitlin has often looked forward to these treats at the end of a night out.

SANDWICHES: A bagel with cream cheese from a decent deli is still one of the best deals in the city, and is a perfectly respectable form of sustenance for anyone on the go. While the freshness and quality of the sandwich counter's meats and cheeses may vary wildly from deli to deli, and spicy mustard is about as crazy as they'll go with the condiments, it's worth remembering that in times of need they'll always be there to put too much mayonnaise on a roll for you.

GREENMARKETS

Caitlin is married to a man from Los Angeles. This actually hasn't been as contentious as many have thought it would be. They agree about most things: L.A. has better weather and Mexican food; New York wins for convenience and culture. They both hate driving and small kitchens. However, there is one matter that remains a battleground: is local produce as good in New York as in California?

Caitlin's husband is not alone is his assumption. Even if you know that New York State has a large farming industry (one-quarter of the state's land is used for agriculture), it's not hard to see those farms in the same remote way as you might see other far-off in-state attractions like Albany, Niagara Falls, and the Buffalo Bills. Yet while it's true that you'll never be able to buy a locally grown avocado here or grow a lemon tree on your roof garden, New York City is within driving distance of ample farmland that yields produce as sumptuous as any farm in the Golden State. But how can your average busy, car-lacking New Yorker take advantage of this considerable asset? That is where the Greenmarket comes in. At Greenmarkets across the city, you can enjoy the region's lush bounty without leaving your neighborhood. Apples are the traditional Greenmarket MVP; they are excellent and plentiful many months out of the year. When they start to fade in the late winter, they're quickly replaced by the amazing early spring vegetables (asparagus, peas, fennel) and herbs, and from there, it's like getting a new toy every week until Labor Day: green beans, peppers, lettuce, corn, cherries, peaches, nectarines, plums, berries, grapes, and tomatoes in every size, shape, and color imaginable arrive one on top of the other throughout the summer. The glorious apples charge in—along with potatoes, brussels sprouts, and maple syrup—right around the time when you think you can't eat another peach. Once you've been seduced by the only-at-the-peak drama of the seasonal offerings, you'll never mindlessly buy a tomato out-of-season at the supermarket again.

It's perennially fashionable to talk about how great shopping at Greenmarkets is. But it's our feeling that all of the vogueish do-gooder hype—Helping farmers! Buying local!—obscures several practical reasons why shopping at Greenmarkets is good for you. The prices are amazing (on many items, substantially less than for comparable imported produce from a supermarket), the offerings unquestionably fresh, and on a nice day, you can't beat the atmosphere. In addition to produce, at many Greenmarkets, you can also get breads, cheeses, jam, honey, meats, and eggs, and even homemade pickles and sauerkraut.

You won't have to go out of your way to shop at a Greenmarket either. When people talk about "the Greenmarket," they are probably referring to the Union Square location, which is the largest, most frequent, and best known. But there are nearly 50 others across the five boroughs. Some are quite small, and others operate on odd days or hours, so it's worth it to put some effort into finding one that suits your taste and schedule. If the Greenmarket around your apartment doesn't have something you'd like, or has inconvenient hours, try one near work or another location you frequent. The CENYC web site has a map with all the market schedules and hours, along with other market information, including a wonderful month-by-month chart of produce at the market.

Part of what's most exceptional about Greenmarkets here is how unexceptional they have become. What the land around our urban mass can produce is amazing; but the markets themselves are now a normal part of the city's consumer landscape, as accessible as any supermarket, and no more exotic than a street vendor. The Greenmarket can easily become a part of your regular grocery routine, no matter where you live. But you'll know you have become a real junkie when you race to your local market every week in March to see if the asparagus is in, and know a good fall apple (Macintosh, Empire) from a winter one (Winesap).

For market locations and schedules, visit www.cenyc.org/greenmarket

Global Groceries

With supermarkets in no short supply and deli penetration nearly total, you'll rarely be stranded for groceries in New York. But there are some things that you just can't find in your local store, no matter how extravagant it may be. People from all over the world arrive and grow up in New York with their own senses of taste and tradition, and it would be a shame if everybody were to forsake his or her culinary heritage in the name of turkey sandwiches, hot dogs, and Kraft singles (even if they are the fat deli deluxe kind). Fortunately for all of us, the city's stronger ethnic communities have refused to do so and have kept their cuisines alive and cooking in these very boroughs.

Of course, it's only too easy to forget that a great number of international cuisines have left permanent stamps on the city's identity. Pizza, bagels, burritos, and General Tso's chicken are by now as familiar to a New Yorker's palate as curry and tea are to a Londoner's—the inescapable gastronomic assimilation of a multicultural city. And beyond those already familiar tastes, even the most blasé New Yorker will admit under duress that few cities in the world can boast such an international culinary landscape. When it's time to eat out, nothing is impossible, whether it's a simple dim sum brunch or an Ethiopian supper. The smart money even knows that to get the best of a region's cuisine you have to go where the locals are, and that an Indian restaurant in the depths of Jackson Heights will probably be better than its cartoon counterpart in the East Village.

When it comes to shopping, however, some New Yorkers are content to think that all the fruits there are on this earth will be found in the produce section at Trader Joe's, and that all the flavors of the world are right there in the Whole Foods spice rack. But to shop this way is to deny yourself one of the city's greatest luxuries: genuine regional grocery shopping. As easy and fun as it is to find what you want in cafés and restaurants, it takes a little more work to stock up on the ingredients you need to create truly international meals at home. And so for those less commonplace elements of the average New York kitchen—rare herbs, forgotten spices, dried noodles, and bizarre-looking fruit—adventurous chefs and homesick ex-pats alike should seek out supermarkets from other lands.

Follow your nose to the denser ethnic neighborhoods and you'll discover street markets, specialty stores, and entire supermarkets selling exactly what you'd find in their intercontinental counterparts. For incredible fresh seafood, harvests of unlikely vegetables, and an overwhelming variety of noodles and rice, try Chinatown's biggest store, the aptly named New York Supermarket hidden under the Manhattan Bridge. If it's Indian herbs and spices you're after, Kalustyan's in Murray Hill is a good choice—but the Patel Brothers outlet in Jackson Heights is even better, and stocks meats and pastries that will make your mouth water. The Sunrise Mart above the St. Mark's Bookstore is the best of several authentic Japanese supermarkets in the city—there are three JAS Marts and two Sunrise Marts in Manhattan alone—filled with infinite varieties of ramen and udon, fresh sushi, dried fish, and a staggering selection of multicolored candy. For a good Russian meal you're almost better off buying ready-to-eat potato and egg salad, beef Stroganoff, pelmeni, and fresh smoked fish at M&I International Food in Brighton Beach than ordering the same at a restaurant in the city. And for Middle Eastern and Mediterranean food, Sahadi's in downtown Brooklyn is the place to go, offering an unparalleled selection of ingredients like spices, nuts, dried fruits, olives, hummus, meats, and feta, and a delicious range of prepared foods, from Greek salads to lamb kebabs and more.

Depending on where you are and what you're looking for, these under-sung outposts of foreign culture can seem like anything from discreet havens of the exotic to baffling arcades of the unidentifiable. But pluck up the courage to give them a try and in one fell swoop you could change your culinary life forever and understand what it means to live in the most cosmopolitan city in the world.

Kalustyan's, 123 Lexington Avenue, at 28th Street, (212-685-3541) www.kalustyans.com

M&I International Food, 249 Brighton Beach Avenue between Brighton 1st Place and
    Brighton 2nd Street (Brooklyn), (718-615-1011)

New York Supermarket, 75 East Broadway, under the Manhattan Bridge, (212-374-4088)

Patel Brothers, 42-92 Main Street, between Cherry and Blossom avenues (Queens),
    (718-661-1112) www.patelbrothersusa.com

Sunrise Mart, 29 Third Avenue, at Stuyvesant Street, 2nd floor, (212-598-3040)

Sahadi's, 187 Atlantic Avenue between Clinton and Court streets (Brooklyn), (718-624-4550)
    www.sahadis.com

PHARMACIES AND DRUGSTORES

New York doesn't have a particularly charming drugstore culture, and that's sad because there sure are a lot of them—whenever any kind of store closes, it's become a bit of a cliché to say that the space will probably turn into a drugstore. The chains dominate, and compete with one another fiercely for each and every customer by opening store after store in one of the most expensive real estate markets in the country. The result is understaffed stores; awkward, sometimes multilevel layouts; uneven selection; and maddening lines. Independents and smaller family-owned chains are few and far between, so count yourself lucky if you live by one, as you'll never be able to get someone to help you find anything—much less look at a rash or decipher an illegible prescription slip—at a Duane Reade.

Still, while we wish we had rosier news—Cashiers with a sense of humor! Selection that can't be beat!—you are going to have to buy your paper towels and multivitamins somewhere, and it's our duty to make sure you are prepared. Good luck.

Bigelow

WHAT IT IS: A historic, old-fashioned chemist with a chi-chi selection of beauty and grooming products and accessories. Bigelow claims to be the oldest apothecary in the country, but today it's more like a boutique where you can get prescriptions filled in the back. If you live in the neighborhood, take advantage of this rare non-corporate pharmacy; if not, it is worth a trip if you need something indulgent and European to make you feel special. If going into Sephora makes you feel depressingly like a marketed-to lemming, buying something at Bigelow will make you feel like a VIP.

WHO'S THERE: Fashionistas picking up Diptyque candles and T. LeClerc face powder. Local moms getting their kids' amoxicillin spiked with grape flavoring.

WHAT'S GOOD: Fancy beauty and grooming products from truly hard-to-find brands. It's also a great place to come for a gift for a girl (or a guy who's into fancy scented candles and soaps). For men, the selection of luxurious shaving products will impress even the most fastidious and well-groomed gent. And there's a large surgical department in the building next door that has a more extensive selection of medical aids like crutches, slings, and braces than most drugstores, as well as some more general good-to-have items (Ace bandages, heating pads).

WHAT'S NOT: Customer service is not as warm as you might expect from a 160-year-old neighborhood institution. And the store's layout may have seemed like a good idea in the 1850s, but the large island with the registers and display cases takes up almost the entire room. If more than one person is waiting to pay, the line snakes into one of the store's two aisles, awkwardly barricading other shoppers—Caitlin was pinned against the Bumble & Bumble hair products for ten minutes during a holiday Friday night rush.

414 Sixth Avenue between 8th and 9th streets, (212-533-2700) www.bigelowchemists.com

CVS

WHAT IT IS: A perfectly decent national chain with a bunch of locations in the city. CVS doesn't have the presence that Duane Reade does, and there's nothing particular to recommend it except that it's reasonably convenient—and not quite as bad as DR. Otherwise, it's pretty much the same as the CVS stores you've been to in other states.

WHO'S THERE: Noticeably more cashiers per store than the competition.

WHAT'S GOOD: The pharmacies. In our experience, the pharmacists here are generally more helpful than they are at comparable chains. Even during busy times, most will take a moment to answer a question or two about a prescription or an over-the-counter purchase. If you have to combine your sundry shopping with drugstore shopping, there are worse places to do it—a lot of CVS branches stock a relatively good range of snacks and kitchen essentials, from ketchup to mayonnaise, candy, and potato chips. Also, because it's a national chain, if you take your prescriptions here, you will be able get refills at any CVS in the country, so it's a good choice for people who travel.

WHAT'S NOT: If there's a difference between CVS branches in New York and elsewhere, it's cleanliness. Explore the farther reaches of a store and you're likely to find grimy shelves and ancient bottles of detergent that have sat gathering dust for years. Some outlets are even carpeted, which is disconcerting.

Multiple locations; see www.cvs.com

Duane Reade

WHAT IT IS: If you've been in the city for more than 24 hours, you've probably seen a Duane Reade. A local mega-chain, Duane Reade has hundreds of stores in all five boroughs and they are mercilessly hard to avoid. Duane Reade could serve as a case study for a class on urban planning: the company has made its pitch to become NYC's official drugstore not only by putting stores in strategic locations (by subway stations, underneath large office buildings, along major cross streets and avenues) but also by adapting the standard one-floor aisle-by-aisle layout to fit the city's quirky offerings of storefront commercial space. Thus you can find Duane Reades in former theaters, shoe stores, and delis, stretched across multiple levels, and into basements. This has given the chain the edge over the nationals in storefront dominance.

Strangely, customers do not seem to figure into the business plan. At best, shopping at Duane Reade is nearly painless; at worst, it's infuriating (you're buying toothpaste in the basement and soap is two floors up), fruitless (the entire vitamin section is empty), and totally absurd (18 people with company shirts on and only one at the cash register—who just left to check a price with the manager on the 7th floor of the store). If Beckett ran a modern-day drugstore, it might be something like this.

WHO'S THERE: New Yorkers, reluctantly. Duane Reade has us in the palm of its hand, and it's nearly impossible to escape its cruel and maddening ways.

WHAT'S GOOD: Chase Bank has ATMs in many branches, and you can't argue with the benefits of a 24-hour pharmacy no matter what the conditions might be like.

WHAT'S NOT: Oh, there are so many choices. But in our opinion, customer service deserves singling out. Stores are shockingly understaffed—even though every store has a line of cash registers at the front, there are never more than one or two people to work at them. The pharmacy—where the savvy shopper knows to go to check out when front-of-store registers are packed—isn't much better. Pharmacists usually won't come out of the drug cave to ring up regular customers, and in some stores, you'd probably have to fake a seizure to get your prescription.

Multiple locations, see www.duanereade.com

Lascoff Apothecary

WHAT IT IS: A good old-fashioned apothecary that has been supplying the Upper East Side with the finest imported cosmetics and pharmaceuticals for more than a century. Beautifully displayed in a wood-paneled room with antique glass cases and cabinets, the supplies at Lascoff overflow with the distinctive looks and smells of exotic washrooms. Rummage through the cupboards and you'll come across welcome oddities that you simply can't find anywhere else in the city, from aggressive licorice-flavored German cold remedies to artisanal Swiss tweezers and authentic English badger-hair shaving brushes. Although it's expensive compared to a CVS or even a Neergaard, lining up for service at the unusually attentive pharmacist's window will take you back to a more civilized age.

WHO'S THERE: Upper East Siders in the know and homesick Europeans who can't live without the bubble bath they use back in the old country.

WHAT'S GOOD: International hygiene. Lascoff stocks a sumptuous range of old-fashioned European soaps, from pastel-colored Parisian slabs to dainty English lavender-scented luxuries and jet-black Greek olive oil bars.

WHAT'S NOT: If the prices don't send you slinking off to the Duane Reade for your wallet's sake, your only potential disappointment could be in the absence of the common essentials you can always find at a larger drugstore. You wouldn't go here for your paper towels.

1209 Lexington Avenue, at 82nd Street, (212-288-9500)

Neergaard

WHAT IT IS: Brooklyn's oldest and finest, Neergaard has carved a niche for itself as a dependable halfway house between your old-fashioned neighborhood drugstore and the larger chains that blanket the city. It has two locations—both in the Park Slope area—and one is open 24 hours a day, 7 days a week. Both take prescriptions over the phone and deliver to your door in the neighborhood. As well as stocking pretty much everything you'd find at a Duane Reade, the stores carry a fine line of slightly grim surgical equipment for rental or purchase and keep a good and fluid selection of random candies by the register.

WHO'S THERE: Aside from the gentle and grateful population of Park Slope, loyal devotees from surrounding Brooklyn neighborhoods who see every purchase from Neergaard as one in the eye for the big chains around the corner.

WHAT'S GOOD: The little things. Whether you're after a certain Japanese moisturizer or are particular about your brand of nail clippers, you need only to ask and the store will probably have it.

WHAT'S NOT: The stores are a little cramped, and don't make the most pleasant places to shop. And Neergaard has been in business in Brooklyn since 1888, and occasionally—just occasionally—you might find a tube of toothpaste or a tin of lip salve that looks like it dates from the last century, too.

454 Fifth Avenue, between 9th and 10th streets (Brooklyn), (718-768-0600); 120 Seventh Avenue, between President and Carroll streets (Brooklyn), (718-857-1600)
www.neergaardpharmacies.com

Ricky's

WHAT IT IS: Ricky's is appropriately hard to pin down. The offerings take the best parts of a drugstore (hair care, cosmetics, body products) and combine them with the resources of a beauty supply store (rows of hairbrushes, make-up brushes, cotton pads, etc.) with quite a few completely unquantifiable items thrown in unaccountably (sexy Santa suits, grow-your-own-Jesus kits). Though there are now locations on Long Island, in New Jersey, and even in Miami Beach, Ricky's is definitely a New York City institution—Caitlin can remember going to the original location on Broadway with her mother to buy hair dye to cover her mom's gray…in pink and purple. (It was the eighties.) Ricky's is a place where you can buy Day-Glo nail polish, fishnets, and eighty kinds of glitter, but underneath the sparkles and feather boas are plenty of worthwhile items that don't assume you're shopping for your inner drag queen. While the salespeople have gotten a little less wild and a little more Diet Coke since the chain's early days, Ricky's remains the most reliably enjoyable—if not necessarily the most practical—errand in town.

WHO'S THERE: Drag queens, make-up artists, stylists, teenyboppers, college students, and little old ladies buying hairnets and rollers. It also sets the city's standards for Halloween costume style, so once a year it's the only drugstore in town that can boast hordes of eager shoppers lined up down the block.

WHAT'S GOOD: Anything that will make you cleaner, prettier, or wilder. Ricky's has a great selection of brands from high to low, mainstream to hard-to-find. The stores seem to stock any kind of hair or beauty product that you could possibly think up—just try finding dry shampoo at a Duane Reade. Costumes and party supplies are also a strong point, especially R-rated ones.

WHAT'S NOT: Anything boring. Ricky's gives a big yawn to unsexy items like cough medicine and paper towels. And while all of the brightly colored, bizarrely organized products may make you feel like you need a dose of Ritalin, you'll have to get your real drugs elsewhere—there's no pharmacy.

Multiple locations; see www.rickys-nyc.com

Walgreens

WHAT IT IS: Walgreens is one of the country's largest chain drugstores, but you wouldn't know it—there are only a handful of locations in New York, many of which are hidden in the farther corners of the outer boroughs. Friendlier than a CVS but as averagely stocked as a Duane Reade, Walgreens is nothing less and nothing more than a decent local drugstore for anyone with a branch in the neighborhood. However, Walgreens has a distinctly national feel that can sometimes make a Manhattanite uncomfortable.

WHO'S THERE: Nobody would go out of his way for a Walgreens, so the clientele is largely local, especially in the outer boroughs where a Walgreens can be the only drugstore in the neighborhood.

WHAT'S GOOD: The prices. While there's not much you can get at Walgreens that you can't get anywhere else, the prices on big brand-name essentials are rock-bottom, and for this reason alone the stores deserve to steal customers from the likes of Duane Reade. **WHAT'S NOT:** Variety plays no part in a Walgreens life. The range of cosmetics and soaps is confined strictly to a few major brands, and even then is not as comprehensive as the chain-store competition, where you might find every single scent of deodorant instead of just two or three.

Multiple locations; see www.walgreens.com

CLOTHING

New Yorkers are constantly on display. Between the amount of people there are here and the amount of time we spend out on the street, we're probably the most frequently looked-at people in the country, if not the world. Looking around streets in neighborhoods like Soho, Williamsburg, and Carnegie Hill, you would be forgiven for thinking that the key to dressing well in New York is personal style. Would that it were that simple. Our clothing must function as more than artfully chosen individual fashion statements. Just as a hiker chooses boots, parkas, and other gear based on the conditions of his expedition, so should the average New Yorker consider weather, anticipated time outside, and estimated distance walking before getting dressed in the morning. Then there are the logistical obstacles of owning and storing clothing in an apartment. Caitlin was once forced to return what she thought was an extremely practical and excellent looking pair of knee-high galoshes because they didn't fit in her closet. Consider yourself warned.

On the other hand, we don't want to put a damper on one of the great pleasures this city offers: exposure to creativity, and an atmosphere that encourages one to express him- or herself through dress. Fashion is a big industry here, and the amount and variety of options for seeing and buying clothes gives every resident opportunity and inspiration for inventing, reinventing, and experimenting with what he or she wears. So we're here to help you get practical, but not so practical that you can't have fun.

With the possible exception of jewelry, nothing you wear should just be about how it looks; that is the recipe for blistered bloody feet, water-ravaged suede, and white pants smeared with immutable black grease from trying to squeeze through closing subway doors. On the other hand, Birkenstocks and North Face fleeces may be comfortable, but they're hard to pull off with most day wear. (It should go without saying that these items never work at night. And actually, if you're over twenty-five and not a sports instructor, we'd strongly encourage you to give that North Face away right now.) The trick, in a sense, is to blend style with lifestyle. Read on.

—————————→ Survival Tips ←—————————

- Edit your wardrobe constantly. You don't have room for anything you don't wear, period.

- Moth balls are cheap, and New York is full of psycho, hungry sweater-loving moths. If the carcinogen smell of regular balls bothers you, get organic ones (available at health food stores and the Container Store), or store sweaters with natural deterrents like lavender, cedar chips, and dried lemon peel.

- Before you plunk down a lot for off-site storage space for seasonal items, consider every possible option within your apartment, no matter how unconventional: above cabinets, under beds raised with risers, in crates stashed behind couches, or under sinks. Some New Yorkers really do use their ovens for shoe storage.

- New York truly offers you the freedom to dress however you want—the only limit is your personal comfort level. But just about every neighborhood and industry has a signature look, and it's certainly easy to begin sartorially conforming without realizing it. The best antidote to keeping your style sharp is people-watching and trolling the stores and streets in all different neighborhoods.

—————————→ Street Shopping ←—————————

You don't need us to tell you that there are many excellent one-of-a-kind stores and boutiques here, but shopping at them can be pricey. One way to manage wardrobe expenditures without sacrificing your style to the chains is to start shopping on the street. Street shopping falls into three general categories. Street vendors are the best for almost-could-be-in-a-boutique items (handmade clothes; shirts and dresses silkscreened with original drawings; handwoven scarves; and gorgeous jewelry). It's not surprising that the best vendors set up their tables in Soho and Nolita. Flea markets are a good place to look for well-priced vintage clothing and jewelry; try the Hell's Kitchen Flea Market on 39th Street between Ninth and Tenth avenues and the Brooklyn Flea at Bishop Loughlin Memorial High School in Fort Greene. Slightly different are artists' markets that exclusively feature local vendors like Artists and Fleas in Williamsburg and The Market NYC on Mulberry Street. (Most flea markets operate only on weekends.) For the best deals, nothing beats stoop sales. In neighborhoods of brownstone Brooklyn such as Clinton Hill and Fort Greene, you can pick up any manner of secondhand treasures for literally pennies. For more on stoop sales, see page 120.

Artists and Fleas, 129 North 6th Street, between Bedford Avenue and Berry Street

(Brooklyn), www.artistsandfleas.com

Brooklyn Flea, Bishop Loughlin Memorial High School, Lafayette Avenue, between Clermont and Vanderbilt avenues, www.brownstoner.com/brooklynflea

Hell's Kitchen Flea Market, 39th Street, between Ninth and Tenth avenues (Saturdays and Sundays), www.hellskitchenfleamarket.com

The Market NYC, 268 Mulberry Street, between Prince and Houston streets, www.themarketnyc.com

---

A QUICK NOTE ON OUR SUGGESTIONS OF "WHERE TO GO":

STYLE IS PERSONAL AND ENDLESSLY VARIED, AND WE WOULDN'T DARE TRY TO INFLICT OURS ON OUR READERS. SO THE STORES, OUTLETS, AND SALES WE MENTION IN THE FOLLOWING SECTIONS ARE RECOMMENDED PRIMARILY FOR THEIR UTILITY: BECAUSE THEY OFFER SOMETHING INDISPENSABLE AT AN UNUSUALLY GOOD PRICE, OR ARE EXCELLENT AND UNOBVIOUS SOURCES FOR A VARIETY OF USEFUL ITEMS.

COATS

WHAT YOU NEED TO KNOW: We wouldn't be good survival guide writers if we didn't remind our readers over and over again how important it is to keep stuff to a minimum in New York. Coats, however, are one apparel category that we wouldn't encourage editing down too much. Not only can temperatures vary widely in this city from season to season—sometimes even from day to day—but small variations in degree can feel disproportionately dramatic when you are spending so much time walking outside in them. A light sweater on a windy day can make a crosstown walk excruciating, for example, while wearing a coat that's too warm on a milder winter day puts you at risk of a rush-hour meltdown on the subway. So it's good to have lots of options of varying weights and degrees of dressiness.

WHERE TO GO: $200 will only buy you about an arm of a parka from most outdoor brands, but Brooklyn Industries offers a couple of styles of warm, down-filled, waterproof coats for men and women each season for a bit less than that. If it's a mild fall, you can save even more money by waiting until they go on sale. Speaking of sales, if you are prepared to dig and elbow, the annual September warehouse sale at Paragon usually has a lot of high-quality winter coats . . . on the first day. Get there early for the best selection of normal sizes and colors. Sample sales are also great places to pick up coats. Also keep your eyes peeled for ones by super-high-end outerwear brands like Moncler, whose coats go for upward of $500 at department and sporting-goods stores.

Brooklyn Industries, multiple locations, www.brooklynindustries.com

Paragon, 18 East 18th Street, at Broadway, (212-255-8036) www.paragonsports.com

SHOES

WHAT YOU NEED TO KNOW: There's a lot to say about footwear; maybe someday we'll collect our opinions into another book. The most obvious point is that New Yorkers walk a lot more than most people in the rest of the country, so if you are new to the city, you should not underestimate how much you'll be working your shoes. And if you have a job that requires you to be on your feet for much of the day (stylist, reporter, photographer), sore feet are an occupational hazard.

The corollary of our shoes doing so much walking is that they also come in contact with the elements of the urban outdoors. Show us an unscuffed shoe here and we'll show you a person who's never stepped out of a town car. In a single day in this city, white shoes will get smudges, a stiletto heel is apt to be snatched by a subway grate, and the thin rubber soles on Chinese slippers may be nearly worn through. Consider the wear and tear a badge of honor, and invest in regular maintenance at your local shoe repair (see page 197).

WHERE TO GO: What's the first thing that pops into your mind when you think "comfortable walking shoes"? The correct answer is sneakers! The area around NYU is serious sneaker country; you can find everything from regular Pumas, Adidas, and Converse at the stores on Broadway, to pricey vintage and limited-edition kicks at specialty sneaker boutiques in Soho and Nolita.

ATHLETIC CLOTHES

WHAT YOU NEED TO KNOW: In many other parts of the country, wearing workout clothing—Spandex, tracksuits, sweatpants—as daywear is acceptable, even considered cool. Not so in New York. Like Paris—where wearing clothes like this in public tags one as an American—in New York, walking around in this type of clothing when not obviously engaging in or en route to some sort of exercise is seen as the mark of an outsider with no personal style. *Très gauche.* So limit your wearing of these items to going to and from your place of exercise, remove promptly after use, and do not even think about keeping your sweats on for brunch, no matter how cute they are.

WHERE TO GO: Paragon has clothing and shoes for every kind of athletic activity a city dweller could possibly partake in (including skiing, camping, rock climbing, and swimming), though its selection for each sport can be spotty and customer service is definitely not pro. Jack Rabbit Sports is small, but real athletes like how knowledge-able (and actually athletic) the staff is. And though it's officially a dance store, at Capezio women can find some top-quality gear (tops, leggings, leotards, even some footwear) for very good prices.

Capezio, multiple locations, www.capeziodance.com

Jack Rabbit Sports, 42 West 14th Street, between Fifth and Sixth avenues, (212-727-2980);

151 Seventh Avenue between Carroll Street and Garfield Place, (Brooklyn),

(718-636-9000) www.jackrabbitsports.com

Paragon, see page 189.

GLASSES (PRESCRIPTION)

WHAT YOU NEED TO KNOW: New York is considerably glasses-friendly, with frames favored by various subcultures from uptown academics to Brooklyn hipsters. Channel a little Woody Allen, invest in a pair of statement frames, and make them a part of your look.

WHERE TO GO: Many eyeglass shops around town have in-store optometrists, which can save you some money. But if you get your eyes checked there, you'll have to get your frames there, too, so if you want to shop around, best to get your prescription from a regular eye doctor, and then explore and compare prices. Flea markets like the ones listed on page 187 are good places to look for vintage frames.

GLASSES (SUN)

WHAT YOU NEED TO KNOW: Nothing out of the ordinary here. Super sunny days occur year-round, even in the dead of winter, so it's best to get a pair that's not so summery looking that it won't seem out of place when worn in February.

WHERE TO GO: If you're prone to losing them, pick up cheap sunglasses from street vendors or at street fairs. Otherwise, department stores like Macy's and Bloomingdale's are the best for trying a ton of styles in all different brands.

Bloomingdale's, 1000 Third Avenue, between 59th and 60th streets, (212-705-2000);
    504 Broadway between Broome and Spring streets, (212-729-5900)
    www.bloomingdales.com
Macy's, multiple locations, www.macys.com

BAGS AND LAPTOP CASES

WHAT YOU NEED TO KNOW: A bit of a Catch-22, but a lovely one for those with a bag fetish. Unlike much of the rest of the country, New Yorkers travel most days without support vehicles, so we need to carry everything we need with us. But because we are running around so much, the bag itself can't be too cumbersome. In the absence of sherpas, you will most likely need some sort of bag to schlep the day's accoutrements.

WHERE TO GO: The options are too varied for us to suggest a few places to fit all needs and tastes, so here we'd rather suggest where not to buy them: on the street. Buying knock-off designer handbags (as opposed to anything handmade on the street, which is entirely different) supports two questionable practices: infringing on a designer's work, and sweatshop labor. On top of that, the bags are poorly made, with flimsy zippers, cheap, easily ripped linings, fake leather, and clasps that easily break. At $40 or $50 each for a bag (sometimes even more), you're better off spending a fraction more for one that will not need to be replaced in two months, will not try your conscience, and doesn't look like what everyone else has.

UMBRELLAS

WHAT YOU NEED TO KNOW: New York gets a fair amount of rain throughout the year, and no season is dependably more or less rainy than another. However, while traditional rainy days aren't unheard of, more common are days that are both dry and wet. In the summer, unexpected (sometimes violent, often beautiful) thunderstorms that last 10 to 15 minutes are common; during other times of the year, rain is more likely to be on-and-off showers than a steady day-long dousing. If it's raining when you leave for work it may be sunny by lunchtime, and vice versa.

WHERE TO GO: Given the capricious nature of NYC rain, carrying an umbrella with you at all times isn't a bad idea. But if you don't like being weighed down by an additional accoutrement, fear not. The street-vendor economy has the market cornered, and even the most unexpected storm won't catch sellers unprepared. The second dark clouds appear in the distance, the trusty $5 umbrellas will magically appear on sidewalks all over the city. If a storm catches you unprepared, listen for the traditional "umbrellaumbrellaumbrella!" sales pitch. Once the storm is over, you won't have to worry about what to do with your sopping wet acquisition, as it'll likely be disfigured, broken, impossible to close, or all of the above. These umbrellas are made to break— that's how vendors keep you coming back.

If you want a stylish one, discount stores like Century 21 and Loehmann's usually have a good selection of pretty designer umbrellas (Lulu Guinness, Nicole Miller) at discount prices, as well as tons of basic Totes in all shapes, sizes, and colors.

Century 21, 22 Cortland Street, between Church Street and Broadway, (212-227-9092);
472 86th Street between Fourth and Fifth avenues (Brooklyn), (718-748-3266)
www.c21stores.com
Loehmann's, multiple locations, www.loehmanns.com

BOOTS

WHAT YOU NEED TO KNOW: Why are so many NYC entryways decorated with a pair or two of rubber galoshes? Because we've got nowhere else to put them! Unless you are lucky enough to move into an apartment with a true foyer closet, you won't have a separate coat closet, and you probably won't want to keep a pair of big, awkward (and sometimes muddy) boots in your regular closet. They're worth the real estate though, as walking through rain and snow will ruin the rest of your shoes pretty quickly. Look for a pair you'll want to show off.

Though it's not really cool to carry your work shoes in a separate bag, we'll admit it's tricky to find good all-weather boots that are passable to wear through the day. The crazier the boot, the fewer outfit options. Solid colors can work with jeans or corduroys, and those with a certain hipster bent can even probably pull them off with a skirt or dress.

Fur-lined galoshes are fashionable and temptingly cozy looking in November, but will get uncomfortable in April. Best only to consider them if you're sure you have room for two pairs in your closet. If you've gotten this far into the book, you know better than to ask us about Uggs.

WHERE TO GO: Right around Union Square are some big shoe stores like David Z and Shoe Mania that stock a range of good city boots from different brands. If you don't have luck at either of those, DSW is also there.

David Z, multiple locations, www.davidzinc.stores.yahoo.net. Union Square location is at 12 East 14th Street, between Fifth Avenue and University Place, (212-229-4790)

DSW, multiple locations, www.dswshoes.com. Union Square location is at 40 East 14th Street, 3rd floor, (212-674-2176)

Shoe Mania, multiple locations, www.shoemania.com. Union Square location is at 853 Broadway, corner of 14th Street, (212-253-8744)

⟶ A Layman's Guide to the Garment District ⟵

People in this city who like clothes love to talk about how "great" the Garment District is in a way that can make the people they're talking to feel guilty about not taking advantage of it. Don't. The truth is that the Garment District (like the Flower District and to a lesser extent, the Diamond District) caters to industry professionals, not consumers. It's possible to "shop" there as an individual, but the stores are there to sell large orders to big customers who know exactly what they're doing.

Fabric stores are what first come to mind when people think of the Garment District. There are dozens of fabric stores scattered around Seventh Avenue in the high thirties and low forties. Some have storefronts, others are located in larger buildings; all have hundreds of rolls of different kinds of fabrics in every color imaginable. If you know exactly what kind of fabric you are looking for and how much you need, you'll be fine. But these are not places you'll want to browse. For one thing, each store has too many different kinds of fabrics—it would be like browsing though a coffee farm to find a certain bean. And then there's the fact that the stores aren't set up to sell to individuals and the layman. There is a distinct code of conduct to fabric shopping in the Garment District, but you won't find it posted on the walls or politely pointed out to you as you shop. Taking fabrics from shelves, cutting your own swatches, and asking questions are all frowned upon. If you go in by yourself, count on being yelled at. Don't count on being helped.

There's more to the District than just the fabric stores though, and that's where the amateur can really benefit. Here are two great, less obvious reasons to visit the Garment District:

TRIM STORES: These are stores that sell all of the bits and bobs a designer needs to spruce up his or her creations. You may never need to dip into their extensive selections of lace, fringe, or appliqués (remember that this is where the pros shop), but they're a great thing to know about if you've lost a distinctive button or need to spruce up a boringly wrapped present. And when rhinestones make a comeback, you'll know where to go!

SALES: Fittingly, the Garment District is also home to a lot of designer warehouses and showrooms. So it follows that this is where many of NYC's famed sample sales happen. Sample sales can be hit or miss—a designer's sale can have a ton of great stuff one month and practically nothing the next—and they're never the most pleasant way to shop. But if you're willing to risk the time, not bothered by stripping in front of strangers, and can brave the merciless, elbowing crowds, jewels can be found. Many a Theory-clad New York woman would be lost without them. You can find out about sales in magazines like *Time Out*, *New York*, and *DailyCandy*; many also have their own mailing lists that you can sign up for if you attend a sale. FYI: at most "sample sales," designers are actually not selling just samples but overstock after all retail orders have been filled. So there is more of a range of sizes, and most of the time, the clothes are from the current season.

REPAIRS

New York City is full of unusual, valuable, and delicate treasures, so not surprisingly, there are an equal number of talented and specialized experts who can fix them. We've found the best of the best, from reweavers who seamlessly repair holes in fine cashmere to electronics whisperers who bring battered and coffee-soaked laptops back to life. No matter how deep the fracture, no matter how obscure the item, if something can be fixed at all, it can be fixed in New York—for a price.

—————→ **Survival Tips** ←—————

- There's no shortage of repair places in this city, but you don't want to trust that Patek Phillippe to just anyone. As with so many things, word of mouth is an excellent way to go here.

- It's not uncommon for a good repairer to say that he or she can't make any guarantees that something can be fixed, especially if it is old, unusual, or if the repair is very complicated. Don't let that scare you away—most of the time things can be fixed, and if the fix isn't perfect, you can see if the repairer will take a bit off the bill.

- If you need something repaired that's not mentioned here, check user reviews on Yelp or CitySearch. While accuracy isn't guaranteed (owners have been known to anonymously post good reviews of their own businesses), a business with a lot of user reviews can give you an idea if it's great or shady before you trust it with your stuff.

- Repairing something is essentially an investment in an item. A good repairperson will usually have an idea of what was paid for it, and depending on its price, will ask you if the repair is worth it. You can't put a price on sentimental value of course, but for everything else, consider whether the investment is worth it before you commit to the work. (This applies to computers, too—if your computer is old, it may not make sense to pay $300 plus labor to replace a hard drive, unless there's something you really need on it.)

CLOTHING (CLEANING)

WHAT YOU NEED TO KNOW: Having a dry cleaner on just about every block is very convenient for the routine cleaning of items that can't be thrown in the washing machine or dryer. But there are also more high-end cleaners that do the cleaning for the fashion houses, socialites, and others who require the best cleaning expertise there is. These kinds of cleaners cost a bit (okay, quite a bit) more than their ubiquitous counterparts, but there's a reason. They use a combination of techniques (including hand-treating, if necessary), and often work on items individually. This is where to go with your most delicate fabrics, antique clothing items, super-deep stains, and special-occasion clothing.

(Not to frighten you, but see page 160 for what to do about getting back a ruined item or when a dry cleaner loses something.)

WHERE TO GO: When her regular dry cleaner made a stain on a satin dress even bigger, Caitlin took it to Meurice, where the staff not only removed the original stain, but completely erased the damage created by the other cleaner. Madame Paulette is another well-known high-end cleaner that we've heard good things about from people who have used it.

Also, organic and chemical-free dry cleaners are popping up all around the city. The cleaning at the ones we've tested is just as thorough; prices, interestingly, are also comparable with their regular chemical-laden competitors. Keep your eyes peeled for one near you.

Madame Paulette, 1255 Second Avenue, between 65th and 66th streets, (347-689-7010)
    www.madamepaulette.com

Meurice Garment Care, 31 University Place, between 8th and 9th streets, (212-475-2778)
    254 East 57th Street, between Second and Third avenues, (212-759-9057)
    www.meuricegarmentcare.com

CLOTHING (MENDING)

WHAT YOU NEED TO KNOW: Professional reweaving is a dying art, but you can still find some old-fashioned practitioners in this city—which is good news if you've got a sweater with large tears or moth holes, as that's not something a regular tailor will be able to fix. Now the bad news: you'll pay a hefty price for this. It can cost $50 or more to fix a single hole (the price will depend on the original weave of the sweater, the color of the yarn, and, of course, the size of the hole). It's also not the speediest work—expect to wait about two weeks for your pieces. Take comfort in the rarefied craftsmanship your garment is receiving, and be patient.

WHERE TO GO: When moths chewed holes in Caitlin's sweaters, she took a few to Superior Reweaving. She was told not to bother with the cheap stuff—cheap cashmere and merino wool—but had two of the nicer pieces fixed for $65 each. Three weeks later, the holes were gone without a trace. French-American Reweaving also has a great reputation—its reweavers have done jobs for high-profile New Yorkers since the 1930s.

French-American Reweaving, 119 West 57th Street, between Sixth and Seventh avenues,
    Room 1406, (212-765-4670)

Superior Reweaving, 41 Union Square West, by 17th Street, Suite 423, (212-929-7208)

SHOES

WHAT YOU NEED TO KNOW: Given the amount of wear and tear that a New York shoe encounters on an average day on the street, it doesn't make sense to be too precious about yours. That said, regular maintenance can easily save you money in the long run, and if you have a good shoe-repair guy here, you can literally wear your favorites until the soles are worn through.

Replacing those soles and heels, along with polishing, are the staple offerings in the realm of shoe repair. Oh, but the fun doesn't stop there. A good repair shop can also craft new straps and strengthen or add padding to make an amazing-looking but ill-fitting pair of boots purchased at a sample sale wearable. Many shoe-repair places will also repair bags and other leather goods, and the best will perform feats of awe-inspiring artistry on favorite soiled pieces. When you have someone you like and trust, it can be easy to get carried away and become a bit of a repair junkie, putting in much more money in maintenance than the item cost in the first place.

Many open on the early side but close around 6 or 7 p.m. and are closed on Sundays.

WHERE TO GO: There are shoe-repair places all over the city, and many look like the kinds of places Vito Corleone might have his wingtips shined after sending someone to sleep with the fishes. Whether you find this particular anachronistic atmosphere comforting or creepy, you shouldn't judge a place by a sign, location, or the atmosphere inside. A shoe-repair place is exactly as good as the guys who work there, so you need to try some out to find one you like. Get some recommendations, then start with simple things like heel replacement before moving on to the fancy stuff.

JEWELRY AND WATCHES

WHAT YOU NEED TO KNOW: Often pricey and dripping with sentimental value, jewelry and watches are items that you'd likely be willing to invest some real money into fixing. So it's a little counterintuitive that this is actually one area where you don't need to be as wary about where you take your pieces: New York is one of the most important centers in the jewelry industry. If you can't get a recommendation from someone, head to the Diamond District.

WHERE TO GO: Take those broken baubles directly to 47th Street. Most people think of the Diamond District as a place to buy engagement rings or where Laurence Olivier's Nazi dentist was recognized by ex-prisoners in *Marathon Man*. But it's also an excellent place to come for jewelry repairs. The direct (and visible) competition keeps prices low, though you should know that haggling is de rigueur. Most specialize in pieces with precious metals and real stones, but some repair costume jewelry, too.

For beaded jewelry, try Beads of Paradise at Union Square. Not only are the staffpeople expert restringers, but they can replace any missing beads from the store's selection of zillions.

Beads of Paradise, 16 East 17th Street, between Union Square West and Fifth Avenue,
 (212-620-0642)

The Diamond District is located on 47th Street, between Fifth and Sixth avenues,
 www.diamonddistrict.org

FURNITURE

WHAT YOU NEED TO KNOW: In this town of movers, shakers, and walk-ups, the reality is that holding on to any piece of furniture for longer than a year or two at a time can be no small feat. When there are so many options for replacing furniture with new stuff, either with a brand-new piece from a home store like ABC or with cheap old objects from Craigslist or a secondhand store, the idea of going to any lengths to repair anything seems almost counterintuitive. There are, of course, carpenters, cabinet-makers, and other professionals around the city who can fix pretty much anything, from a legless stool to an antique bookcase. But skilled labor is expensive, and for the time and money it takes to repair something—with the possible exception of priceless family heirlooms—you might be better off dumping the old and buying something new.

WHERE TO GO: With such a spectrum of potential specialization, it's best to let your fingers do the walking in the world of furniture repair, and look up local carpenters online or in the Yellow Pages. But there are a few places that stand out from the rest, either for generous prices or sheer workmanship. The brilliant Williamsburg Chair Repair Company does exactly what it's supposed to: bring in anything from an antique La-Z-Boy to a rusting bench and its repairpeople can do something with it for a reasonable price. Joseph Biunno, an antique restorer in the Flower District in Manhattan, can repair anything from vanities to jewelry boxes for much less than you'd expect to pay if you went through a high-end antiques store. And Little Wolf on the Upper East

Side not only handcrafts beautiful woodwork from scratch, it also repairs shelves, cabinets, and bookcases—often improving them with beautiful detail in the process.

Joseph Biunno Ltd., 129 West 29th Street, between Sixth and Seventh avenues,
(212-629-55630) www.antiquefurnitureusa.com

Little Wolf Cabinet Shop, 1583 First Avenue, between 82nd and 83rd streets, (212-734-1116)
www.littlewolfcabinetshop.com

Williamsburg Chair Repair Co., 161 Clymer Street, at Bedford Avenue (Brooklyn)
(718-387-4211)

COMPUTERS

WHAT YOU NEED TO KNOW: No matter where you live, whether it's been dropped or spilled on one too many times, has been mysteriously riddled at the airport by a trip through the X-ray machine, or ravaged by an evil file-eating virus, it sucks when computers break. It also always manages to happen at the worst time possible, and we won't even go into whether or not you've been backing up, so you'll want someone fast and good. We'll get right to the point.

Many service centers specialize in either Macs or PCs, so before you schlep your laptop over to a shop for the first time, be sure to find out. If you have a desktop, consider someone who makes house calls. Centers that have been in business for a few years will often have more experienced technicians than upstarts. If you have a Mac, you might be tempted to take your ailing machine to an Apple Store's comfortingly named Genius Bar. Before you do, know that the Genius Bar takes reservations—and you should definitely make one. The last thing you'll want to do when you're pulling your hair out is to wait in line for an hour while the single technician tries to explain how to load songs onto an iPod to a bunch of Dutch retirees on holiday. (You can make the reservations online at www.apple.com.) If the Genius Bar is booked (a not-infrequent occurrence), or if none of the locations are convenient for you, any Apple Authorized Service Center will give exactly the same kind of service, minus the lines and commotion, and if your computer is not under warranty, the prices should be comparable.

WHERE TO GO: Many of the city's most fashionable Mac users swear by TekServe for the quality of service and the quirky small-town-meets-high-tech atmosphere. We like Digital Society, where the technicians look like they could star in a Kevin Smith movie, but are unusually pleasant, and are the best at explaining the problem to you in words you can understand. (They also have a fabulous and appropriately laidback return policy on items purchased in the store.) Both TekServe and Digital Society are Apple Authorized Service Centers, and have been in business for over a decade.

Funnily enough, Caitlin's PC suddenly malfunctioned right around the time she was working on this section. Some quick online research on a borrowed desktop brought her to Amnet Data Solutions, a repair and data-recovery center in Midtown with a lot of write-ups, both favorable (successful) and lukewarm (pricey). While it certainly wasn't cheap (nor was the staff as charming as the guys at Digital Society), it was fast—amazingly fast. She had an estimate (and a detailed description of the necessary work) within an hour of dropping the computer off, and it was ready to be picked up by the end of the day. Even better, the store stuck to the price in the estimate when she went to pick it up. Bottom line is that computer repairs are almost always going to be disappointingly pricey, so best to judge a place on speed and quality of work. For this Amnet gets our approval. (They repair Macs, too.)

Amnet Data Solutions, 226 East 54th Street, between Second and Third avenues,
  (212-935-9200) www.amnetdatasolutions.com

Digital Society, 60 East 10th Street, between Broadway and University Place, (212-777-3093)
  www.digsoc.com

Genius Bars, located inside Apple stores, multiple locations, www.apple.com

TekServe, 119 West 23rd Street, between Sixth and Seventh avenues, (212-929-3645)
  www.tekserve.com

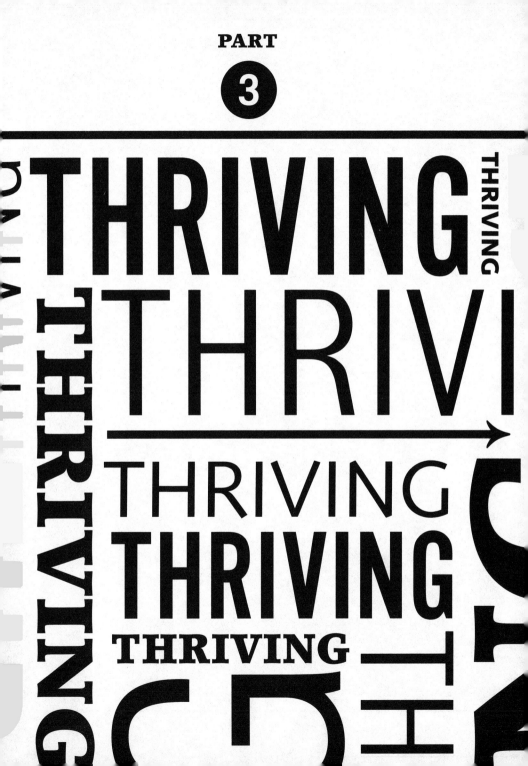

THRIVING

MAKING FRIENDS

One of the things that newcomers often struggle with is how to make friends in New York. The volume of people here makes the traditional routes—joining teams and clubs, going to free events—less appealing (it can be a bit overwhelming to try to figure out whom to chat with at a book reading with 300 attendees). Plus, the cultural pressure to stuff one's schedule until it bursts at the seams—on top of the 60- and even 80-hour work weeks that are the norm in many industries here—mean that many people you meet will seem impenetrably busy.

On the other hand, New York boasts an unusually large amount of unavoidable interpersonal interaction. Instead of commuting alone in their cars to work, and driving through banks, cleaners, and even coffee shops, New Yorkers must do all of these things in public, out in the open. This is a city where you bump into people you know, and get to know the people that you regularly pass by.

The key, we think, is to take the obligatory intermingling one small step further. While we're not suggesting that you try to pick up a date on the subway (though we know one married couple who met on the D train), there are plenty of promising opportunities for friendship mere blocks from your door, and ones that don't require anything more from you than showing up to something you are invited to. Without too much effort, you can get to know people whose personal orbits cross your own.

→ Thriving Tips ←

- Go to everything you are invited to, even if it sounds strange, or you don't know anyone or don't know how to get there. As one five-year New York veteran originally from Minnesota, put it, "If you say no, you'll stop being invited. And why would you want to sit in your tiny apartment every night anyway?" At worst, you'll get a few boring outings with free food and drink. At best, you'll come away with an adventure, new friends, good stories, or all of the above.

- One friend can be a key to many. Don't underestimate the potential of friends of friends whom you meet at parties or other group gatherings. Get their contact info and arrange to get together independently. It's not poaching as long as you both remain friends with the common friend.

- Friendships are the best-kept secrets of randomly selected roommates. While living with someone you are already friends with can test the limits of an existing friendship, many a long-lasting friendship has blossomed out of a Craigslist setup. Be open to it.

HOME SWEET 'HOOD

Right outside of your apartment building is a wealth of people who live or work in the neighborhood, and frequent the same local businesses and spend a good deal of time on the same streets as you do. Already that's a group of people you have more in common with than any number of friends you already have. A strange sort of paradox about New York is that while it can be hard to make friends with your actual neighbors (people who live in your building), it is often quite easy to make friends with the people just outside it.

Neighborhood friends have a unique value beyond companionship: they also make you feel happier about where you live. Really. These friendships connect you to your neighborhood (a nice thing to feel, even if your 'hood is not the one you dreamed of living in); they're the basis for future nostalgic yearning when you do move on; and they make you feel like a part of this city we share is yours. Caitlin's cherished neighborhood buds include cleaners that ask after her family, an architect whose office was next door to a building she lived in, gym friends, and a sommelier who works at the wine bar downstairs from her apartment.

There can also be practical benefits to having friends in the neighborhood. We know a writer, for instance, who has her packages shipped to the dry cleaner on the corner because she doesn't have a doorman to sign for them. Neighborhood friends also come in handy if you need someone to pick up your mail, feed your pets, or water plants while you are away.

Neighborhood friends fall into two general categories: local residents and local workers. Local residents are the people at the gym, dog run, and coffee shop; they're usually on a similar schedule as you, so you will probably spend a bit of time around them before a chat is initiated. Local workers may take a bit more reaching out to on your part, but you also have more of a choice of who you cozy up to. Start by exploring the neighborhood and considering the offerings. Then try a bunch of places and see what clicks. Once you've found your local (or locals), try to go a bunch of times in a short period, be open to chatting, and be patient. It can take many frustrating weeks of ordering the same thing at the same time each morning at your local coffee bar, but your persistence will be rewarded on the day when the formerly surly barista finally cracks a smile and has your regular order ready by the time you hit the register.

One small warning: Like any friendship, a neighborhood friendship takes work, and one thing to remember is that if you do become friends with someone who you interact with every day, you should be friends with the person . . . every day. If you don't think you want to have a long conversation with the guys at the juice bar every morning, it may be best to just keep things cordial with them. On the other hand, a few moments shooting the breeze every morning with someone you've come to know and like is a sacrifice well worth making in the name of friendship, or even just being a nice person. So, we'll say choose your friends wisely and leave it at that.

BUDDIES BY PROFESSION

New York is one of the few major cities in the world where the notion of districts designated by profession still exists in spades. While the Fulton Fish Market has sailed for the Bronx, and the Meatpacking District has been filleted down to a few rows of refrigerated warehouses, there still remains a sense in the city of neighborhoods belonging to one industry or another. Things aren't quite as simple now as they were a century ago, when an able-bodied seaman new in town could head for the taverns by the South Street Seaport and expect to find work and affinity among the other old salts. But each profession has its circle, and every crew has its stomping ground, and sometimes knowing where things go on is the first step toward getting to know the people who are involved. So whether you're looking for new buddies in the city and you want to stay close to your own, or you're looking for work in a particular field and you want to make some friends on the inside, it pays to know what happens where.

The suits and wallets of Wall Street have made the Financial District their own: there isn't much to do down there unless you work in finance, but if you're part of that world (or if you want to be) its high-class restaurants and old-school dives are the right places to rub shoulders with everyone from ambitious yuppies to drunken executives. It's a similar story in Midtown, where office workers from lawyers to accountants unwind in well-trodden old pubs, upscale restaurants, and crowded cocktail bars. Gramercy and Flatiron are favored by the media, where publishers, agents, and less cut-throat businessmen congregate in old taverns and hip restaurants to gossip with one another and have indulgent lunches with clients. And although young artists tend to *live* in Williamsburg, Dumbo, or the more affordable areas in Brooklyn and the Lower East Side, Chelsea remains essentially the "art district," with a mass of studios, workshops, and galleries occupying its old warehouses and factory buildings. Even apart from the openings that crowd the neighborhood every Thursday night, the overwhelming presence of art keeps a steady crowd of artists and art-lovers passing their time between the galleries, cafés, and bars here.

KEEPING UP

←→

It's said that you can tell a lot about a person by the newspaper he or she reads. In New York, this rule doesn't really apply—plenty of card-carrying *Times* readers will discreetly take an extended peek at the *Post* or the *Daily News* when it crosses their path, while no self-respecting English *Guardian* reader would be caught dead touching the *Daily Mail*. It's not that we're more open-minded, it's more that New Yorkers are media sluts, with loose morals and heady appetites. Moreover, in New York, news really falls into two categories: news outside the city and news inside the city. Not surprisingly, the latter can inspire as much journalism as the former. New Yorkers in turn have shown an impressive tolerance for the amount of reading they can stomach on the subject of their home turf. The result is a staggering regular barrage of city-centric information, including real news coverage; articles and essays that cover (or sensationalize) every aspect of city life; and listings, write-ups, and reviews of every happening from Far Rockaway to Staten Island.

The bounty has its advantages. Namely, it can help you keep on top (or at least, give a peripheral view) of what's going on. If you wanted, you could map out an entire week of eating, shopping, entertainment, and transportation with the Sunday *Times* and a copy of *Time Out*, and still have plenty of good stuff left to do the following week. Also, city-centric publications compete desperately for your discerning eyes, and many are free or practically free.

Aside from the general publications, plenty of places have their own newsletters and listservs that should be subscribed to according to your interests. If you are a real film buff, for example, you will surely want to sign up for the online newsletter for the Film Forum, the calendar for the IFC Center in the West Village, and the mailing list for BAMcinématek. With so much going on all over the city, it's impossible to keep on top of every venue and happening, so getting info directly from the sources you are most interested in is a good strategy to avoid accidentally missing a limited-time event.

A word of caution: One can easily become a slave to his or her chosen publications, so it pays to edit your list wisely. While each of the outlets below offers a unique perspective and value, getting them all is a recipe for an overwhelming amount of paper and media clutter. Struggling to keep up with the influx of information into your home and inbox is no way to live, not least because it keeps you from actually doing things. You know you've gone too far when you're turning down invitations because you have to get through the previous week's Metro sections.

The *New York Times*

WHAT IT IS: We won't delve into its merits as compared to newspapers in other major cities, or as a pinnacle of international journalism. You don't read the *Times* just to find out about things that are going on in New York, of course, but it is technically a local paper. The Metro, City, Real Estate, Dining Out, House and Home, Styles (and to a lesser degree, the Arts and Leisure) sections are all NY-focused. It should go without saying that the reviews, articles, and profiles in the *Times* are more substantive than any you'd find in places like *Time Out* and *New York* magazine; on the other hand, the *Times* doesn't provide the same easily accessible utilitarian listing information of when, where, and how long, and it's less likely than those other publications to cover anything outside the mainstream at all. Read the *Times* to pique your interest, rather than rely on it to tell you what to do.

WHO READS IT: Depends what you mean by *reads*—getting the paper and reading it are two different questions. That said, the *Times* is the most reputable paper in town, and its large and diverse group of followers reflect that.

WHAT'S GOOD: All web services are now free, which means you can search for articles from as far back as 1981 free of charge, and you can bookmark any article in an online Times File (you'll need to register for a free online account to do this). This is a great way to keep track of a restaurant from a particularly vivid review or a longer article that mentions a few places you'd like to check out. (The City section sometimes has features on neighborhoods or different themes and will list a bunch of different things to do around that area.)

WHAT'S NOT: Reading the *Times* every day is a challenge, and many have been defeated by the volume of content and paper that demands to be consumed. You know you've lost the battle when you start "saving" sections to catch up on the next day. Our advice is to invest in a weekend subscription or just buy the Sunday paper, dedicate a few hours to it, discard promptly, and supplement that during the week with the online version.

The *New York Times*, www.nytimes.com

New York Post/New York Daily News

WHAT THEY ARE: The *New York Post* and the *New York Daily News* are the two publications that compete for the tabloid readership, but for all intents and purposes they may as well be the same paper. While they both cover some important national and international news—albeit in a suitably brief and aggressively editorial fashion—it's the gossip pages, the local horror stories, and the enormous sports sections that pull in the punters. One of the popular distinguishing features of the *Post* is its "NYPD Daily Crime Blotter" page, where the paper lists murders and violent crimes daily—by borough. Enough said.

WHO READS THEM: The tabloids appeal equally to the blue collars and blue blazers of the city. The sexy/gory stories of local calamity and the unrivaled sports coverage keep the former happy, while what editorial content there is has a distinctly conservative leaning that lures upstanding Republicans away from that liberal rag, the *Times*.

WHAT'S GOOD: The headlines. Bad Heir Day? Ike 'Beats' Tina to Death? Hicks Nix Knicks in Six? Not even a staunch left-wing intellectual with passionate views on the importance of the press can resist a good pun, and the *Post* and the *News* can dole them out like nobody else. The *Post*'s classics were even collected and published under the title of an all-time favorite, *Headless Body in Topless Bar*.

WHAT'S NOT: The shameful feeling you get after reading them, with cheap ink all over your fingertips and a renewed hatred for society—similar to the feeling you get after an especially greasy, drunken, lukewarm McDonald's binge.

New York Post, www.nypost.com; *New York Daily News*, www.nydailynews.com

Metro/AM New York

WHAT THEY ARE: The two interchangeable free tabloids that are handed out at subway entrances. The content of both includes brief articles on international and local news, some business and sports coverage, and leisure pages with limited dining, arts, health and beauty, and home coverage. The only discernible difference between the two publications is in design concept: *Metro* goes for a sleek and Euro aesthetic, with a fashionable green-and-orange color palette, while *AM New York* has more of a *Post* grown-up workingman feel to it.

WHO READS THEM: Commuters who can't avoid them.

WHAT'S GOOD: The chance that you'll find out about something or some place worthwhile while you are on your way to work, for free.

WHAT'S NOT: The target readership is too broad for the papers to cater to any one interest group, but at the same the time, they're small, and the allotted section space doesn't allow for more than a sampling from all across the city. Thus, you might happen on an interesting tidbit, but they shouldn't be counted on to deliver an exhaustive daily report of what's out there.

Metro, **www.ny.metro.us;** *AM New York*, **www.amny.com**

The Village Voice

WHAT IT IS: Once considered Norman Mailer's greatest legacy, *The Village Voice* has lost significance over the years, though it's still a quality rag. A free paper you can pick up in stores or from boxes on the street, the *Voice* retains a trace of the rebelliousness with which it was founded, and remains a liberal paper that is by and for the younger people in the city. With a relatively hip editorial voice, consistently excellent reviews, and the most thorough music and movie listings you can find anywhere, it's a good train-ride read and a useful paper to grab when you want to find something to do.

WHO READS IT: Everyone reads the *Voice* from time to time, though it's most popular among kids in the East Village and people waiting around in bookstores, bars, and diners.

WHAT'S GOOD: The music reviews are uncannily good, written as they frequently are by enthusiastic indie-lovers who are really in it for the love. Dan Savage's candid "Savage Love" column, in which he tackles the raw sexual problems of people across the nation, entertains everyone who can face it, and possibly educates them, too. And the letters pages remain among the most honest and open forums of public opinion in the city's press.

WHAT'S NOT: There's no news, per se, and if your tastes run wide of the beat/punk/indie scenes, you may only be able to stomach a handful of articles in each issue.

The Village Voice, **www.villagevoice.com**

Time Out New York (*TONY*)

WHAT IT IS: The official "What's on?" authority in the city. *Time Out* isn't necessarily the best of the bunch—and there is a youthful slant that might make you feel like a bit of a fogey reading some sections after you've turned twenty-five—but it's a reliably good way to find out what's new and what's happening.

WHO READS IT: Just about everyone who does things. Young and old, rich and less than, all flock to *Time Out* at least once in a while. It should be said that a subscription to *TONY* is not necessarily a prerequisite for actually doing anything—plenty of people who get *Time Out* have never made it to a single free concert or restaurant during opening week. Nevertheless, a subscription to *TONY* is as essential an accessory as an unlimited-ride MetroCard for those who desire to make the most of the city.

WHAT'S GOOD: Getting weekly updates of the new restaurants, bars, stores, plays, etc.—all compiled and delivered to your door. Whereas the breadth and volume of limited-time happenings—the concerts, the readings, the sales—can be overwhelming and even anxiety inducing, you can feel informed without the pressure by reading about the less transient offerings, such as the museum exhibits and gallery shows, restaurants, bars, and stores that you might get to someday . . . maybe.

WHAT'S NOT: A magazine redesign has confusingly lumped the shopping, health and beauty, and travel together into a section called "Seek," and thrown some other regular features (a dating column, fitness tips, a home décor page) in as well. The mix seems contrived and not particularly user-friendly. Who wants to read about bad breakups when looking for shiatsu?

Time Out New York, **www.timeout.com/newyork**

New York magazine

WHAT IT IS: *New York* magazine combines some of the usefulness of a *Time Out* with a more, shall we say, distinctive editorial voice. Feature articles don't really delve deeply so much as twist the screw on the concerns of the city's upwardly mobile class. *New York* definitely plays on New Yorkers' obsessions with themselves and reinforces the notion of NYC as the center of the universe. This isn't entirely a criticism—in our opinion, *New York* has its fingers on the pulse of its narrow readership far more than *Time Out* does, and it knows what buttons to push.

WHO READS IT: *New York* magazine is the guilty pleasure of New Yorkers who wouldn't be caught dead reading *Us Weekly* but can't stop themselves from reading about the latest school-admissions controversy or the seamy secret lives of the kids who work at Trader Joe's.

WHAT'S GOOD: The reviews (food, shop, music, art, books, movies, etc.) are an informational middle ground in substance between the listing-driven publications and the fine journalism of the *Times*. *New York*'s web site is also an excellent resource for restaurants, bars, and shopping info; in addition to brief write-ups and addresses, it lists other relevant info like hours, closest subways, and the ever-so-useful cross streets.

WHAT'S NOT: The dirty feeling you get after you've read an article about the sex antics of NYC private schools kids.

New York, **www.nymag.com**

The New Yorker

WHAT IT IS: *The New Yorker* has been an institution of the culturally minded city-dweller since it was founded in 1925 and, despite going through unpopular patches in the 1980s and 1990s, has remained a bastion of thoughtful commentary and good writing ever since. It's a *New York* magazine for the older crowd and for those with higher brows when it comes to their weekly reading matter. There are listings in the front of what's going on around town, from movies to galleries, music, readings, theater, and hot restaurants, but the tone is more serious than *Time Out* or *New York*, and highlighted selections are more likely to be operas and ballets than club nights in Greenpoint. The magazine boasts an impressive roster of literary writers and political commentators, with serious essays, short stories, and intelligent if sober reviews making up the bulk of each issue.

WHO READS IT: Highbrows across the city buy it, media types across the city subscribe to it, but reading the whole thing wouldn't leave time for much else in the week—and we suspect a large percentage of its readership buys it solely for . . .

WHAT'S GOOD: . . . the cartoons and the cover illustrations.

WHAT'S NOT: The reviews can verge on the pretentious, even when the subject is as accessible as *The Sopranos* or Mary J. Blige. And unless you fall squarely into *The New Yorker*'s mature and refined demographic, you can't rely too heavily on its listings to let you know what's fun from one week to the next.

The New Yorker, **www.newyorker.com**

Manhattan User's Guide (MUG)

WHAT IT IS: This informative electronic daily started in 1992 as a monthly newsletter; it shifted to the web in 2003. *MUG* covers everything from restaurant and store openings and happenings around town to round-ups on specific services and resources (rug and carpet cleaning, charity donations, etc.). It often includes short essays on local architecture or forgotten city heroes and occasional eloquent rants on moving companies (there appears to be vendetta against U-Haul), civil liberties, or the *New York Times*—and delivers a single story to subscribers' inboxes every morning, Monday through Friday. It sounds a little random, but it works perfectly. Much of *MUG*'s content—whether it's a brief on the Brooklyn-Queens Expressway or a recommendation for an eco-friendly pest control service, for instance—covers issues you really won't come across anywhere else without a lot of effort, but still manages to be readable and relevant. Along with its smart breadth of coverage, *MUG*'s unwhimsical tone and patently populist editorial slant make it hands down the best source for useful, expert information about the city.

WHO READS IT: Serious New Yorkers. *MUG* is not all fun and games, and serves New Yorkers who *really* live in this city. By that we mean people who do need to get furniture reupholstered, figure out how to register to vote in a primary, and may need to file a complaint with an obscure city agency at some point.

WHAT'S GOOD: While *MUG* covers events around the city to a certain degree, its real strength is in its cut-and-dry service pieces on things like repairs and cleaning, community service, and matters of local bureaucracy.

WHAT'S NOT: *MUG* archives are free, but the search feature on the web site is a bit primitive, which can be frustrating when you're trying to find a certain piece on mini-storage, jury duty, or pet adoption. Better to archive all the pieces you may want to go back to on your own e-mail.

Manhattan User's Guide, www.manhattanusersguide.com

Daily Candy

WHAT IT IS: The original version of the popular consumption-focused daily e-mail publication that now has editions in cities across the country (as well a slew of shameless imitators). For those unfamiliar with the concept, each edition consists of a single 150-word piece about a single restaurant, store, or product. The subject of the piece is always new, and is almost always local, though it does occasionally cover topics like books or music. The tone is unfailingly (and charitably) characterized as whimsical, but it's tacitly acknowledged that one doesn't read *DC* for the quality of the prose. Many local businesses literally owe their lives to *Daily Candy*, as the focused "coverage" that is sent out to its highly coveted and targeted demographic generally produces better results; (purchases, attendance, etc.) than a listing in the publications mentioned previously; it provides vital support to businesses in NYC's impossibly tough market.

WHO READS IT: Girls, women, chicks . . . No boys allowed.

WHAT'S GOOD: Even though the writing is flimsy, to its credit, *DC* has managed to keep its editorial integrity despite the fact that it must be bombarded by more publicist solicitations than any operation in the city. Somehow, it still manages to uncover new and off-beat gems like off-the-beaten path boutiques in Brooklyn, environmentally friendly cleaning services, and cheap, quality manicures. *Daily Candy* seems to take pleasure in not totally catering to the officially stated demographic interests. Every once in a while, choices veer from its glossy mainstream path, and it shines a light on surprising topics like a DJ academy and places to take tap-dancing lessons.

WHAT'S NOT: *Daily Candy* is extremely popular, which means that anything listed will subsequently be mobbed. While this is great news for the listees, it can be bad news for readers. The sample-sale roundups are the worst—if a sale has been on *DC*, bring your elbow and shin guards because it's going to be a battle.

Daily Candy, www.dailycandy.com/new_york

juli b.

WHAT IT IS: A *Daily Candy* derivative, with a bit more substance and a (tiny) bit less whimsy. Though it covers exactly the same beat in an almost identical format, the tone of *juli b.* is subtly more upscale, more "uptown." (It has a seasonal Hamptons edition, if that tells you anything.)

WHO READS IT: Pretty much the same people who read *Daily Candy*.

WHAT'S GOOD: Because the content is presented in a more straightforward way than that of *DC*, it provides more informative basics than *DC*. For instance, if both do pieces on the same restaurant (a common occurrence), you'll get more details on the food, décor, chef, and ambience in the *juli b.* version.

WHAT'S NOT: If you're getting *Daily Candy*, there'll be a bit of overlap. Choose *juli b.* if you prefer Madison Avenue to Williamsburg.

juli b., www.julib.com

GOING OUT

←→

Going out to eat and drink in New York City can be anxiety provoking for even the city's most characteristically blasé residents. Will there be a wait? Will I get a reservation? Will it be as good as I thought it would be? Will the place be too busy, too empty, too loud, too quiet, or just too awful? The hassle can be enough to tempt one to retreat to one's own apartment with a lifetime supply of delivery menus.

Fear not. Going out is supposed to be fun, and that it can easily be. You need not be rich, well-connected, or even particularly imaginative to get it right. Never forget that this is a city of infinite possibilities and boundless creativity. A combination of open-mindedness, a sense of humor, and a spirit of adventure will yield rewards, just as it does when looking for an apartment or browsing the "Around Town" listings in *Time Out*. More specifically: Waits can be worthwhile and even pleasant in the right circumstances, but so can eating at the bar, finding a nearby Plan B, or taking that 6:00 or 10:30 p.m. reservation on occasion. An impromptu three-course meal at 3 a.m. is a magical way to end a night on the town, and a barbecue on your stoop opens up the door for all kinds of fun that private backyard parties can never achieve.

Let's be clear: by "going out," we're not talking about street food, a slice of pizza, or takeout. All of these options can be excellent local dining experiences, and you don't need any more guidance from us than that you should take advantage of them whenever the impulse strikes you. What we are dealing with here, however, are the social occasions that require at minimum the desire to spend time in a specific place that is not your home while eating, drinking, and having fun. We are talking about bars and sit-down restaurants, places to have parties, and possibly reservations and advance planning. In the spirit of the old "teach a man to fish" proverb, we are not telling you exactly which places to go to ensure a great time for every occasion, but rather advising on how to get what you want from the multitude of interesting, eclectic, and delicious choices. You can have your extravagant meal—or great party or perfect clandestine midnight snack—and eat it too, so to speak.

FIRST DATES/ROMANTIC EVENINGS

WHAT YOU NEED TO KNOW: With a reputation that precedes it in the countless movies, novels, television shows, and comic strips that have glorified the city's every corner, cab seat, hotel, and skyline view, New York has a lot to live up to as a romantic backdrop. But to the uninitiated, New York might seem at first glance no more than a spotty adolescent, fidgeting in the shadows of such urban Don Juans as Paris, London, or Rome. Unless you're part of the tuxedo-and-red-rose crowd—for whom dinner and dancing in a Midtown ballroom and a carriage ride back through the park is still the thing—you'll have to accept that romance in New York, like everything else, has to be sought out among the crowds, the traffic, the bodegas, and the subways. In fact, whatever your preconceptions, the act of seeking out a secret place among the bustle and grime for the perfect meal or a lustful drink only makes a romantic night that much sweeter. Whether your tastes are inclined toward champagne and oysters in a cozy French bistro or galvanizing cocktails in a red-lit saloon, there are places for every kind of romantic all over the city.

WHERE TO GO: Finding a really pleasant place for a quiet romantic drink in the city can be tough, particularly on weekends, so it's always a good idea to head off the beaten path and look for something quaint. Angel's Share on Stuyvesant Street in the East Village is a good choice—a Japanese cocktail lounge with a speakeasy feel hidden upstairs beside a bustling yakitori restaurant. Robin des Bois in Cobble Hill has a good wine list and one of Brooklyn's most romantic gardens, and is a perfect place for a date when it's warm enough to sit and sip wine outside. And if you want to go upscale, head to one of the roof bars around Manhattan—the Gansevoort, the Beekman, and the Peninsula are three hotels with the most romantic views of the Hudson, the East River, and Central Park respectively.

If you're comfortable enough with your date to retain sobriety and look for a romantic meal, try smaller places, the intimate spots that are hidden from the view of the marauding masses. Marlow and Sons in Williamsburg is one of the authors' favorites: warm and cozy with an open fire in the winter and tables outside with views of the river in the summer. Peasant in Nolita is one of the city's best restaurants for any occasion, but the downstairs annex is particularly romantic. Reservations aren't taken and the long old wooden tables are communal, so you end up sharing your romantic meal with similarly minded company. And Café des Artistes on the Upper West Side is one of the city's hidden treasures: a tiny restaurant with room for about a dozen diners, we're yet to find a sexier and more intimate place to bond over a meal and a bottle or two.

Of course, not every date has to be in a bar or a restaurant. Take a walk through one of the parks, with an ice cream in summer or a hot chocolate in winter. Take a bottle of wine and a blanket to the waterside parks in Dumbo or Long Island City and watch the city's lights flicker across the river as night falls. Head down to Battery Park or the Chelsea Piers and watch the sun set. Or just pick a movie to see at one of the city's fancier theaters, like the Landmark Sunshine or the Ziegfeld. Sometimes the easiest or most obvious things to do in the city can be the most romantic.

Angel's Share, 8 Stuyvesant Street, between 9th Street and Third Avenue, (212-777- 5415)

Beekman Tower, 3 Mitchell Place, at First Avenue, (212-355-7300)
    www.thebeekmanhotel.com

Café des Artistes, One West 67th Street, at Central Park West, (212-877-3500)
    www.cafenyc.com

Hotel Gansevoort, 18 Ninth Avenue, at 13th Street, (212-206-6700) www.hotelgansevoort.com

Landmark Sunshine Cinema, see page 43

Marlow and Sons, see page 99

Peasant, see page 56

Peninsula Hotel, 700 Fifth Avenue at 55th Street, (212-956-2888) www.newyork.peninsula.com

Robin des Bois, see page 79

Ziegfeld Cinema, 141 West 54th Street, at Sixth Avenue, (212-307-1862)

BREAKFAST/BRUNCH

WHAT YOU NEED TO KNOW: Gone are the days when the first meal of the day was the most important. For most New Yorkers, breakfast is just another thing that has to happen between waking up and getting to where they need to be that morning: yogurt and granola at home, a bagel from the deli on the way to work, or just an extra helping of half-and-half in their coffee. While there are diners in every neighborhood where you can always get a decent full breakfast, delis across the city carry everything for a breakfast on the go, from croissants to oatmeal, breakfast sandwiches, and fruit.

Come the weekend, however, New Yorkers indulge en masse in the ritual of brunch. Brunch is taken seriously here: it's as much a mark of a good weekend and as universal a social occasion as going out to eat and drink on a Friday or Saturday night.

It's also vital to the city's constitution—a long, drawn-out meal (often involving alcohol) that acts as recovery from a hard week, restorative hangover cure after a big night out, and farewell indulgence to the weekend all at once. As well as the many hundreds of diners around town that offer everything from vegetarian omelets and waffles to lumberjack specials of pancakes, eggs, and three kinds of pork, most serious restaurants that wouldn't be open for breakfast during the week also compete for the brunch crowd with morning menus of their own.

Even with so many places to go, the demand for brunch is high, so unless you want to wander the streets with the hungry herds it's worth having a few ideas in mind. Some restaurants whose great reputations for brunch verge on cliché, such as Balthazar, certain hotels uptown, and Five Points, even require reservations for a table on a Sunday morning. But in general, your best bet is to decide where to go before you set off and, if you're eating with a big group, to be prepared to wait a little while for a table. (Tradition dictates you do your waiting at the bar with a Bloody Mary.)

WHERE TO GO: Any restaurant worth its salt for lunch and dinner will have a brunch menu to match, and often it'll retain something of its evening ambience in the morning too—so every time you come across a place you like, make sure to see if it serves brunch and give it a try. Patois, the wonderful French restaurant in Carroll Gardens, opens early on Sundays to serve a great menu of provincial variations on brunch, and with free mimosas and a wood fire crackling in the hearth it is the perfect place to while away a winter afternoon. The addition of eggs is ostensibly the only thing to distinguish the fantastic brunch menu at Freeman's from its dinnertime counterpart, and the restaurant is as bustling and lively (albeit even scruffier) on a Sunday morning as it is on a Thursday or Friday night. The aptly named Diner in Williamsburg gives you the menu of a sophisticated new American restaurant with the tin ceiling and red leather banquettes of a freeway diner. And for a breakfast with a flavor of its own neighborhood, get the legendary dim sum brunch at the Golden Unicorn in Chinatown or head up to the M&G Diner in Harlem to join the well-dressed after-church crowd for the best soul food in the city.

Balthazar, 80 Spring Street, between Crosby Street and Broadway, (212-965-1414)
    www.balthazarny.com

Diner, see page 99

Five Points, 31 Great Jones Street, between Lafayette Street and the Bowery,
    (212- 253-5700) www.fivepointsrestaurant.com

Freeman's, Freeman Alley, off of Rivington Street, between the Bowery and Chrystie Street,
    (212-420-0012) www.freemansrestaurant.com

Golden Unicorn, 18 East Broadway, at the Bowery, (212-941-0911)
    www.goldenunicornrestaurant.com

M&G Diner, 383 West 125th Street, near St. Nicholas Avenue, (212-864-7326)

Patois, 255 Smith Street, at DeGraw Street (Brooklyn), (718-855-1535)

GROUP DINNERS

WHAT YOU NEED TO KNOW: Group dinners—by which we mean a meal out with six people or more—are probably tricky to plan anywhere. But they can be especially fraught in New York, where the infinite dining options multiply the logistical complications exponentially. Every restaurant has its own policy on reservations and offerings for groups, and the nicer the place, the more rules there will be, while the smaller the place, the more difficult it can be to bring a group in at all.

A rather general rule of thumb for a medium-size restaurant (one with more tables than you can count on two hands, but fewer than a hotel banquet hall) is that twelve people is the maximum you can expect to be accommodated at a regular table. (It could be more at a family-style restaurant, less in a quirky, six-table joint in the Village.) With more than twelve guests, you will start to run into private rooms, a set menu, or both. However, some restaurants have semiprivate areas set off from the regular dining room but not actually in separate rooms; some have space in the dining room with one long table that is saved for large parties, or that is usually used as a communal table but can be saved for groups. Some places won't mind pushing together a long line of tables; and some restaurants that say they don't take reservations at all will unofficially reserve some space for a large group, depending on the night. So if your group is bigger than twelve, you can probably find somewhere that will take you . . . but it will require a bit more persistence. Finally, perhaps this is common sense, but you should always make a reservation with a true group. Five is the limit we would try to pull off without a reservation, maybe six in a pinch.

WHERE TO GO: We advise casting your net wide, cuisine-wise. Chinatown is an excellent destination to consider for group dining—family-style food, big tables, reasonable prices. Restaurant options there abound, and most will not require a VIP connection to get a group reservation. Indian, Moroccan, and Mexican restaurants are other crowd pleasers that this city has plenty of, and a pub with a decent kitchen is a good idea for a large and potentially rowdy group in any town.

HOT RESTAURANTS

WHAT YOU NEED TO KNOW: The New York restaurant scene defies conventional logic. There are quirky no-frills joints that are as hard to get into as any upscale four-star restaurant. Some restaurants that have been open for years remain impossible to penetrate during normal dining hours, while others disappear as soon as the foodies have turned their attention away, and then are reincarnated a few months later in a different culinary or aesthetic model. The one rule of thumb is that no matter what it is, how odd the concept seems, or in what part of town it's in, if people are talking about it, it'll be mobbed. Remember, this is a city where people spend hours in line for cupcakes, and that supports one restaurant serving only rice pudding, another that only serves mac and cheese, and another that serves only desserts made of tofu.

Common sense will tell you that if you have your heart set on eating at a hot restaurant and don't know someone who knows someone, then you either have to be willing to wait for the crowds to die down, or be willing to go at an abnormal mealtime. Lunch can be an opening, as can eating at the bar, though neither of these tricks is exactly a secret.

New York's volume of restaurants does offer one dining perk that other cities lack: the number of alternatives to any hot spot. There are more restaurants here than any eater could ever go through, so if you can't get reservations to one place that has recently gotten rave reviews, we guarantee there's a place with a similar menu and comparable atmosphere where you can. If you show up somewhere only to be told that the wait is more than two hours, you're not stranded there. Any neighborhood that has one restaurant that people flock to has several others nearby, and you and your companions are at most a quick walk from another great dining destination (another advantage we have over our friends in driving country). What you find could be more pleasant or tasty than the massively hyped one, and discovering a great place on your own is, in our opinion, a bigger accomplishment than getting into a place that everyone is talking about.

A final note: Some very trendy and/or respected restaurants don't take reservations. If you really want to go to any of these, all you have to do is swallow your pride and get there early (as in, within the first half hour after they open for lunch or dinner).

WHERE TO GO: Many of the publications we listed in "Keeping Up" have restaurant reviews and previews. But most pieces run when the restaurant is about to open or is already up and running, so by the time you read about it there, it's already too late to beat the crowds. To really be on the cutting edge of the NYC dining scene, go online.

NY-based blogs and web sites such as Eater, Grub Street, and The Strong Buzz are good places to find out what's opened, what's closed, what's coming up, and what's good.

Eater, www.eater.com

Grub Street, www.nymag.com/daily/food

The Strong Buzz, www.thestrongbuzz.com

RESTAURANT WEEK

WHAT YOU NEED TO KNOW: New York does two Restaurant Weeks a year, one in late January and early February, and one in late June and early July. Both "weeks" are actually two weeks long, though they don't include the weekends. During Restaurant Week, participating restaurants offer a prix-fixe three-course lunch or dinner or both, and the price is the same at every restaurant. Thus, you can in theory have lunch at Gramercy Tavern for less than $25 or dinner at any of Jean-Georges's restaurants for $35.

We have mixed feelings about Restaurant Week. On one hand, some people we know swear by it, literally marking their calendars for when the list is released, and then working OpenTable like they're trying to get tickets to a concert. To them, it's an affordable way to have a really, really nice meal, which is true. On the other hand, since Restaurant Week is all prix-fixe, you're getting a more limited menu than you would at a normal time. If you are an adventurous eater, this isn't so bad, but if you have any dietary restrictions, Restaurant Week is not the time to ask the kitchen to make you a special plate. And, of course, because it's such a good deal, it requires advance planning, and competing with the rest of the city. Many restaurants offer the deal at lunch only, and the places that do offer dinner fill up very quickly, so consider clearing your calendar for a nice long lunch that week. And while restaurant reservations are usually not our style, we'd definitely recommend them for Restaurant Week, no matter where you go.

WHERE TO GO: Visit www.nycvisit.com a few weeks before Restaurant Week to see the list of participating restaurants. If you've got your heart set on specific places, act fast and be flexible with the times and days. OpenTable, the reservations web site, also has the list of participating restaurants, and you can book at many of the restaurants through the site (for those that you can't book through OpenTable, you should call for reservations).

OpenTable, www.opentable.com

PARENTS, IN-LAWS, AND THE LIKE

WHAT YOU NEED TO KNOW: Make no mistake: New York is a crowd-pleaser. All of us at one time or another face the difficult prospect of visits and checkups from parents, relatives, in-laws, and the like. Anyone moving here from somewhere else immediately becomes the pride, shame, envy, or skeleton of the family, and therefore warrants regular investigation from loved ones and former guardians of one kind or another. Whether it's anxious parents flying in from the sticks, a wealthy and impressionable aunt popping down from upstate, or blue-eyed, white-toothed New England in-laws here to make sure you're looking after their little princess, the city has something to suit every occasion. With all its bars, restaurants, sights, and sounds—and the implicit gravitas of being the greatest city in the world—New York caters better to the ingratiating host than any other city on the planet. You just need to know how to work it.

The first thing to do is to consider the occasion and work out the appropriate mood. Whatever the event, extremes are always a risk, so think twice before you make reservations at Lucky Cheng's, no matter how much you think Uncle Walter might like it. In general, occasions for which you're hosting away from home mean you're called upon to assert a certain impression, whether it's the noble portrait of a struggling artist on the breadline or the crisp-pressed image of a sophisticated Wall Street executive, so explore a little and find an environment to suit. Strangers to the city are the easiest to host—sacrifice your resident's pride and take them somewhere famous and touristy. Anybody with a sharper knowledge of New York, however, should be treated with more care: do a little research and take the person somewhere he or she hasn't been before, somewhere off the beaten track that will send your guest home in awe at how well you know this crazy town. It goes without saying that you should bear in mind above all your company's taste and do your best to complement it.

WHERE TO GO: While we wouldn't be so bold as to suggest where to break the news of your engagement/divorce/hiring/firing to your parents/in-laws/aging benefactors, we can lay down some helpful general guidelines and point you in the direction of some personal favorites. When money is no object, whether you're a high-flier impressing the in-laws or an underpaid bohemian with generous relatives, a popular option is to follow a meal at an expensive downtown restaurant like Perry Street or Blue Hill with a trip uptown to the opera at the Met or a concert at Carnegie Hall. For shoestring budgets or to play the salt-of-the-earth card, take them to Arturo's for pizza or a humble meal at a respectable diner, and suggest a walk across the park with a coffee afterward. For friends and relatives who don't mind going touristy, consider dinner in the Rainbow Room at the top of Rockefeller Center, a table at Cipriani in Grand Central overlooking the beautiful concourse, or a meal at River Café gazing out across the river at the Manhattan skyline. To impress upon someone your infinite knowledge of the eclecticism of the city, go for an Ethiopian meal at Ghenet on Mulberry Street, an Indian feast at the Jackson Diner in Jackson Heights, an aperitif of vodka and caviar at the Russian Tea Room in Midtown, or a tower of scones and clotted cream at Tea and Sympathy.

Arturo's, 106 West Houston Street, at Thompson Street, (212-677-3820)

Blue Hill, 75 Washington Place, between Sixth Avenue and MacDougal Street,(212-539-1776)
  www.bluehillnyc.com

Carnegie Hall, 57th Street and Seventh Avenue, (212-247-7800) www.carnegiehall.org

Cipriani Dolci, Grand Central Station, West Balcony, (212-973-0999) www.cipriani.com

Ghenet, 284 Mulberry Street, between Prince and Houston streets, (212-343-1888)
  www.ghenet.com

Jackson Diner, 37-47 74th Street, near 39th Road (Queens), (718-672-1232)

Lucky Cheng's, 24 First Avenue, between 1st and 2nd streets, (212-995-5500)
  www.planetluckychengs.com

The Metropolitan Opera, Lincoln Center, see page 67, www.metopera.com

Perry Street, 176 Perry Street, at West Street, (212-352-1900) www.jean-georges.com

Rainbow Room, 30 Rockefeller Plaza, 65th Floor, (212-632-5100) www.rainbowroom.com

River Café, 1 Water Street, near Old Fulton Street (Brooklyn), (718-522-5200)
  www.rivercafe.com

Russian Tea Room, 150 West 57th Street, between Sixth and Seventh avenues,
  (212-581-7100) www.russiantearoomnyc.com

Tea & Sympathy, 108 Greenwich Avenue, between Jane and Horatio streets, (212-807-8329)
  www.teaandsympathynewyork.com

BAR PARTIES

WHAT YOU NEED TO KNOW: Bar parties in NYC are not just the province of heirs and heiresses, those with unlimited bank accounts, and VIPs of uncertain origins. People far less fancy than your humble authors host their birthday parties, bachelor and bachelorette fetes, holiday celebrations, and the like in the cozy booths, comfy couches, and simple tables of public drinking establishments. With the exception of celebrity-owned clubs and of-the-moment lounges, most bars in the city are happy to reserve some space for a group with a little bit of notice, and if you're lucky, will even throw in a couch or two. (And you should reserve, particularly on a weekend night—it may seem like there are far too many bars in the city for them all to be packed, but remember that no bar would be able to stay in business in this town if it wasn't busy on a Saturday night.) However, while a bar won't charge the host for the space, some do require the host to guarantee a minimum on drinks, or to purchase a certain number of bottles of alcohol for a table. If you don't want to do this, you should be able to find an alternative with a little bit of calling around. Generally, the less flashy the place, the less likely it is that you'll be charged. One thing to consider when planning a bar party is if your guests will have a hard time getting in, might be turned down at the door, or will have to wait in a long line to get in.

Many bars with good group seating do a brisk business during the office Christmas party season, so if you want to have your party anytime between Thanksgiving and New Year's, start calling early.

WHERE TO GO: The best way to find a bar to have a largish gathering at is to think of places you have been before, cross off the ones that you had a hard time getting into, and then either call and ask what they can do for parties or check their web sites. Many bars with good group seating areas mention it on their web sites, along with their policies on how to reserve space. Pubs, places that have been around forever, and bars with multiple levels in untrendy neighborhoods and/or with gardens (in nice weather) are all good places to start.

PARTIES IN PARKS

WHAT YOU NEED TO KNOW: Having a party or a picnic in a city park can be an economical and spacious alternative to a house or bar party, albeit one that requires a bit more thought and effort on the set-up leg. The city requires permits for gatherings of more than 20 people in any park; while in practice you probably would not get busted for not having a permit if a couple of people show up with unanticipated plus ones, getting a permit isn't a bad idea even if your group is definitely going to be smaller. The permit also guarantees you a certain reserved space, so if you don't have one, you may have to move the announced location if there's already a group there, or try to kick people off it (which may be impossible if they have the permit for the place you chose).

The downside of getting a permit is the hassle of getting one. You have to apply for one at least a month in advance (it takes between 21 and 30 days to be processed). You can apply for the permit online on the Department of Parks and Recreation's web site, but you have to pick it up from the permit office in the borough you are applying in or include a self-addressed, stamped envelope for them to mail it back to you. There are no rain dates, and you can't have alcohol.

WHERE TO GO: Central and Prospect Parks are the first that come to mind, but you can have a party in any city park, and the less popular the park, the more likely it is that you'll be able to get the spot you want.

Department of Parks and Recreation, www.nycgovparks.org. To find a list of parks, click on "Find a Park" under the "Your Park" menu. To apply for a party permit, click on "Special Events" under the "Permits & Services" menu.

BARBECUES

WHAT YOU NEED TO KNOW: A beach chair and a fire-escape grill are traditionally how true New Yorkers enjoy their rites of summertime. We feel duty-bound to warn you, however, that it is technically illegal to barbecue on a fire escape or roof in NYC. There are actually several different laws at work here: First, it's illegal to keep anything on a fire escape because of the possible obstruction. Second, you cannot grill within ten feet of any combustible surface, material, or building. So gardens and yards are okay, as are terraces longer than ten feet, and roofs that have been treated with a fire-retardant material. All that we'll add to this is that this law is impossible to enforce, many people don't know about it, and a crackdown on illegal grills would make about as much sense as trying to enforce a ban on chewing gum on the subway. If you do choose to embark on clandestine grilling, however, charcoal is the way to go. Not only is a charcoal grill safer to use than gas in a semienclosed area like a fire escape or terrace, but while the guy at the deli will look the other way when you pick up a bag of charcoal, a propane purchase is riskier because it's also illegal to bring propane itself into any building in NYC, refill a tank in the city, or transport a propane tank through a tunnel or over a bridge.

You can 'cue in the city crime-free, and without even necessarily having to invest in your own grill, at one of the 50 designated grill areas in NYC parks. The grill areas all have public BBQ pits, but you can also BYOG. You only need a permit if your group is over 20 people (see previous section), but if you don't have one, know that the public pits and any nearby picnic tables get claimed early in the day on weekends during prime BBQing season. (No barbecuing is allowed under trees.)

Interestingly, it's also legal to barbecue on NYC sidewalks, so long as you are not under a tree and are obeying the ten-foot rule. Of course, if you are having a gathering, there's definitely a privacy issue, and potentially some logistical ones, too (pedestrians and dogs come to mind), but on the other hand, what better way to endear yourselves to your neighbors than a burger on the house! Besides, anyone can have a have a barbecue in his backyard, but it takes a certain amount of joie de vivre to grill your meat on the street.

WHERE TO GO: The list of public grill areas in NYC parks is available online at the Department of Parks and Recreation web site.
Department of Parks and Recreation, www.nycgovparks.org (Click on "Things to Do" and choose "Activities and Facilities.")

LATE NIGHT

WHAT YOU NEED TO KNOW: Late-night dining falls into two categories: refueling and true sit-down meals that happen to occur after midnight. For the former, there is no shortage of 24-hour diners, pizza places, and delis, all offering fast, filling, economical options at all hours. But this is New York, after all, and the city that never sleeps does not let its night owls down. New York is full of places where our chefs, actors, graveyard shifters, and others for whom midnight meals are a regular occurrence can dine comfortably and not feel a bit out of place.

During the week, you're covered in much of Manhattan and Brooklyn until 12 a.m, and until 2 a.m. on weekends, though the sleepier the neighborhood, the slimmer the pickings. Thus the Upper East Side has fewer options than the East Village, but Times Square is a goldmine. Generally, though, it shouldn't take more than a couple of minutes to find somewhere serving dinner at 10:30 p.m. on a Tuesday. In fact, it could be a great opportunity to get a meal at some hot spot that doesn't have a table at 8 for the next four months.

After 2 a.m. on weekends, your options narrow a little, though there are still plenty of choices. Two is when many restaurants close, but bars with kitchens and restaurants with lively bar areas often keep their kitchens open with a more limited menu until 4 a.m. After four, some of these close, so this is when you need to know of a good 24-hour restaurant.

WHERE TO GO: First, remember that there's a difference between a restaurant that is open late (midnight on weekdays and 2 a.m. on weekends), and one that's open around the clock. Of the former, Blue Ribbon Brasserie in Manhattan is a long-standing late-night favorite of many of the chefs and other late-night dining aficionados. It's open until 4 a.m. seven days a week. (FYI: the Brooklyn location does not keep the same hours.) For the latter, in addition to the countless all-night diners, the bistros L'Express and French Roast are good options to know about. Both can be pretty loud during regular dining hours, so they're actually more pleasant late-night. The sixty-five-year-old Ukrainian diner Veselka is still a favorite among the post-clubbing crowd. It's good for a hearty meal (pierogies, kielbasa) and if you need to wake up rather than head to bed, as the light is bright and harsh.

Blue Ribbon Brasserie, 97 Sullivan Street, between Prince and Spring streets,

> **(212-274-0404) www.blueribbonrestaurants.com**

L'Express, 249 Park Avenue South, at 20th Street, (212-254-5858) www.lexpressnyc.com

French Roast, 78 West 11th Street, at Sixth Avenue, (212-533-2233) 2340 Broadway,

> **at 85th Street, (212-799-1533) www.frenchroastny.com**

Veselka, 144 Second Avenue at Ninth Street, (212-228-9682) www.veselka.com

→ Our Favorite . . . ←

Place to take a first date: **PEASANT**

Restaurant for dinner with parents or in-laws: **ETATS-UNIS**

Place for lunch with a rich uncle: **GRAMERCY TAVERN**

Bar for a birthday party: **4TH AVENUE PUB**

Place for an outdoor birthday party:
THE CIRCLE LINE'S SUNSET "HARBOR LIGHTS" CRUISE

Restaurant for a group dinner:
PUBLIC (fancy); **ALTA** (casual); **AVENUE A SUSHI** (crazy)

Late-Night Eatery: **BIG NICK'S**

Restaurant bar to eat at: **TELEPAN**

Restaurant that doesn't accept reservations: **MARLOW AND SONS**

4th Avenue Pub, 76 Fourth Avenue, between Bergen Street and St. Mark's Place
    (Brooklyn), (718-643-2235)
Alta, see page 47
Avenue A Sushi, 103 Avenue A, between Sixth and Seventh streets, (212-982-8109)
Big Nick's, see page 68
Circle Line "Harbor Lights" Cruise, Pier 83, by 42nd Street and the Hudson River,
    (212-563-3200) www.circleline42.com
Etats Unis, see page 64
Gramercy Tavern, 42 East 20th Street, between Broadway and Park Avenue South,
    (212-477-0777) www.gramercytavern.com
Marlow and Sons, see page 99
Peasant, see page 56
Public Restaurant, 210 Elizabeth Street, between Prince and Spring streets,
    (212-342-7011) www.public-nyc.com
Telepan, see page 68

SPORTS

⟵⟶

GYMS

What NYC lacks in expanses of outdoor space to run around in it makes up for in options for indoor workouts, ranging from deluxe health clubs to outlets of gym chains to proudly no-frills operations that you can join for as little as $20 a month.

New York Sports Club (NYSC) is the Starbucks of gyms—it's got the most locations around the city (over 50 across the five boroughs, plus several dozen more in New Jersey, Long Island, and Westchester), and is a reliably middle-of-the-road fitness center identical to its Boston, D.C., and Philly counterparts. However, though the set-up and décor are as cookie-cutter as it comes, the vibe in individual gyms reflects the neighborhood: for example, the Midtown locations are crazed during and right after work; the Upper West Side outlets offer babysitting and plenty of midday classes; and the ones in Murray Hill feel like university fitness centers.

NYSC's chief rival is Crunch. Crunch has far fewer locations—twelve in Manhattan, two in Brooklyn, and none in the other boroughs—but several are clustered around the East Village/Soho area, so if you live around there and like having access to a bunch of clubs, it's a good option. (Though NYSC does have locations there as well.) Crunch competes for a similar demographic as NYSC, and its rates are pretty much identical, but it tries very hard to project itself as a cooler gym. (So there's pole dancing, but no babysitting.) For that reason, the membership skews younger and tends to be bit more homogenously hipster; you're more likely to see tattoos on the treadmill there than at any other chain gym. One difference between the two is that while NYSC offers different membership rates depending on whether you want access to only one club or all clubs, Crunch memberships are all-access, so you can't save any money if you just want to go to one of its clubs.

Equinox is on the deluxe end of the chain gyms; if NYSC is Starbucks, then Equinox is like Le Pain Quotidien: its offerings and ambience are a step up in fanciness, but in its soul, it's still a chain. Still, while the touches may not be personal, they're certainly comfortable. Instead of massage rooms, there are day spas; locker rooms resemble hotel bathrooms; and the "juice bars" have suspiciously calorie-laden offerings like pressed panini. Not surprisingly, these creature comforts don't come cheap: Equinox rates are roughly double those of Crunch and NYSC. If you like your fitness tough, sweaty, and a little smelly, Equinox's fluffy-towel-fancy-lotion approach is probably not for you.

You won't find either pole dancing or panini at New York Health and Racquet Club. HRC is the old-guard of NYC gyms, having been in the business since "fitness clubs" were the province of men of a certain class. Its current incarnation is a bit of an odd mix of old-fashioned white-collar clubbiness and twenty-first-century fitness. All locations have pools (see page 240), three have racquet ball courts, and there are a host of off-site member amenities like access to a tennis club, a beach club, a golf club, and even a private Health and Racquet Club yacht that does four cruises a week through the summer—all of which make it seem like HRC is trying to position itself as the urban alternative to a country club. However, if you like to swim or play squash, or find the *Bonfire of the Vanities* vibe exhilarating, it could be for you. (Beware, though, that this gym has a bit of a reputation for smarmy membership practices, even within the famously smarmy gym industry.)

The sports complexes of Chelsea Piers and Asphalt Green both include all the regular fitness offerings of other gyms, along with larger-scale facilities that only gyms in locations as inconvenient as these could house. Both have gorgeous pools, sprawling fitness centers, and a lot of classes and organized fitness programs; Chelsea Piers also has an indoor track, a rock-climbing wall, and a boxing ring, plus a full spa and sundeck. These both fall on the high end price-wise, and probably are only interesting if you live nearby and/or are interested in one of their less common offerings. If you just want machines and classes, they're not worth the extra investment—or the extra crosstown blocks.

On the other end are lower-profile chains like the scrappy Dolphin Gym, beloved by members for its dirt-cheap membership fees. Aside from that admittedly noteworthy perk, there is nothing in particular to recommend Dolphin. The gyms are essentially rooms with lots of fitness machines; only a few offer classes. There are two locations in Manhattan, four in Brooklyn, and three in Queens. A few more dollars a month can get you a membership to Bally, which has a couple of Midtown Manhattan locations and a few more in Brooklyn and Queens. Bally is like NYSC with an even less sexy marketing approach, but it costs about half as much.

Community centers are another option. The YMCAs in the city vary greatly in their fitness offerings and condition of their facilities: some look like they haven't seen a new piece of equipment since the Depression, but quite a few have state-of-the-art machines and classes not unlike those you'd find at Crunch or Equinox. The Jewish

Community Center on the Upper West Side also has a beautiful fitness center, including a good-size pool—if you live anywhere near there, stop reading now and join! Y memberships can be a good deal, but the fees vary from branch to branch, and some are nearly the same amount as a private gym. On the other hand, you get additional non-fitness benefits by joining a community center, so if there's one by you, it's not a bad idea to check it out before committing to a regular gym.

The final option is city recreation centers. There are about thirty centers across the five boroughs, which, among other features, have fitness offerings. These offerings vary from location to location, but most have weight and cardio equipment, locker rooms, and some classes. Some also have indoor pools, boxing rings, indoor tracks, and other amenities; you can check out the offerings at specific centers at the Department of Parks and Recreation web site. Not only are the rates far less than any private gym or even a community center ($50 for locations without pools; $75 for locations with pools), but you also don't have to worry about getting scammed by any sly membership representatives.

For information on membership for any of the gyms above, you must visit a location. More information on the gyms and locations can also be found on their web sites.

Asphalt Green, 555 East 90th Street, between York and East End Avenues, (212-369-8890)
    www.asphaltgreen.org

Bally, multiple locations, www.ballyfitness.com

Chelsea Piers, 23rd Street and the Hudson River, (212-366-6666) www.chelseapiers.com

Crunch, multiple locations, www.crunch.com

Department of Parks and Recreation, multiple locations, www.nycgovparks.org (go to the
    "Things to Do" tab and click on "Indoor Recreation Facilities")

Dolphin, multiple locations, www.dolphinfitnessclubs.com

Equinox, multiple locations, www.equinoxfitness.com

Jewish Community Center, 334 Amsterdam Avenue, at 76th Street, (646-505-4444)
    www.jccmanhattan.org

New York Health and Racquet Club, multiple locations, www.nyhrc.com

New York Sports Club, multiple locations, www.nysc.com

YMCA, multiple locations, www.ymca.org, www.92y.org, or www.edalliance.org

REAL SPORTS

RUNNING

Not surprisingly, Central and Prospect parks are popular places to run. In Central Park, you can do long runs through the park on the drives (up to six miles), and shorter runs along the bridle paths and around the reservoir. In Prospect Park, there's the 3.5-mile loop on the Park Drive, which you can extend by taking paths that branch out at different junctions. The drives in both parks are only open to cars during morning and evening rush hours on weekdays (the times are different in each park), so they are vehicle free most of the day and all weekend long. (However, both drives are also popular with cyclists, so watch out.) FYI, both parks are officially closed between 1 and 5 a.m. every day.

The path along the west side of Manhattan is an alternate route many runners like, because of the views across the Hudson—you can run the length of Manhattan from Battery Park up through Riverside Park. The downside is that it's completely flat, which some runners might find boring, and can get pretty jammed on nice weekends (there aren't many lanes, and some are designated for cyclists). If you're not training, the scenery is nice, but it's probably not the route to choose if you've got a pace to keep up (at least not on the weekends). You can also run across the Brooklyn Bridge, and there are locals who do regular weekday runs across it, to or from work. But the exhaust fumes aren't pleasant, and you can forget about it on the weekends—too many tourists.

If you want to race, you should absolutely join the New York Road Runners Club (NYRR). The club holds more than 50 races a year around the five boroughs, and membership grants you discounted entry fees in those races. There are races of all different distances, in different locations, for all different causes and occasions. A couple of runners we know mentioned the Grand Prix, a series of five half-marathons, one for each borough; runners who complete all five get a trophy. In addition, NYRR holds clinics, classes, and lectures that are free or discounted for members, and through them you can find a running partner or a group to run with regularly. The annual membership is $40 for one year, $69 for two years.

With an NYRR membership, you are also eligible for guaranteed entry for the New York Marathon. NYRR members who complete nine qualifying races in a calendar year and volunteer to work at one are guaranteed a spot in the following year's marathon. (You can check which ones are qualifying races on the NYRR web site.) The trick is that you have to actually be a member for two years—the year you do the qualifying races, and the following year for the marathon—and you have to become a member or renew your membership by January 31 of each year. Also, those with guaranteed entry do still have to send in a marathon application, and they have to remember to do it by May of that year's marathon. Despite the fine print, if you're interested in running the marathon, this is the best way to do it; the alternative is to enter the general lottery, and risk being turned down.

There is also a Brooklyn Road Runners Club. This isn't a Brooklyn branch of NYRR; it's a separate running club that holds a few weekly runs, most in Prospect Park. It puts on a handful of races during the year, but it's more of a running club. If you live in Brooklyn and just want some people to run with, or want to find a couple of routes, this a great way to do it; if you want to race, you might be interested in the training runs and the running community, but you'll want to join NYRR too. You can try any Brooklyn Road Runner runs for free, and if you decide to join, membership dues are $20 per year.

A cool running activity, particularly for people who don't run regularly or don't want to do evening runs alone are the Niketown runs. These are free group runs that meet at the Niketown store on 57th Street Tuesday and Thursday evenings at 6:30 and Saturday mornings at 9. The runs start with a group stretch, then break into groups of 3-, 5-, and 7-mile distances along the Central Park drives. These runs give you the safety benefits of running with a group without actually having to join one; it's also a convenient way to run outside after work on a weeknight, because there is an area where you can safely leave your stuff in the store. Plus, afterward there's food! (Runners are also provided with reflective vests, which are especially useful on winter nights, when it's already dark.) In Brooklyn, Slope Sports also holds free group runs a few times a week. There are light runs on Wednesday nights, long runs on Saturday mornings, and speed workouts on Tuesday nights. All runs meet at the Grand Army Plaza entrance of Prospect Park; you can find out more details and routes at Slope Sports' web site.

Brooklyn Road Runners Club, www.brooklynroadrunners.org

New York Road Runners Club, 9 East 89th Street, between Fifth and Madison avenues, (212-860-4455) www.nyrr.org (for information on the New York Marathon, call 212-423-2249 or visit www.ingnycmarathon.org)

Niketown, 6 East 57th Street, between Fifth and Madison avenues, (212-891-6453), www.nikerunning.com

Slope Sports, 70 Seventh Avenue, between Lincoln and Berkeley Places (Brooklyn), (718-230-4686) www.slopesports.com

TENNIS

Permits are the first thing to know about if you want to play tennis in New York. There are few private courts in the city, and hourly rates are as much as $100 for court time and thousands of dollars for season passes. In contrast, there are more than 500 city tennis courts, and the $100 permit allows you one hour of tennis per day every day on any of the courts (or two hours per day for doubles play), for the entire tennis season, from early April through late November. If you are a more intermittent player, you can also purchase single-play tickets for $7 each. However, like all good deals, there's a little bit of fine print. The Department of Parks and Recreation only issues a certain number of permits and single tickets, and they do sell out, so you should try to get one as soon as they become available in mid-March for the upcoming season. You must apply for new permits in person at a permit office (there's one in each borough) or at Paragon Sports. Don't forget to bring a photo ID. (Once you have a permit, you can renew online, but you still have to remember to do it each spring when permits become available.)

Once you've got the permit, you can play anywhere, but the savvy NYC tennis player knows that not all courts are created equal, and, most important, thinks beyond Central and Prospect Parks. Those courts are by far the most popular, so much so that you need advance reservations, an arduous process that involves buying additional $7 reservation tickets at the permit offices, and then making a reservation up to 30 days in advance. For those who prefer their tennis to be a bit more carefree, there are many other options. For instance, one tennis player we know thinks the best courts in the city are the ones at Frederick Johnson Park, at 150th Street and Adam Clayton Powell Boulevard. The park's eight courts were renovated within the past ten years, and they also have lights, which not all city courts do, so you can play at night. You can find the full list of court locations on the Department of Parks and Recreation web site, organized by borough. (None of the other city parks require court reservations as Central Park and Prospect Park do.) Confusingly, the list of indoor courts includes mostly private tennis centers that the city tennis permit doesn't cover, but the list of outdoor courts will show all the parks with city courts, and the number and type of court each has.

Almost all of the city courts are "hard courts." If you like to play on clay, your best options are the Riverside Clay Tennis Association (RCTA) courts. These ten red-clay courts are located in Riverside Park, but are actually maintained by the RCTA, not the city. (You still need the city permit or a single-play ticket to play on them, though.) Other options—particularly if you don't have a permit—are the courts at the USTA stadium in Flushing Meadows Corona Park, better known as the home of the U.S. Open. Aside from the few weeks in August and September when the Open is on, the courts are open to the public year-round (there are 9 indoor courts as well as 22 outdoor courts), and the rates are very reasonable compared to other private courts (as little as $18 an hour for indoor courts or $16 for outdoor courts). Reservations for court time can be made by phone up to two days in advance.

Department of Parks and Recreation, www.nycgovparks.org (click on "Activities and Facilities" under the "Things to Do" menu)

Paragon Sports, 867 Broadway at 18th Street (212-255-8036) www.paragonsports.com.

Riverside Clay Tennis Association courts, Riverside Park (Around West 96th Street and Riverside Drive), (212-870-3078) www.rcta.info

USTA Billie Jean King National Tennis Center, Flushing Meadows Corona Park (Queens), (718-760-6200) www.usta.com

⟶ Tennis's Little Brother ⟵

Every great sport has its younger siblings: baseball has softball, the horses have the greyhounds, golf has its wayward youngster mini—and tennis has ping pong. In the 130 years since its creation over a drawing-room table in Victorian England as an after-dinner distraction, table tennis has outgrown its older brother (and its elitist infancy) to become an Olympic game and, second only to soccer, the most popular sport in the world. Too long tarnished with the rowdy reputation of pool, darts, skittles, and the other backroom bar sports, ping pong has experienced a renaissance in New York in recent years and can now be enjoyed at every level and by anyone, from casual amateurs to pro am league competitors.

There are places to play table tennis all over the city, ranging from professional facilities with accomplished instructors and Olympic-standard equipment to more casual neighborhood halls and game rooms in cafés and bars. For serious players and ambitious amateurs, the two best places in the city are the New York Table Tennis Federation (NYTTF) and the Manhattan Table Tennis Club (MTTC). Training ground for the prestigious NYU college team, the NYTTF has a huge space in Chinatown where a monthly membership price of $75 entitles you to play on its immaculate tables as much as you like, and $45 buys you a lesson from a pro instructor. The MTTC offers similar deals in a slightly smaller but equally well-equipped facility uptown, with tables available both for walk-in players and students to the in-house professionals.

If you're not quite ready for professional instruction and local league competition, a better bet is to look up one of the city's many neighborhood table tennis halls. Notoriously under-advertised and often tricky to find in a basement or on an upper floor, table tennis clubs are often good spaces with reliable equipment and an atmosphere that is geared toward playing at your own level. Our favorite is the Brooklyn Table Tennis Club in Coney Island, which is as fun to play in for a first-timer as it is for a more experienced player.

If all you're looking for is a quick bat back and forth while you're out on the town, there are tables in many of the city's coolest bars and clubs. Our favorites are the Fat Cat on Christopher Street, where you can play with a drink in your other hand while you listen to live jazz, and Southpaw in Park Slope, where people congregate around the table even while a gig goes on in the background. And for the ultimate New York table tennis experience, check out a Naked Ping Pong party. Naked Ping Pong holds weekly events in a loft in Tribeca where people can drink, mingle with trendy downtown kids, and then challenge each other to a contest at one of the several tables around the room. The parties attract an unusual mix of hipsters and pros, drinkers and players, and—as is always the way with table tennis—everybody seems to have fun when they get paddles in their hands.

Brooklyn Table Tennis Club, 1100 Coney Island Avenue (Brooklyn), (718-421-2200)
   www.bttclub.com

Fat Cat, 75 Christopher Street, at Seventh Avenue, (212-675-6056)

Manhattan Table Tennis Club, 2628 Broadway at 100th Street, (212-864-7253)

Naked Ping Pong, www.nakedpingpong.com

New York Table Tennis Federation, 384 Broadway, between White and Walker streets,
   (212-966-2922) www.nyttf.com

Southpaw, 125 Fifth Avenue, between Sterling and St. John streets (Brooklyn),
   (718-230-0266) www.spsounds.com

CYCLING

There are numerous inherent logistical challenges to owning and riding a bike in NYC: walk-up apartments, long stretches of inclement weather, traffic and unsympathetic drivers, and scarcity of storage space. Yet, despite these deterrents, there are many cyclists here, ranging from intermittent lap riders, to amateur racers and true weekend warriors who spend their Saturdays going on 60- or 70-mile rides.

The parks are the place to start. Central and Prospect Parks are the big cycling hubs, and the most popular spots to bike in the city, but they're more than places to ride. They're where you can meet other cyclists of all different levels, find out about other rides and groups, and become initiated to the local cycling scene. Weekdays and off-season are the nicer times to ride, especially if you want to go fast—they're also the best times to catch the better cyclists. On weekends from spring through fall, it's a lot more crowded, and a lot more dangerous—not only are there more cyclists, but there are more people in general to watch out for.

Once you've gotten to know the parks a bit, you'll probably want do more than ride around in circles. The New York Cycle Club (NYCC) is a good place to find out about local rides, and to find people to ride with. The club offers a ton of group rides at all different skill levels year-round; rides are all free, though you have to become a member to have access to the full ride bulletin. (Membership is less than $20 for the year, and pays for itself pretty quickly if you take advantage of the discounts at all the bike stores in the area.) It does list some rides on its web site so you can try out a few before you commit to joining. The web site also has a "ride library," with routes for hundreds of well-tested rides in NYC, Long Island, Rockland and Westchester Counties, and as far upstate as the Catskills. Another very cool thing about the NYCC is the free clinics it offers each spring called Special Interest Groups or SIGS. SIGS are held in three different categories of difficulty, and each concentrates on taking the riders to the next skill level (the toughest group finishes with a 108-mile ride), and introducing cyclists to some particulars of NYC-area riding. The A group is for experienced riders, but the B and C groups welcome true novices to cyclists who are just new to the city. The SIGS start in March and most meet every Saturday until May.

The NYCC has plenty of advanced, serious, and arduous rides, but there's no racing; experienced athletes who are interested in racing should acquaint themselves with www.nyvelocity.com. Though the articles and the comment fields are the primary draws for regular readers, the site also has some ride listings, profiles of many local teams, and info on upcoming races. However, if you are actually going to race, you will also need to become a member of the CRCA (Century Road Club Association). The CRCA oversees all of the local races, most of which happen in Central Park very early on weekend mornings.

There's also the Kissena Velodrome (aka "the track of dreams") for those brave/crazy enough to consider track racing (races that take place around a track, on bikes with no brakes and only one gear). Originally built for the 1964 Olympic trials, the 400-meter track recently reopened after two years of renovations, which included a deluxe repaving of the track, and the addition of bleachers and a couple of safety enhancements for these daredevil racers. At the regular weeknight races from late April through September, competitors zoom around the banked ovals at super-high speeds. Not surprisingly, bike messengers do really well.

Century Road Club Association, www.crca.net
Kissena Velodrome, Kissena Park, Flushing (Queens), www.kissena.info
New York Cycle Club, www.nycc.org

SKIING/SNOWBOARDING

Snow in the city is either a non-event (white stuff coming out of the sky that disappears when it hits the ground) or a few hours of pristine white powder followed by weeks of crusty black wedges piled up by the curb. For local winter sports enthusiasts, the East Coast skiing model—the quaint New England ski resort—may seem impossibly out-of-reach, or at least a dishearteningly complicated event that requires a car, a massive drive, and at least a night's lodging. Think again. Not only can you get to plenty of ski areas in three hours or less, but you can also go skiing on a day trip. (And you don't even need a car!) And, lest one forget that New York (state) has hosted the winter Olympics not once but twice, just about five hours away is Lake Placid, a ski town that has more winter sport cachet than any of its New England competitors. You can't take a luge run or skate on an Olympic ice rink anywhere in Vermont, now can you?

If your starting point is NYC, a good rule of thumb is that the skiing gets better the farther you go away from the city. Two hours will get you the bare minimum: small mountains, and the least amount of natural snow. Three to four gets you some higher peaks, better trails, and probably even a cute ski town nearby to stay in. If you're willing to invest more than five hours, then you can make it to places like Stowe in Vermont and Whiteface (the mountain that was used for skiing in the Olympics), some of the top slopes in the east, and home to enough grueling trails to please even an elite Colorado ski snob.

Hunter Mountain is the most popular destination for day-trips, and the easiest to get to. True, Hunter is no Aspen—or even a Whiteface—but it does offer perfectly decent skiing less than two hours from the city. Many ski and sporting goods shops in the city offer regular bus service to and from Hunter every weekend that there's snow, and sometimes once or twice during the week. The cost runs about $70 or $80 for transportation and lift ticket; some offer options for rentals, and transportation-only for people who have season passes. (Some of these places also offer bus trips to Vermont, but they leave at three and four in the morning.)

The downside of Hunter's easy accessiblity is that it's crowded. An alternative is Windham, also about two hours away, but less overrun than Hunter. Some of the places that do bus trips to Hunter do trips to Windham as well, as it's also a feasible day trip to and from NYC.

Across state lines, Vermont is the traditional Eastern ski-getaway destination, but it's pretty far from the city—at least five hours. But there is also fine skiing in the Massachusetts Berkshires (Butternut for example), which is only about a three-to-four hour drive. The snow is usually better than at places closer to the city, and it's less expensive than the fancy, better-known resorts in Vermont.

Butternut, Great Barrington, Massachusetts, (413-528-2000) www.skibutternut.com

Hunter Mountain, Hunter, New York, (800-486-8376) www.huntermtn.com

Stowe, Stowe, Vermont, (800-253-4754) www.stowe.com

Whiteface Mountain, Wilmington, New York, (877-SKI-FACE) www.whiteface.com

   (Also visit www.lakeplacid.com)

Windham Mountain, Windham, New York, (800-754-9463) www.windhammountain.com

ROCK CLIMBING

There are several indoor climbing walls in Manhattan where experienced climbers can join or go for the day, and beginners can take lessons. You have to pay a premium for many large-scale activities in the city, but climbing is actually surprisingly affordable, and almost all of the climbing walls offer day passes, so you don't have to make a substantial investment to try it once. Whether you're new or experienced, the City Climbers Club is a good place to start. The home gym at the West 59th Street Recreation Center is kind of a hub for climbers in the city, and the membership and day rates are very reasonable ($15 for a day pass, $250 for the year). The gym is slated to be under construction at press time, but there are other options. The wall at Chelsea Piers is the largest in the city, but it's also on the expensive end ($50 for a day pass; $1,500 annually). The wall at the North Meadow Recreation Center in Central Park is a steal ($5 day pass; $200 annually), but it's a small wall and the hours are restrictive. In between is the wall at Manhattan Plaza Health Club ($20 day pass; $1,400 annually, which includes use of the entire health club; a student membership is also available). Dedicated climbers can find out about news in the local climbing world on www.climbnyc.com. (The site also has useful descriptions of area climbing walls.)

There actually happens to be excellent real rock climbing nearby as well. Really! (We were surprised, too.) The Shawangunk Ridge is a major destination for climbers, even ones who live far from NYC, but if you're new to climbing, you can also take lessons there. The Gunks, as they are known, are located about ten miles outside of New Paltz. (New Paltz is 90 miles north of the city.)

Chelsea Piers, see page 230 (climbing wall, 212-336-6500)

City Climbers Club, 533 West 59th Street, between Tenth and Eleventh avenues (inside the
   59th Street Recreation Center), (212-974-2250) www.cityclimbersclub.com

Manhattan Plaza Health Club, 482 West 43rd Street, at Tenth Avenue, (212-563-7001)
   www.mphc.com

North Meadow Recreation Center, inside Central Park at around 97th Street, (212-348-4867) www.centralpark.org

Shawangunk Ridge (The Gunks), New Paltz, New York, (845-255-4911) www.gunks.com

SWIMMING

Swimming is one of the most challenging activities to do regularly in the city. Pools take up a lot of space and are expensive to keep up, a bad mix for a New York City business model.

If you are a dedicated year-round swimmer, start by considering the good pools, even if they aren't the most convenient, because the bad ones can be really bad. Though some pools have pretty steep membership fees, others are quite reasonable, and if you like swimming enough to do it regularly, you're not going to want to do your laps in a dingy two-lane ten-meter bathtub with 85 other people at the same time.

A hidden gem on the city's dismal aquatic scene is the pool at Stuyvesant High School. This high school in lower Manhattan generously shares its pool and other gym facilities with the community. Not only is it a nice pool, but it's a bargain to use: the pool-only membership is $300 per year. The pool is open to members evenings and weekends during the school year, which is only a deal breaker if you're a professional swimmer, are unemployed, or need to swim during the day on weekdays for some reason. (During the summer, when school isn't in session, the hours are longer.) If you live or work anywhere near Tribeca, look no further.

It would be nice if other schools were as generous with their facilities, but for the most part, they're not. While Stuyvesant is one of the very few high schools in the city with its own pool, many of the colleges and universities here have them, but most don't share. One exception is Caitlin's swimming nemesis, NYU, but it's an exception with an asterisk. There are a very limited number of community memberships available for NYU's Coles Gym, and they're only available to people who live in Community Board 2. The community memberships come in the form of 12-visit punch cards for $100 each, so the price per use is reasonable, but the more you swim, the more it'll add up.

Asphalt Green has the pool that swimmers really covet; theirs is the only private Olympic-size swimming pool in Manhattan, with eight luxurious lanes for laps. The downside is its location: 90th Street and the East River. To get there from the nearest subway is a workout in itself, and in the winter, the walk back after a swim, with wet hair and the wind off the river, will weed out the less dedicated athletes for sure. Another pool that swim junkies like to whisper about is the one at the Manhattan

Plaza Health Club, which has a translucent retractable roof, a perk that will be appreciated by any local swimmers accustomed to doing their laps in windowless basement tubs. It's not Olympic, but at 75-feet it's a decent size for a pool in the city. Memberships are intentionally reasonable (Manhattan Plaza was built as subsidized housing for artists), and day passes are available. The JCC and Chelsea Piers are also single-location operations with lovely pools, but neither offers day passes and membership isn't cheap. If you live in the area, they're attractive options; if not, tack transport time and hassle onto the fees.

If none of those pools are convenient, your best bet is probably to join a gym or a Y that has one, or use the ones at the city's recreation centers. But research your options carefully, because some pool options are far inferior to others. For instance, three New York Sports Club locations have pools. But the ones in the 49th & Broadway and 91st and Third locations are tiny (both four lanes only and under 20 yards). The Kips Bay location has a nice one, but it's outdoors, so it is open only from Memorial Day to Labor Day and requires a separate membership. On the other hand, all New York Health and Racquet Club locations have pools, though some are much smaller and grungier than others. The same variety holds true with the YMCAs, as well as the city's recreation centers. As we said in the gym section, the city rec centers are the best fitness deals bar none, and we know people who happily swim at the pools at the Carmine Street and Metropolitan Avenue locations. But not all centers have pools, and again, some are much nicer and newer than others. Bottom line is that finding a pool to join will take some work, and there's a big range in price and facility quality that doesn't necessarily correlate the way you would think. Do your homework.

It's not nearly as hard to find a place to swim here when it's warm enough to do it outdoors. There are 52 outdoor city pools across the five boroughs, which are open to the public for free from late June through Labor Day. Swimmers starved from the city's meager year-round rations can feast come summertime: there are Olympic-size pools (the Astoria pool is actually one of the largest swimming pools in the country), pools with diving areas, and pools with morning and evening lap sessions. Swimming at the city pools isn't entirely carefree—the pools can get very crowded, there are many restrictions on what you can bring on the pool deck (no food, no newspapers, no clothing other than a swimsuit and a white T-shirt), and the hours are limited (they also all close for at least one hour right in the middle of the day for pool cleaning). But they are generally clean, there are a lot of them, and they're free. If your objective is exercise, then it's probably best not to rely entirely on these pools, as they are seasonal and can get very crowded. If your objective is relaxing and cooling off, then forget those other pools that you have to pay for, and jump right in.

Asphalt Green, see page 230

Chelsea Piers, see page 230

The Community Center at Stuyvesant High School, 345 Chambers Street, at West Street,
(212-267-9700) www.communitycenteratstuyvesanthighschool.org

Department of Parks and Recreation, see page 230

Jewish Community Center, see page 230

Manhattan Plaza Health Club, see page 230

New York Sports Club, see page 230

New York Health and Racquet Club, see page 230

NYU Coles Gym, 181 Mercer Street, between Bleecker and Houston streets, (212-998-2020)
www.nyu.edu/athletics

YMCA, see page 230

⟶ That's a funny-looking bat . . . ⟵

Moving to a new country entails many challenges, and settling in a new environment means missing a lot about the place you came from. Although they may not be the first thing you think of, sports and the games people play are a big part of the cultural divides that make life in one city different from another. But moving to New York is a different story. With so many cultures having left such deep impressions on the city's character, there are reminders everywhere of the places and cultures people left behind to come here, and the same community spirit that keeps the city's cuisines so authentically international keeps its sports fields that way, too.

Would you believe that the fastest-growing sport in New York City is cricket? England's finest export, cricket has long been the most popular sport of many countries of the former British Commonwealth, and with such dense West Indian, Pakistani, Indian, and Sri Lankan communities in Brooklyn and the Bronx, the game has spread across the city. There are several cricket clubs around town—from serious organizations such as the New York Metropolitan and District Cricket Association to more relaxed neighborhood clubs—and fields in all five boroughs, helpfully detailed with a wonderful educational video about the game on the Department of Parks and Recreation web site. The best place to go to get involved is Van Cortlandt Park in the Bronx, which lights up with men in whites in the summer months and is the most enjoyable place to play as well as to sit and watch—which, as any fan of the game knows, is more than half the fun.

Another European export that never really found universal popularity in America is rugby. A dirtier and less tactically oriented precursor to football, rugby is beloved by burly men around the world from Ireland to New Zealand. Thanks to the lasting influence of immigrant cultures in the city, the sport still has a real presence in old-school organizations such as the New York Rugby Club and the Metropolitan New York Rugby Football Union, and in the playing fields of Brooklyn, the Bronx, and Queens. To get involved with playing regularly, the best thing to do is to roam around the bigger parks on a weekend and find people playing to talk to about local leagues and clubs.

And finally, the great European street sport of *boules*—otherwise known as *pétanque*, and interpreted only slightly differently by the Italians as *bocce*—has become one of the most popular and accessible summertime games for New Yorkers. Besides the street courts that are assembled every July for the Carroll Gardens Bastille Day celebrations, there are boules courts in parks all around the city, and even in a handful of bars in Brooklyn. The very serious and very French Pétanque Federation of America (FPUSA) has its headquarters and holds training games in Washington Square Park and plays tournament games in Bryant Park, but there are informal courts in Central Park and in the neighborhood parks of downtown Brooklyn, too.

Department of Parks and Recreation, see page 230
Metropolitan New York Rugby Football Union, www.metnyrfu.org
New York Metropolitan and District Cricket Association, www.nymdca.com
New York Rugby Club, www.newyorkrugby.com
Pétanque Federation of America, www.labouleny.com

HIKING, HUNTING, CAMPING, AND FISHING

The New York City region itself has no fewer than seven state parks, and they're closer than you might think. Some feel quite urban (East River State Park in Brooklyn, and Riverbank along the upper west side of Manhattan), but at others, you'd never know that that a city of 10 million people was, well, right there. It's not like you can go camping on the banks of the East River, but you can go fishing at Gantry Plaza State Park in Long Island City, or birding at the Jamaica Bay Wildlife Refuge. The latter is part of Gateway National Recreation Area (so it's not actually a state park), which is made up of three units covering Brooklyn, Queens, Staten Island, and Sandy Hook, New Jersey. Gateway has beaches, hiking trails, marinas, and more, and all three units are accessible by public transportation—though we personally wouldn't recommend that. Driving (or biking) is much more direct.

Once you cross over the city lines, the options for outdoor recreation multiply. If you know a bit about the geography of New York State, it should not come as too much of a surprise that you can do pretty much any outdoor activity you can imagine within a few hours of the city. There are mountain ranges, great lakes (and two Great

Lakes), rivers and river valleys, and, of course, Niagara Falls. Most of the activity offerings take place within state park areas, so if you are looking for a place to go camping or hiking or anything like that, they're a good place to start. The New York State Office of Parks, Recreation, and Historic Preservation divides the state into eleven regions, which gives you some idea of how vast the terrain is. Here's another way of thinking about it: the Adirondacks encompasses a full third of the state's entire land area.

Closer to home, the Catskill, Palisades, and Taconic areas have plenty to offer besides convenience to and from NYC. (They can all be reached in about two hours or less, and there are plenty of areas that you can get to on Metro-North or by bus.) The Taconic region runs along the east side of the Hudson River; the Palisades runs along the west side of the Hudson; and the Catskill Mountains are just northwest of the Palisades. Between them, there are plenty of opportunities for camping, hiking, hunting, fishing, rock climbing, bird watching, swimming, boating, cross-country skiing, snowshoeing, and general outdoorsiness. You can search for specific activities and compare the offerings at different parks on the New York State Office of Parks, Recreation, and Historic Preservation web site.

Gateway National Recreation Area, www.nps.gov/gate

Metro-North, see page 152-153

New York State Office of Parks, Recreation, and Historic Preservation (Riverbank,

    East River State Park, and Gantry Plaza State Park), www.nysparks.state.ny.us

INSIDE EDITION

$\longleftrightarrow$

The single greatest advantage a resident New Yorker has over his transient neighbors is the knowledge of those little perks and pitfalls that can only come with time and experience. It could be serendipity, it could be trial and error, or it could be because you took a wrong turn on a block you'd never seen before. But however it comes, knowledge of the city can make all the difference between out-of-town green-horns and true-blue New Yorkers. And to save you years of groping around blind in the wilderness of a strange city, here's a short list of our favorite insider secrets to give you that local edge.

GALLERY OPENINGS IN CHELSEA ARE FREE—and in addition to admission-free art, many serve free wine, beer, and even snacks sometimes. Head to Tenth Avenue in the twenties any Thursday between 6 and 8 p.m. and just look for the crowds.

ASK WHAT'S PLAYING ON THE BIG SCREEN. The movie theater on Second Avenue and 12th Street used to be a Yiddish playhouse, and seeing a movie on screen one, which is in the main auditorium, is like seeing a movie in an opera house. The other screens, however, are unusually tiny. You can't tell what screen your movie is playing on if you buy your tickets online, but if you call the box office or buy your tickets there, they'll tell you which movie is playing on "the big screen."

MANY FARMERS AT GREENMARKETS DISCOUNT THEIR OFFERINGS AT THE END OF THE DAY. Prices start dropping about an hour before the market officially closes, a little earlier in the winter at markets that stay open all afternoon (check the web site for official hours of each market). The closer to closing time you get, the more you can haggle, or get some bonus items thrown in. An added plus on weekends is that late afternoons are often a less crowded time to visit.

DO A LITTLE HAIR MODELING AND YOU CAN GET YOUR HAIR CUT FOR FREE OR CHEAP. What this entails is letting your hair be cut at a salon by either a stylist-in-training or a new stylist (someone who has completed training but is just starting to work on his or her own). Policies vary from salon to salon, but most will allow you to come regularly, and some places will let you suggest the kind of cut and how much to take off. Many also offer color and styling. (Though beware that the ones that don't offer styling may not do more than a very basic blow-dry after your cut is over.) Though you are getting your hair cut by a newbie, all studios fear bad word of mouth like the plague and will fix your cut for free with a professional stylist if you aren't happy with it. A few to look into: The Model Project at Bumble & Bumble (cuts are free and tipping is not allowed, but you first have to attend one of its weekly "model calls" to determine which cut or cuts you are eligible for); Dop Dop Salon ($35 for a student cut; $50 for color); Antonio Prieto (offers cuts, styling, and color at two trainee levels that start at $45); and the Aveda Institute (cuts are $20; color starts at $25, and depends on the type of service; it also offers student spa services for super cheap).

Antonio Prieto Salon, 127 West 20th Street, between Sixth and Seventh avenues, (212-255-3741) www.antonioprietosalon.com

Aveda Institute, 233 Spring Street, between Varick Street and Sixth Avenue, (212-807-1492, extension 2) www.avedainstituteny.com

Bumble & Bumble Model Project, 415 West 13th Street, between Ninth Avenue and Washington Street, 6th Floor, (866-7-BUMBLE) www.bbumodelproject.com

Dop Dop Salon, 170 Mercer Street, between Houston and Prince streets, (212-965-9540) www.dopdop.com

ANYONE CAN GET HIS OR HER OWN BENCH IN CENTRAL PARK. It costs $7,500, but it's good for a lifetime, and includes an engraved plaque with the dedication of your choice. You can also get the same deal for a bench in Prospect Park for only $5,000. The same goes for street signs with your name on them—but you probably don't have that kind of money . . .

GET DISCOUNT THEATER TICKETS WITHOUT STANDING IN THE TKTS LINE. At broadwaybox.com, you can find discount codes for just about any show—Broadway, off-Broadway, even supposedly sold-out shows—that you can either use to purchase online or print out and bring to the box office for purchase. Discounts range from 25 to 50 percent or more off the face value of the ticket (about the same as what TKTS offers), but unlike TKTS, you can buy them in advance, and there's a larger availability of shows.

SNAG THAT COVETED TABLE. Every weekday, *New York* magazine calls ten hot restaurants to see if they've got a table at 8 p.m. and posts the results (who's got room, who doesn't) on Grub Street, its food and restaurant blog. The daily Grub Street e-mail (which you can subscribe to for free) goes out around 5 p.m., and "Two for

Eight" is always the top item. If you act fast enough, your prize is a prime-time, prime table for two, and all the bragging rights that go with it.

GET FREE WI-FI. NYC may be an easier place to steal a Wi-Fi signal than more spread-out cities, but it's still frustrating and ethically questionable; meanwhile, offering free Wi-Fi in coffee shops and restaurants never really caught on, and in any case requires cash for endless coffees and all the heartburn that comes with it. Luckily, many public spaces offer those valuable invisible signals for free. On a balmy day, for instance, you can surf gratis at hot spots in many NYC parks, including Union Square, Washington Square, Battery, Riverside, Bryant, Flushing Meadows, and several areas within Central and Prospect Parks. (The Department of Parks and Recreation web site has a list of the locations and a map of their coverage areas, as does www.wifisalon.com.) If the weather's not conducive to surfing outdoors, head to the Financial District, where the Downtown Alliance has strung up Wi-Fi like Christmas lights, encompassing many pleasant spots like the Winter Garden and the atrium at 60 Wall Street; it maintains a full list of hot spots on its web site. An organization called NYC Wireless is working on a project to get free Wi-Fi available all over the city; it currently has 145 deployed hot spots (though only a handful of these are monitored to ensure that they are running correctly).

Department of Parks, www.nycgovparks.org
Downtown Alliance, www.downtownny.com
NYC Wireless, www.nycwireless.net

A NUMBER OF THE CITY'S FANCIER BAKERIES REDUCE THE PRICES OF THEIR SWEETS AND PASTRIES AT THE END OF THE DAY, turning outrageous indulgences into mere trifles. Try Café Falai on Lafayette or the Falai Panetteria on Clinton Street, Amy's Bread in Hell's Kitchen, the West Village, or in the Chelsea Market, and Balthazar Bakery on Spring Street. For more virtuous deals, check the "yesterday" jars at Angelica Kitchen's take-out kiosk on East 12th Street for vegan muffins, cookies, rolls, and the like.

Amy's Bread, multiple locations, www.amysbread.com
Angelica Kitchen, see page 43
Balthazar, 80 Spring Street, at Crosby Street, (212-965-1785)
  www.balthazarbakery.com
Café Falai, 265 Lafayette Street, at Prince Street, (917-338-6207) www.falainyc.com
Falai Panetteria, 79 Clinton Street, at Rivington Street, (212-777-8956)
  www.falainyc.com

IMPROVE YOUR BODY ON A BUDGET. Yoga is not exempt from NYC's sphere of fanciness, and you'll pay a price—currently around $20 a class—to do your downward dogs next to Sting, Russell Simmons, or Maggie Gyllenhaal. But there are also some deals to be found, particularly if you are just starting out. Almost all yoga studios will offer some kind of introductory deal—a great one is YogaWorks' two weeks of unlimited yoga for $30. While gyms and other fitness operations also often have specials for new members, yoga's particular charitable side can also be seen in the offering by some studios of "community classes" or other occasional classes at a discounted rate. At the East Village studio Yoga to the People, all classes are pay what you wish, with a suggested donation of $10. The YogaPass is also an amazing deal, if you don't mind traveling around the city. For $75, you get a book of passes good for multiple classes at more than 100 studios all over Manhattan, Queens, and Brooklyn. Each pass corresponds to one studio; most studios offer two free classes per pass, but some offer up to four, or an unlimited number of classes in a week—so your $75 investment can buy you 200 or 300 classes. The passbooks come from the American Health and Fitness Alliance, which also offers similar deals for gyms (the FitnessPass) and Pilates, Gyrotonic, and Alexander Technique (the PilatesPass).

Yoga to the People, 12 St. Mark's Place, at Third Avenue, 2nd Floor, (917-573-9642)
   www.yogatothepeople.com
Yogaworks, multiple locations, www.yogaworks.com
For more information on the YogaPass, FitnessPass, and PilatesPass,
   visit www.health-fitness.org

CHURCHES AND CATHEDRALS ARE THE PROUD AND SECRETIVE OWNERS of some of the city's prettiest and most peaceful gardens. While some keep their gates locked to anyone but the Sunday service congregation, most of the time they're quiet and empty because people just don't think to go hang out in a churchyard on a sunny afternoon. St. John the Divine on Amsterdam Avenue has an ornate, winding garden that hosts peacocks in the warmer months. The Church of the Holy Trinity on the Upper East Side has a tiny and picturesque garden and is largely untouched save by the older European Yorkville community. And the General Theological Seminary in Chelsea is the pick of the bunch: there are deck chairs in the beautiful garden out back, and in summer you might even find a set of croquet mallets leaning up against a tree so you can knock balls around the lawn in traditional summer fashion.

Church of the Holy Trinity, 316 East 88th Street, between First and Second avenues,
   (212-289-4100) www.holytrinity-nyc.org

General Theological Seminary, 175 Ninth Avenue, between West 20th and 21st streets, (212-243-5150)

Saint John the Divine, 1047 Amsterdam Avenue, at 112th Street, (212-316-7490)
    www.stjohndivine.org

THE ONLY THING COOLER THAN KNOWING THE BEST BARS IN TOWN IS KNOWING THE SECRET BARS IN TOWN. Ever since the days of Prohibition, secrecy and disguise have brought a certain cachet to bars around the city. These days, masking a bar as something else is more of a vanity than a necessity, but that's not to say it isn't just as fun. Now New York is a big place, it changes all the time, and watering holes can come and go like trash in the wind that blows down Broadway. Keep your eyes and ears open and you're bound to hear about hot new places opening and closing from month to month all over the city. But at the time of publication, a handful of hidden bars seemed like they'd be around for a while—so check them out while you can, and flash your insider's knowledge of downtown Manhattan when you do. Back Room on the Lower East Side is the only place we've ever seen with a door genuinely concealed in a bookcase. Happy Ending, a veteran of the secret circuit, disguises itself as a Chinese deli with a seedy cellar on Broome Street. La Esquina is ostensibly a Spanish diner on Kenmare, but make it past the pretentious bouncer and there's a whole other world through the kitchen downstairs. And Little Branch, an unmarked cocktail bar on Seventh Avenue, is a sweeter and only mildly less exclusive cousin of international uber-secret Milk and Honey.

Back Room, 102 Norfolk Street, between Delancey and Rivington streets, (212-228-5098)

La Esquina, 114 Kenmare Street, at Lafayette Street, (646-613-7100)
    www.esquinanyc.com

Happy Ending, 302 Broome Street, near Forsythe Street, (212-334-9676)
    www.happyendinglounge.com

Little Branch, 20 Seventh Avenue South, at Leroy Street, (212-929-4360)

Milk and Honey, 134 Eldridge Street, near Broome Street, www.mlkhny.com

EVERY DAY, THE CHEFS IN TRAINING AT L'ECOLE, THE RESTAURANT OF THE FRENCH CULINARY INSTITUTE, PUT THEIR SKILLS TO THE TEST AND OFFER VERY REASONABLY PRICED LUNCHES AND DINNERS TO HORDES OF WILLING GUINEA PIGS. A three-course prix-fixe lunch costs just $26.50, while a four- or five-course supper is only $39.95. The menu is limited—like variables in an experiment—but the food is almost always superb, and it's the cheapest full French meal you can get in the city.

L'Ecole, 462 Broadway, at Grand Street, (212-219-3300) www.frenchculinary.com/lecole

GETTING OUT OF TOWN

⟷

To the millions of tourists who visit New York every year, the city is a dense urban fantasy of skyscrapers, department stores, yellow cabs, and crowded subways. To a certain *Sex and the City* faction, Manhattan is the be-all and end-all, an island of fashion, food, culture, and cool whose coast may as well be the edge of the world. But to residents with their wits about them, New York is the perfect place to be not only because of what's in it but because of what's around it.

Living in any city can be exhausting in one way or another, and living in one of the busiest and most compact urban environments in the western world can really take it out of you. Even in a city where the parks of the five boroughs, the rivers around Manhattan, the beaches of Brooklyn, and the therapeutic powers of designer shopping are always within reach, people need to get away for a while. And even a city with as much to offer as New York can't compete with the coast and the countryside when it comes to fresh air, natural beauty, and open space.

Travel in any direction from the heart of the city and in a matter of a couple of hours you can pass from the suburban to the rural and downright bucolic, and end up anywhere from the rolling hills of the Berkshires to the dramatic landscape of the Hudson Valley, and from the unlikely sands of the Jersey Shore to the exclusive beaches and country clubs of the Hamptons. Once you get over the New Yorker's fear of leaving the city limits, there's a whole world to explore—and all it takes to get there is a quick look at the train schedules. So whether you're looking for a cheap night out in a city nearby, a weekend away in the peace and quiet of the country, or a weekend by the beach in summertime, the hardest part is choosing where to go.

THE HAMPTONS

WHAT IT IS: As if you don't know . . . A couple of hours up the coast from the city, beyond the suburbs of Long Island and across the sound from Connecticut, the Hamptons are a summer playground for well-to-do New Yorkers, a community of summer homes, seaside hamlets, and country clubs extending along the beautiful South Fork of Long Island. Strictly speaking, the Hamptons include Southampton, Westhampton, and East Hampton, the three largest towns along the coast. But in spirit the Hamptons run from Southampton to Montauk at the farthest tip of the Fork, taking in Bridgehampton, Sag Harbor, East Hampton, Amagansett, Springs, and a host of other hamlets along the way.

With a lineage of wealthy residents that has run the spectrum of celebrity, from Spielberg to Seinfeld, Pollock to Pelé, and Martha Stewart to Roger Waters, the Hamptons are definitely the poshest of Long Island's summer resorts. While Sag Harbor and the smaller hamlets retain some of their salty authenticity as fishing villages, the larger towns feel like a cross between the New England countryside and Madison Avenue. There are at least four Ralph Lauren stores in Southampton alone, and elsewhere high-end jewelry, clothes, and interior design shops rub shoulders with fresh fish restaurants, boating emporia, and age-old taffy stores.

For those lucky enough to be in the loop, the Hamptons are a heavenly home away from home where there are friends in every town and houses to visit all along the coast. For everybody else, the Hamptons are an expensive but beautiful haven from Manhattan with a New York City mentality and a celebrity cachet—and miles of peaceful, beautiful beaches. If you can't spend your summer idling between country clubs, mansions, and golf courses, there are plenty of other fun things to do—all the trappings of a good seaside resort are here, from fishing trips to boats and bikes for hire.

WHO'S THERE: The rich, the famous, and those sun-seeking New Yorkers who wish they were more of either. It's true that the Hamptons—particularly the more exclusive extremities such as Montauk and Bridgehampton—are traditionally the preserve of celebrities and New York aristocracy, many of whom own houses along the coast and pick up and move here for the summers. There is also quite an artistic heritage in the Hamptons: before its transformation into the posh resort it is today, the area was a peaceful retreat for artists and writers such as Jackson Pollock, Willem de Kooning, and Joseph Heller. A healthy extension of the Manhattan art scene still exists today in a handful of small galleries and in the private collections of certain residents. But with a range of accommodations all across the Fork, from small motels to seaside inns, the Hamptons are relatively accessible to the average New Yorker too—the chino and boat-shoe count is high year-round, but in summer, at least, the sloppy city flip-flop brigade balances things out a little.

WHAT'S GOOD: The beaches. However strong your loyalty to the beaches of the five boroughs, there's no denying that the beaches of the Hamptons are the best you can get short of a flight down the coast. The sands are softer, the water is cleaner, and the waves feel bigger than anywhere from Fire Island down to the Jersey Shore—East Hampton beach was voted by National Geographic as one of the world's five most beautiful in the world. The relative exclusivity of the New Yorker's summer colony means the beaches don't suffer the curses of overcrowding, wanton barbecuing, children screaming, and radios blaring that blight the shores of Long Island and Brooklyn—and if you are sharing the sand with anybody else, there's a good chance the person is famous. Country club elitism aside, a summertime stint cycling from beach to beach in the Hamptons is an invigorating reminder that there's more to the Atlantic coast than Coney Island, and that the perfect peace and childlike pleasure of the seaside is much closer to the city than you think.

WHAT'S NOT: Hamptons nightlife isn't worth the salt the Atlantic washes up along its beautiful shores. With the exception of the potentially obnoxious "share" crowd—group investors who rent a house out there and take turns jetting up from the city on weekends—most people who go to the Hamptons go to escape the noise and bustle of New York nightlife, and so aren't even tempted by the cheesy clubs and overpriced restaurants that have appeared in the larger towns. Instead, three other kinds of clubs share primacy here: the yacht club, the country club, and the golf club. The Hamptons are a hotbed of upper-middle-class, upper-middle-aged elitism, where private beaches, fabulous clubhouses, and magnificent mansions abound. But if you're not riding the coat-tails of a genuine Hamptons socialite, there's little here beyond the seaside itself to satisfy the tastes of the urbane New Yorker. Stray too far from the chinos and taffy stores of the towns and you risk running into the real world of 7-11s, freeways, and less glamorous suburban housing developments that occupy the country between the Forks. Our advice: go for the beaches, the baked clams, and the bike rides around the coastal countryside, and don't expect too much else.

HOW TO GET THERE: The first rule is to book early—accommodation in the Hamptons is limited, and the nicer hotels and guesthouses fill up fast in the summer. Once you have somewhere to stay, the Long Island Railroad runs a regular service from Penn Station all the way to Montauk (with express services to the Hamptons in the holiday season), which makes good time and is a beautiful ride along the coast. But the most convenient way to travel is by bus. Two coach companies share the responsibility of shepherding New Yorkers daily to and from the Hamptons: the Jitney and the Luxury Liner. Although, as its name suggests, the Luxury Liner is a swankier ride—the seats are leather, there are fewer seats and there's more legroom, and every bus has a free "buffet" of chips, mineral water, and newspapers at the back—there's little difference in price. Both bus services run more frequent and—importantly—later schedules than the train, and have pick-up and drop-off points up and down the East side of Manhattan and in Brooklyn, making them better options for weekenders looking to make the most of their time. Both train and bus services make stops in the key towns along the coastline, and car services are easily available to take you to your motel—sorry, your *mansion*—when you get there.

Hampton Jitney, (212-362-8400) www.hamptonjitney.com

Hampton Luxury Liner, (631-537-5800) www.hamptonluxuryliner.com

Long Island Rail Road, see pages 152-153

CHINATOWNS OF THE EAST COAST

WHAT IT IS: Second to crispy duck—and possibly third to the celebrations at New Year—the Chinatown bus is the single greatest service the Chinese community has conferred upon its fellow Americans. The Chinatown bus runs comparably cheap and amazingly frequent services between the East Coast's thickest Chinese enclaves, in New York, Boston, Philadelphia, and Washington, D.C. (and indeed to other major cities across America, beyond the reach of the weekending New Yorker). A small-time local operation turned ramshackle national enterprise, the Fung Wah bus (to give it its proper name) is a fine example of successful urban entrepreneurial spirit: affordable transport for the poorer immigrant communities made possible by competing directly with Greyhound and other bus companies.

Not every break from the city need be a break from the urban: Boston, Philadelphia, and D.C. are all great places to visit, whether you're popping over for a walk around and a meal or looking to be a tourist and see the sights from the White House to the Tea Party. Getting off in the Chinatowns of each leaves you pretty well positioned to explore the cities—and it's fun enough to see a new Chinatown, anyway. On the Chinatown bus, the tickets are cheap, the trips are quick, and the schedules run pretty much from dawn to midnight, making weekend or even day trips to three of the most interesting cities within reach of New York easy and affordable.

WHO'S THERE: Chinese people, students, and travelers on a budget. The crowd on almost every bus is predominantly Chinese, which can make for an interesting ride if you don't speak the language. The extreme affordability means you might travel alongside some unsavory types—but then, you wouldn't ride a Greyhound for the company, either.

WHAT'S GOOD: The Fung Wah bus is very, very cheap: tickets to Boston are around $12; to Philadelphia, $15; and to D.C., $25. The only cheaper option is to hitchhike.

WHAT'S NOT: The price you pay for the cheapest bus on the East Coast is a certain sacrifice in standards of travel. Safety rules and regulations are cloudy on the Chinatown bus, and accidents seem to happen with greater frequency than on other services. If there is a problem and you're an English speaker, you may find yourself surrounded by Chinese people who can't help you out. And there have been unusual stories of unscheduled stops and suspicious luggage transfers . . . but for that money, who cares?

HOW TO GET THERE: The principal pick-up and drop-off point for the Fung Wah bus in the city is at the intersection of Canal Street and the Bowery, but there are drop-off points in Midtown, Brooklyn, and Queens as well. And while you can buy tickets online, it's just as easy—and more spontaneous—to buy one from the screaming lady under the Manhattan Bridge with a reel of stubs in her hand the size of a barrel.
Fung Wah Bus, www.fungwahbus.com

N.B. The success of the Chinatown bus business model has spawned the creation of some other reasonably priced non-Chinese competitors offering bus service to these same destinations. Most of these position themselves as the "classier" alternative by playing up the, er, English fluency of their drivers and staff, and some in-bus amenities like Wi-Fi, electrical outlets for portable electronics, and complimentary bottles of water. These companies include DC2NY and BoltBus.
BoltBus, www.boltbus.com
DC2NY, www.dc2ny.com

ATLANTIC CITY

WHAT IT IS: The Vegas of the East Coast and the inspiration for the original Monopoly board, Atlantic City is New Jersey's most famous casino resort and a legendary den of vice and iniquity. It's also a popular place for summer seaside vacations, built alongside some of the state's prettiest sandy beaches and with one of the longest and most beloved boardwalks in the country. A famous venue on the stand-up-comedy circuit and full of amusement arcades, theaters, and malls, it's equipped with enough entertainments beyond gambling to cater to every crowd from kids to stag parties and senior trips.

Although it's said to be improving, Atlantic City can also be rough in parts. Half of Atlantic City is made up of glittering strips of hotels, casinos, bars, restaurants, and storefronts, while the other half is decrepit, underdeveloped, and generally unsafe for idle consumption. The outer suburbs of the surrounding Atlantic County continue to be pretty much untouched by the transient crowd visiting the city itself, and there's little reason beyond the beautiful coastline to leave the city limits once you get there (see page 257 for "The Jersey Shore"). But Atlantic City is a fun place to explore if you stick to the right tracks, and has an atmosphere all its own.

WHO'S THERE: Like a watered-down Las Vegas, the mainstay crowd at Atlantic City is an eclectic mix of families on package vacations, rowdy stag and bachelorette parties, and a range of gamblers from the lifelong compulsive to the amateur at leisure. It's cheaper and grittier than Las Vegas, and so attracts a younger and sometimes seedier crowd to the casino side, most of whom come from nearby parts of New Jersey and Pennsylvania. But its proximity to New York, Philadelphia, and other big cities on the East Coast means it's also a popular day or weekend destination for savvy urbanites who want to slum it for a night or two.

WHAT'S GOOD: Blackjack! It's a better bet for the casual gambler than the cheesy reservations in Connecticut, and with a wide range of hotels from fancy casino resorts to small motels, it's a cheap and easy way to indulge in some light vice away from the increasing moral cleanliness of post-Giuliani New York. If you want to win back your rent on roulette and shamelessly take in a topless revue, this is the place for you.

WHAT'S NOT: Bust! Although there are a lot of shopping and eating options, and although the beaches are huge and sandy, there's nothing here aside from the casino lifestyle that New Yorkers can't get better at home or on a more scenic trip up Long Island. If you don't want to lose your lease at the poker table, you're better off leaving Atlantic City alone.

HOW TO GET THERE: Atlantic City has its own airport, and moderately priced flights leave daily from LaGuardia. New Jersey Transit operates regular train services to and from Atlantic City from Penn Station in Midtown. But the popular option for one-nighters and weekenders is to drive—it's a quick trip, there's plenty of parking, somebody has to stay sober, which tends to inhibit wanton gambling, and there's something romantic about driving back up the coast to New York from Atlantic City late at night with your winnings burning a hole in your pocket.

New Jersey Transit, see pages 152–153

HUDSON VALLEY

WHAT IT IS: For many less adventurous New Yorkers, the Hudson is just the river that runs alongside Manhattan, a moat protecting the great castle of the city from the barbarian hordes of New Jersey and beyond. To anyone of a more explorative nature, the Hudson is a monumentally beautiful river that has carved a stunning valley down through the rocky countryside, creating some of the most dramatic landscapes on the East Coast and garnering immense historic significance along the way. Home at various times over the past few centuries to Algonquin Indians, British and Dutch settlers, Colonial revolutionaries, a celebrated president, and an entire school of landscape painters, the Hudson Valley is a wonder of natural beauty that also happens to be steeped in American cultural history.

Named for Henry Hudson, the disappointed seventeenth-century English explorer who went looking for a passage to the Pacific and ended up in Albany, the river moves more or less due north of the city, past the Bronx and the New Jersey Palisades and up into the rocky and forested hills of the valley. Historic buildings and pretty towns dot the landscape on either side of the river all the way from Nyack, just north of Yonkers, to Catskill and Hudson itself. Beyond Franklin D. Roosevelt's home at Springwood and the Rockefeller house and gardens at Kykuit, the valley has a distinctly artistic heritage that includes Washington Irving's home at Sunnyside, Thomas Cole's Cedar Grove in Catskill, and Olana, the house Frederic Church built especially to afford himself the views of the valley he most wanted to paint. And beyond the legacy of the Hudson Valley School and the collections of the Newburgh and Garrison museums, the valley has become a quiet new home for modern and contemporary art, at the Dia:Beacon and the Hudson Valley Center for Contemporary Art at Peekskill.

With far fewer options for overnight accommodation than the city's neighboring seaside resorts, the Hudson Valley is better suited to a day-tripper than a weekender. Excepting the spots of historic interest, the towns along the valley aren't much to look at; but in between the houses, gardens, galleries, and museums that stand testament to New York's powerful past, there is amazingly beautiful countryside and some great places to walk, ride, fish, and picnic a day away.

Cedar Grove, 28 Spring Street, Catskill, NY, (518-943-7465) www.thomascole.org

Dia:Beacon, 3 Beekman Street, Beacon, NY, (845-440-0100) www.diabeacon.org

Hudson Valley Center for Contemporary Art, 1701 Main Street, Peekskill, NY, (914-788-0100) www.hvcca.org

Kykuit, Route 9, Sleepy Hollow, NY, (914-631-3992) www.hudsonvalley.org

Olana, Route 9G South, Hudson, NY, (518-828-0135) www.olana.org

Springwood, 4097 Albany Post Road, Hyde Park, NY, (845-229-9115) www.nps.gov/hofr

Sunnyside, West Sunnyside Lane, Tarrytown, NY, (914-631-8200) www.hudsonvalley.org

WHO'S THERE: The farther you travel straight up the Hudson, the deeper you reach into the provincial world of upstate New York. As beautiful, serene, and historic as the Hudson Valley may be, it's still among the least commercial and most straightforwardly bucolic retreats immediately available to the average New Yorker. Aside from the artsy crowds—young and old, contemporary and classical—there is a strong hiking, camping, and foliage contingent, and the odd summer-homer who prefers the river to the sea. But for the most part, especially farther from the city and beyond Poughkeepsie, the Hudson Valley is the peaceful preserve of upstate New Yorkers who play host to nature-loving sophisticates from the big smoke downriver.

WHAT'S GOOD: The river, stupid! Exploring the Hudson Valley is one of the easiest ways to get out of the city and into New York's countryside—just riding the train up from Grand Central to Poughkeepsie alongside the water is beautiful enough, and when you finally pick a place to get off and explore, the landscape is by turns peaceful, intoxicating, and dramatic. If hiking, boating, and fishing aren't enough for you, then you can always use the river as a guide for a tour of some of the key monuments to New York's political, social, and artistic history.

WHAT'S NOT: Anything else. The Hudson Valley is gorgeous, and it's great for any nature-loving New Yorker who wants to get out into the fresh air or for anyone interested in the historic buildings and galleries along the way. But for something more typically engaging, be it good food or a great place to spend the night, you're better off looking to Connecticut or Long Island, where it's easier to combine rural respite with more tangible amenities than fresh air and the undying spirit of Colonial revolution.

HOW TO GET THERE: While driving is easy and affords you a greater choice of destination, the Metro-North Railroad service that runs up the valley from Grand Central to Poughkeepsie is the most attractive option for the typical pedestrian New Yorker. The train stops close to all of the valley's most historic attractions, from the Dia: Beacon to Thomas Cole's house at Cold Springs, and it's easy enough to get off anywhere and find your way to a pretty spot by the river or deeper into the countryside. If you have a specific location in mind that isn't a stop on the Metro-North, or if you're going beyond Poughkeepsie up to Catskill or Hudson itself, it's worth taking the time to scope out local transportation and find out whether you want to bring a bike with you to ride where you want to go, or whether you'll need to take a bus or a local train for a stop or two to get there. But whatever the weather, the train ride itself is worth taking for the spectacular views across the Hudson alone.

Metro-North, see pages 152–153

THE JERSEY SHORE

WHAT IT IS: Traditionally, moving to live in New York means adopting a snobbish attitude toward its neighbor, the Garden State across the Hudson. That the "bridge-and-tunnel" crowd are vilified is fair enough; Bruce Springsteen is still talked about as the state's greatest export to date; and it's true that once you live in New York there's little reason to venture out into Hoboken, Trenton, Newark, Jersey City, or the other towns that look to the city from beyond the water. But look a little further and you'll find that there is more to New Jersey than tollbooths, 1980s rock music, and unpleasant industrial landscapes: there are beaches, and lots of them.

Although it reaches all the way south to Cape May, the stretch of the Jersey Shore that's most realistically accessible to a sun-seeking New Yorker extends from Sandy Hook down through Manasquan to Long Beach Island, alongside Monmouth and Ocean Counties in New Jersey. This stretch of the shore takes in some twenty-odd separate seaside communities, ranging from the posh to the plain, all joined together by miles of uninterrupted sands and beautiful open ocean vistas. The farther south you go, the prettier it gets, and Long Beach Island is a highlight: separated from the mainland by the beautiful Barnegat Bay, the thin strip of sand is surrounded by water, extremely picturesque, and more peaceful than the rowdier beaches up the mainland.

What distinguishes the beaches of the Jersey Shore from their Long Island counterparts is the near-constant presence of boardwalks, and all the fun they entail. In a sense, the Jersey Shore is an extended Coney Island, with almost all its beaches lined with some of the longest and most celebrated boardwalks in the country, and those are in turn dotted with fairground rides, amusement arcades, hot-dog stands, ice cream stalls, bandstands, and all the trappings you could hope to find in a seaside resort. Each area has its own character, so it's easy to find a part of the shore that feels right for you, whether it's one with fewer amusements and a more local vibe or a busier stretch seething with people and all the fun of the fair.

WHO'S THERE: The Jersey Shore crowd is a mixed bag of beachgoers from the major ports of call within reach of its soft white sands. Aside from North Jersey locals—of which there are many—a lot of people from New York and Philadelphia drive down in the summertime in search of a fun alternative to the beaches of Long Island. And the excitement of the boardwalks attracts a younger crowd than the silence and solitude of the Hamptons—you can expect to hear a lot of music, smell a lot of food, and have sand kicked in your face by kids playing ball games all over the beaches.

WHAT'S GOOD: The beaches themselves are fantastic: huge, white sands with waves good enough for surfing, bays peaceful enough for fishing, and undisturbed views of the Atlantic Ocean. But the real perk of the shore is the atmosphere. Although there are quiet stretches (particularly on Long Beach Island, where there is no boardwalk) and you can pass a day in the sand without saying a word to anybody, there are so many amusements up and down the coast, from shuffleboard games and carousels to outdoor movies and concerts, that a summertime jaunt to the Jersey Shore can feel like spring break—in a good way.

WHAT'S NOT: Depending how far down you go, the journey can sap a good chunk out of a sunny day—and the local reception to "bennies," the visiting crowds from New York and Philadelphia, can be a little frosty when you get there. And if crowded boardwalks and strains of Springsteen blowing over the ocean winds aren't your cup of tea, you're better off heading north to the quieter beaches of the Forks and the Hamptons.

HOW TO GET THERE: The quickest way to travel down the Jersey Shore is by car, which allows you to pick a spot along the coast and park for the day relatively easily—and which allows you to drive across the causeway to Long Beach Island, which isn't served by public transport at all. If you're without wheels, there are train and bus routes between Penn Station and Atlantic City, which run through Philadelphia and from which you can take local bus routes to individual towns and beaches along the shore. But the most fun way to travel is by boat: get up at dawn on a summer weekend and hop on the SeaStreak ferry from 34th Street on the east side of Manhattan, which will drop you off by the pristine beaches of Sandy Hook in a little over half an hour.
SeaStreak, www.seastreak.com

THE NORTH FORK

WHAT IT IS: The North Fork is—literally—the flip side of the Hamptons. Long Island splits into two "forks" around Riverhead, about 80 miles east of the city; the Hamptons are on the South Fork, while the other side is known simply as the North Fork. While it has the same beautiful scenery and refreshing air that the farther reaches of Long Island are famous for, the North Fork is the opposite of those famously fancy towns to the south in pretty much every other way. It's also very different from what is known as the "North Shore," where the Roosevelts and the Vanderbilts had their estates. The North Fork is farm country, not Gatsby country. Instead of nightclubs, boutiques, and glorious mansions, there are cornfields, farmstands, and vineyards.

Since the North Fork has never been colonized by the local gentry in the way that those other two areas have, it is a different kind of place to visit. The North Fork feels truly calm, and even sleepy. There are inns and B&Bs and some new upscale boutique-style hotels, but not enough that you'd have to worry about bumping into someone you know (or famous) at the farmstand the way you might in the Hamptons. The North Fork is also home to Long Island's wine industry, and while it's proudly not a well-oiled tourist trap like Napa, there are vineyards to tour, tasting rooms to frequent, and fine wines to sample around town.

At the easternmost tip is the town of Greenport, where you can catch a ferry to Shelter Island; if you have a car (or a bike), you can drive right across Shelter Island and catch the ferry to Montauk on the south side of the island. If you've never been to either the North Fork or the Hamptons before, consider staying on the North Fork: it's cheaper, and you can easily go back and forth between the two if you have a car. (You can also get summer shares and seasonal rentals here for a bit less than across the bay.)

WHO'S THERE: The North Fork has a seasonal weekend contingent, but it keeps a lower profile than the Hamptons people. Here, summer residents do their best to blend in with the locals, farmers, and the occasional NYC ex-pat business-mogul-turned-winemaker.

WHAT'S GOOD: Bike riding and vineyard tours are two North Fork activities that can work together, if you plan your trip well. Long Island's famously flat terrain makes it a great place for leisurely rides, and the vineyards are hard to miss—remember, you're on a long, narrow fork. (FYI: bikes are allowed on LIRR.) The North Fork

Table & Inn in Southold is worth the trip alone—but think like a New Yorker and make reservations for both the inn and restaurant way in advance. There's also decent outlet shopping at the Tanger Mall in nearby Riverhead.

North Fork Table & Inn, 57225 Main Road, Southold, NY, (631-765-0177)
www.northforktableandinn.com
Tanger Outlets Center, 1770 West Main Street, Riverhead, NY, (631-369-2732)
www.tangeroutlet.com/riverhead

WHAT'S NOT: There's no ocean. The beaches are either on the sound or the bay in between the forks, so they aren't as nice as the "ocean beaches" on the South Fork. Also, most beaches aren't public, so you need either to obtain a town permit or pay a day fee to visit them.

HOW TO GET THERE: If you are spending a few days and want to do some exploring or venture over to Shelter Island or the South Fork, you'll want to have a car. If you don't want to get a car, stay in Greenport and definitely rent or bring a bike. Greenport has an LIRR station, the Shelter Island Ferry, and it's the North Fork's major hub, such as it is. There is a new boutique hotel (the Greenporter), and restaurants, shops, art galleries, and the water are all within walking distance. The Ronkonkoma line of the LIRR makes stops at a couple of other North Fork towns, and the Hampton Jitney has a North Fork line (which also has a stop at the outlets in Riverhead).

The Greenporter, 326 Front Street, Greenport, NY, (631-477-0066) www.thegreenporter.com
Hampton Jitney, see page 252
LIRR, see pages 152–153
Shelter Island Ferry, (631-749-0139) www.northferry.com

THE BERKSHIRES/WESTERN MASS.

WHAT IT IS: If there were a scale of destination poshness, with the Hamptons on one end and, say, the Jersey Shore on the other, the Berkshires would fall about in the middle. The area has a particularly New England (though not Boston) flavor; it's rural, but not provincial, which makes it an attractive destination for city folk who want a break from the fast pace, but do not want to dine at a Red Lobster. The area is famously beautiful—mountains, valleys, lakes, farms, foliage, you name it—but it's also full of arts and culture, and as many visitors are attracted to the area for its museums and performing-arts festivals as they are for hiking, biking, and skiing.

Nearby, there's also the Pioneer Valley (called "arguably the most author-saturated, book-cherishing, literature-celebrating place in the nation" by none other than the *New York Times*), and North Adams, a formerly depressed mill town experiencing a major cultural revival—and the tasteful tourist-centered trappings that go with that— thanks to the successful contemporary art museum, Mass MoCA.

Mass MoCA, 1040 Mass MoCA Way, North Adams, MA, (413-MOCA-111) www.massmoca.org

WHO'S THERE: There are New Yorkers with second homes here, but they're out-numbered by Bostonians, year-round locals, and students (there are about a dozen colleges between Williamstown and the Pioneer Valley, including the five in the Amherst/Northampton area alone). In the summer, the area is bustling with actors, dancers, and musicians from Tanglewood, Jacob's Pillow, and the theater festivals, as well as the tourists who come to see them.

Jacob's Pillow, www.jacobspillow.org

Tanglewood, www.tanglewood.org

WHAT'S GOOD: The quality and variety of arts and culture offerings would be amazing in any location, but is particularly staggering for a rural area more than an hour from the nearest major city. For instance, while some vacation areas might have a single theater or musical festival for a few weeks each year, the Berkshires has Tanglewood, the Williamstown Theater Festival, Jacob's Pillow, and Shakespeare on the Mount. In the visual arts, Mass MoCA is overtaking DIA:Beacon as the new trendy destination museum for the NYC art crowd. Its popularity and critical success (the museum has held some important exhibitions, such as the first indoor installation in the U.S. by Jenny Holzer) have transformed the entire area around the museum into an unlikely artist mecca. There's also the Clark Museum in Williamstown, known for its collection of impressionist and post-impressionist paintings, the famous Williams College Museum of Art, and some smaller museums (the Norman Rockwell Museum in Stockbridge; the Eric Carle Museum in Amherst). Plus bookstore upon bookstore upon bookstore . . .

Another perk about the area for an NYC-based traveler is that there are a ton of charming places to stay—it would be harder to find a chain motel than a cool little inn here. There are well-known places like the Red Lion in Stockbridge; modest B&Bs in historic houses; and newer country inns catering to the art crowd, like the Guest House at Field Farm and Porches, by Mass MoCA. Though all of these places have plenty of sweet amenities, none are exorbitantly expensive, and all are significantly cheaper mid-week or off-season.

Clark Museum, 225 South Street, Williamstown, MA, (413-458-2303) www.clarkart.edu

Eric Carle Museum, 125 West Bay Road, Amherst, MA, (413-658-1100)
www.picturebookart.org

Guest House at Field Farm, 554 Sloan Road, Williamstown, MA, (413-458-3135)
www.guesthouseatfieldfarm.thetrustees.org

Norman Rockwell Museum, 9 Glendale Road, Stockbridge, MA, (413-298-4100) www.nrm.org

Porches, 231 River Street, North Adams, MA, (413-664-0400) www.porches.com

Red Lion Inn, 30 Main Street, Stockbridge, MA, (413-298-5545) www.redlioninn.com

Williams College Museum of Art, 15 Lawrence Hall Drive, Williamstown, MA, (413-458-9017)
www.wcma.org

Williamstown Theater Festival, www.wtfestival.org

WHAT'S NOT: While it's possible to get to certain towns by train or bus, it's difficult. Service is infrequent, and bus trips often involve a layover at the scary bus station in Springfield. Plus, once you are in the area, you'll miss out on a lot if you don't have a car to get from place to place. Best to save this trip for when you've got access to a vehicle.

HOW TO GET THERE: The Berkshires is a three-hour drive from NYC; the Pioneer Valley and North Adams are between three-and-a-half and four hours. There are a bunch of route options, some more scenic than others. The prettiest is the Merritt Parkway that covers a short stretch of Connecticut; it's a small road with lots of trees, and is especially nice in the fall when the leaves are changing.

CONNECTICUT

WHAT IT IS: True-blue New Yorkers would be forgiven for thinking of Connecticut as one long, rich suburb; the state you drive through "on the way" to New England; or not really thinking of it at all. But Connecticut has one particular perk for New Yorkers: it's got lots of pretty things that are easy to get to.

Connecticut has plenty of rural and scenic parts for NYC-escapees, and small as the state is, there's still a bit of diversity of terrain. The two closest parts of Connecticut (and the easiest to get to from the city) are Fairfield and Litchfield counties. Fairfield County is a little closer, and encompasses the southwestern part of the state, along the Long Island Sound; Litchfield is in the northwestern part of the state that borders Massachusetts to the north and New York's Dutchess County to the west. If you want beaches, and coastal maritime-y towns, choose Fairfield County; if you want quaint inns, lakes, and farms, head to Litchfield. (Both also have a respectable number of antiques stores and fancy houses to ogle.) Each county has many cute little towns and villages, but there are also a lot of fancy suburbs that don't hold any interest for a visitor (as well as some rougher parts, see "What's Not"), so it is better to plan your trip around a specific destination (a beach, an inn, etc.) than to just choose a town blindly and start looking for the sand or a farm or antiques stores.

There's another reason New Yorkers go to Connecticut that has nothing to do with pastoral beauty . . . gambling! Foxwoods, which is near Hartford, is actually (and rather surprisingly, we think) the largest casino in the world; there's also Mohegan Sun, which is less than ten miles away. Both are under three hours from NYC, accessible by public transport, have thousands of hotel rooms, and all the slot machines and roulette tables you could dream of.

Foxwoods, Ledyard, CT, (1-800-FOXWOODS) www.foxwoods.com
Mohegan Sun, Uncasville, CT, (1-888-226-7711) www.mohegansun.com

WHO'S THERE: Depends where you are. There are blue-blood residents around the tony suburbs; white-collar office workers in Hartford and Stamford; New Yorkers with second homes in some of the towns along the coast and in Litchfield County; perky college kids around New Haven; and gamblers by the casinos—but these diverse contingents rarely mix with one another.

WHAT'S GOOD: Connecticut gets a bad rap sometimes as being just a fancy suburb, but parts of it have the same charming, rural, visitor-friendly vibe as more traditional

New England destinations in Vermont, Massachusetts, and New Hampshire—and it takes two hours less time to get to them. Connecticut beaches are similarly overlooked. While there isn't an actual ocean, nice beaches and fine water exist along the sound. One Connecticut native we know compared the Long Island Sound to an armpit, with the beaches getting nicer the farther down (well, east) you go. Cove Beach in Stamford is where they start getting decent; if you hold out all the way to Old Saybrook (which is farther out along the coast, in Middlesex County, beyond the Metro-North line), you'll get a boardwalk, better water, and sand. For golfers, there are public courses in Stamford and Fairfield that are nicer than the ones you'll find in Westchester and only a few miles (or train stops) farther away.

WHAT'S NOT: Cities are not this state's strong suit; they range from seriously unattractive to shamefully depressing (Hartford, for instance, has one of the lowest per capita incomes of any city in the U.S.). New Haven is the most charming, but coming for a New Yorker, the food, theater, and culture will probably seem a bit dinky to go out of one's way for. (An exception is the Pilot Penn Tennis tournament, held each August at Yale's tennis center. It takes place right before the U.S. Open, and you can see a lot of the same players there, in a smaller venue, for a lot cheaper.)
Pilot Penn Tennis, www.pilotpentennis.com

HOW TO GET THERE: The Fairfield area is easy to get to on Metro-North; there are stops at a dozen coastal towns between Greenwich and Bridgeport on the New Haven line. Many of these towns are close enough to the city that you could take a day trip to the beach, maybe stopping for dinner in Greenwich on the way back. (There are also car and passenger ferries in Bridgeport and New London that you can take back and forth from Long Island.) If you are driving, taking the Merritt Parkway (see page 262) instead of one of the bigger roads will make the drive feel like a part of the trip.

For Litchfield County, you really need a car. It's definitely possible to do this as a day trip, but since this is an area known for its inns and B&Bs, it's one to consider an overnight stay for.
The Bridgeport and Port Jefferson Ferry, www.bpjferry.com
Metro-North, see pages 152–153
New London Ferry, www.longislandferry.com

—————————→ **Foliage and Apple Picking** ←—————————

When Caitlin was in college in Massachusetts, she always looked forward to the trip back home for fall break in October, when she could see the leaves changing color from the window of the Greyhound bus. Fortunately, there are other places besides along the highway where you can see the foliage. The New York State tourism web site does an online fall foliage report with weekly updates, so you can find out where peak color is. The leaves start turning in the middle of the state, around the Adirondacks, in late summer and reach peak color in late September; expect peak color in areas close to the city in November.

In our opinion, no one who lives in the city should ever be eating a supermarket apple, especially in the fall. The Greenmarkets are overflowing with them well into the winter, and there's a reason that they're considered a regional specialty. But if you're a real apple fanatic, then you should take an afternoon to go apple picking. The New York Apple Association web site lists many "u-pick" orchards within two hours of the city, in any direction you want to go. Time the trip with peak foliage, and you've got yourself a perfect fall afternoon.

New York Apple Association, www.nyapplecountry.com

New York State Tourism Web Site, www.iloveny.com

AIRPORT STANDINGS

When you're taking a trip home for Thanksgiving, to Miami for a break from winter, or a European vacation, you'll have to branch out into the airports. New Yorkers are fortunate to have access to three, but those with limited experience may not know how different they are from one another. Here, we award first, second, and third place to our local airports.

FIRST PLACE: JFK

Okay, JFK isn't perfect. Not by a long shot. But it is often the lesser of all evils. Let's consider each category one by one. First, getting to and from: JFK is much more convenient than Newark for anyone who lives in Brooklyn, Queens, the Bronx, and almost all of Manhattan (except for Tribeca). But it also handily beats LaGuardia, which though closer, lacks the AirTrain, which is key if you want to get to the airport both efficiently and affordably. If you need a cab, there is a flat fare of $45 plus tolls, which isn't cheap, but it's a bargain compared to the $70 or so you'll pay to and from Newark, and a metered fare to LaGuardia can be nearly that much if there's a lot of traffic. Advantage JFK.

Next, service. LaGuardia, being only a domestic airport, can't even compete with JFK's worldwide offerings. But JFK also beats Newark, because as the top international airport in the U.S. (17 percent of all international-bound passengers in the U.S. go through JFK, more than any other airport), it's got more flights to practically anywhere in the world. And JFK is not skimpy on domestic options—it's the hub of JetBlue, for example—especially transcontinental ones.

Finally, airport experience. Despite being by far the busiest of the area airports (and one of the busiest in the country), it doesn't feel like there are more lines, glitches, and delays than the others. For food and shops, it's definitely ahead of grungy LaGuardia, and generally about even with Newark. But the JetBlue terminal (which has, among other offerings, a sushi bar, a Papaya King, and a spa) knocks it one tick ahead— and the new terminal (scheduled to open in late 2008) promises to be even better.

JFK AirTrain, see page 153

SECOND PLACE: NEWARK

Newark doesn't have the international cachet of JFK, and of course it's technically in New Jersey, but it does have its place in the NYC-area repertoire. While it's rarely the most convenient option, it's still accessible, and so it can be useful to have another area airport option when you are looking for a flight. (Particularly if you like to fly Continental—Newark is its hub.) And though it's a poor choice if you need to take a car or a cab, Newark does have an AirTrain, which makes it potentially more convenient even than LaGuardia.

Newark AirTrain, see page 153

THIRD PLACE: LAGUARDIA

On paper, LaGuardia seems very attractive—it's close to the city, and it's the smallest of the of area's airports, which, if you follow the conventional wisdom, would suggest that it's less susceptible to delays than a behemoth like JFK. When possible, however, resist the temptation. Flying in and out of LaGuardia is the air-travel equivalent of commuting in a place like Los Angeles or Atlanta: if you're going at an odd hour and everything is running smoothly, it's not so bad. But if you go at a normal time, the traffic is unbelievable, and things never really run smoothly—just as an accident on one freeway can set off massive delays on a host of other routes, a bad patch of weather in the Midwest can mess up LaGuardia's overpacked schedule for the rest of the day. LaGuardia also has a nasty habit of trying to cut its losses on a busy day by spontaneously canceling flights. In fine weather conditions, a morning flight has a decent chance of leaving reasonably close to scheduled take-off time. But because of how crowded the take-off and landing schedule is, afternoon and evening flights are frequently delayed because of traffic alone; throw in a little drizzle, or God forbid a full-blown storm, and you should just hope that your flight leaves at all.

Taking a cab to or from LaGuardia is not as crippling as the other airports, though watch out for rush hour: the $20-to-$30ish fare can climb to $40 if there's a lot of traffic. And even this comparative bargain is not much consolation for the fact that the public transport options are dismal. There's no AirTrain, and while you can take a city bus to LaGuardia, we wouldn't recommend it. The single Manhattan option (there are a few Queens buses that make stops at the airport) is the M60, which leaves from Morningside Heights, and makes stops in Harlem. The bus trip to the airport is about an hour; with the time getting to the stop, waiting for the bus, and then getting to your terminal, you should probably allow two hours just to get to the airport. The best option is the New York Airport Service. Its buses leave about every 20 to 30 minutes, stopping at Port Authority, Penn Station, and Grand Central, and then at each airport terminal. The trip takes between 45 minutes and just over an hour depending on which stop you get on at, and the cost is $12 one way or $21 round-trip. (New York Airport Service also has buses to JFK.)

M60 Bus, www.mta.info

New York Airport Service, (212-875-8200) www.nyairportservice.com

⟶ A note on Islip ⟵

Islip Airport (or MacArthur Airport) has experienced a recent rise in popularity among some newer New Yorkers and those who visit them, much to the confusion of many people who have lived here for a while, who would never consider it a "local airport." The cause for this misguided vogue is that Islip is the only NYC-area airport (if you can really call it that) with direct service from Southwest Airlines. People who love Southwest Airlines (and there are people who really love it) think Islip must be some great untapped resource, and that a little more travel time to and from the airport is a small price for its flexible booking policies, cheap tickets, etc. Perhaps. But before you succumb to the temptation of a good fare, no change fees, or a relative waiving a ticket voucher in front of your nose, know this: Islip Airport is seriously far from NYC. To put it into numbers, it's about 50 miles from the city; nearly a two-hour trip on the LIRR (you take the train to Ronkonkoma, and then a cab or a shuttle for an additional charge to the airport itself); and a car service into the city (remember there are no cabs!) is at least $100. In other words, you could easily spend as much getting to or from the airport as you would save on the ticket, for many times more aggravation and minutes spent in transit. Don't say we didn't warn you.

TAKE A DAY OFF

⟵⟶

Ask New Yorkers what's great about living in the city and they'll probably tell
you that there is more to do here than anywhere else in the world. And they'd be right:
with so many shops, museums, galleries, parks, theaters, bars, waterfronts, clubs,
restaurants, gyms, cafés, and delis to choose from, it's hard to imagine anybody
having the chance to be bored in this town. But one of the ironies of life in the city is
that with so much to do, it can be difficult to remember how much *else* there is to do.
You'd be surprised how many people find themselves doing the same things every
weekend, or every time they have a few hours to themselves. People have favorite
neighborhoods to spend time in, favorite places to eat, favorite places to shop, favorite
trees to fall asleep beneath—but it can take a bit of willpower to break the mold and
go looking for new favorites. To really make the most of time to yourself in the city, the
important thing is to keep an open mind, keep your eyes open and your ears to the
ground, and to be on the lookout for something new.

When Jacob first arrived in New York from London, a combination of insurmountable jet lag and temporary unemployment meant he spent a couple of months
getting up incredibly early in the morning and spending his days finding ways to pass
time between looking for work and a more permanent place to live than his friend's
sofa bed. What seemed at the time like a harrowing test of financial and spiritual
endurance soon became, once he had found a job and an apartment, one of the most
fondly remembered periods in his time as a New Yorker. This was the time he had to
really explore the city, to travel around the boroughs to places he did not yet know
he'd never set foot in again, to stumble upon neighborhoods that would one day be
called home, and to get a sense of every aspect of city life.

Take mornings, for example. For the vast majority of New Yorkers, mornings are
a routine blur marked by the unwelcome buzz of an alarm clock, the untimely house
music of a gym, a barista's voice calling out your order at a coffee shop, and the sound
of the subway doors closing behind you on the way to work. But rise at dawn one day
and you'll see an entirely different city. In the busier parts of this city that never sleeps,
early mornings are the quietest times: people out late are only just getting to bed, people going to work haven't quite gotten up yet, and the streets are quieter than they will
be for twenty-four hours. There are strange sights and sounds all across town that
you'd usually sleep through: the arrival of the meat trucks at the few stock houses in

the Meatpacking District; the quiet return to Sheepshead Bay of midnight fishermen with their daily haul for the restaurants of Brooklyn; horses being exercised up and down Riverside Park; and the eerie silence of no traffic on the usually busy avenues of Manhattan.

The best way to spend a morning in New York is to walk around and explore neighborhoods you only know in their waking forms—or neighborhoods you don't know at all. Walk across Prospect Park and watch the dog run fill up and the joggers roll in. Stroll down the East River and enjoy the sunrise across Long Island. Take a coffee to Battery Park and watch the last of the night's industrial boats leave the harbor. Travel up to City Island and eat fish for breakfast. Ride the cable car to Roosevelt Island and walk across to Long Island City in the sunshine. Or be the first person in a nice diner as the sun comes up and the smell of bacon wafts in from the kitchen.

Our advice is, if you're unemployed or are master of your time, get up early and enjoy it; and if you work every day, there is no sweeter feeling than deciding at the last minute to turn away from the subway and keep walking to a day of freedom. Experience a full morning in New York and by bedtime you'll feel like you've lived two days instead of one.

The same goes for nighttime, too. As only New York really can, the city has a fully functioning and entirely civilized nocturnal life that needs to be explored to be enjoyed (as well as a decidedly uncivilized one, if that's your thing). In the livelier neighborhoods, and particularly in Manhattan, there are enough twenty-four-hour delis and diners, enough late-night movie theaters and bars, and even enough Apple shops, American Apparels, and bookstores open to keep the city's night owls busy from dusk to dawn. Deciding on a whim to go see a midnight movie at the Sunshine on Houston Street is as much fun as skipping work to catch one in the morning. Walking across Central Park lit up by the bright lights of Midtown can be as beautiful and restorative as watching the shadows of the trees grow at dawn. And stepping out to pick up a newspaper and some groceries is as easy to do at three in the morning as it is five hours later when the rest of the neighborhood is doing the same.

In between morning and night lies the entire expanse of the day. Traditional business hours are perhaps the most the challenging time to convince oneself to seize the day, but also potentially the most rewarding. If you are between jobs, be sure to tear yourself away from the hunt for at least one full weekday—believe us, if you don't, you'll regret it once you are working. If you work at home or make your own hours, take a break somewhere between 11 and 4 and see the city like a Broadway actor, a stay-at-home parent, or a producer on a morning show. Have a long solo lunch somewhere with a lovely atmosphere and a nice prix fixe. Visit MoMA on Monday and have

Les Demoiselles D'Avignon all to yourself. (Even most of the tourists think that it's closed!) Experience the simple camaraderie of sharing a midday movie with some of the city's dedicated cinophiles—and remember that the film buff you are sitting next to just might be Woody Allen or Spike Lee. Go to Staten Island, or the Cloisters, or Queens' Chinatown, or anywhere else that you haven't made it to since you've lived here. As both Jacob and Caitlin know from stints of unemployment and jobs with unconventional hours, there's a wonderful atmosphere in areas of NYC outside of the business and tourist hubs that you can only experience off-hours. Don't miss it.

Morning, noon, or night, any time spent without the daily grind of work, free from any impositions beyond the primal necessities of sleep and food, should be regarded in New York as a golden age and enjoyed as if it were an unexpected vacation. In fact, more than in most cities in the world, New Yorkers are known to take vacations without going anywhere. New York is a busy place, and New Yorkers tend to be busy people. Whether it's through the routine of work, the neighborhood you live in, or the circle of friends you keep, almost everybody can grow into a comfortable niche of New York life—and in a place where you can find pretty much whoever and whatever you want wherever and whenever you want them, it's easy never to look beyond that. The trick to keeping your curiosity alive is to let yourself be surprised: take some time off and go somewhere new without leaving the city, see something you've never seen before, and you'll soon find yourself doing something fun you never expected to—and knowing more about the city than you did before.

Things You Don't Do Now That You Live Here

It takes a certain kind of person to come to New York and ride a hop-on-hop-off bus around the city. To take the "Real Kramer's Seinfeld Tour" and eat at the Seinfeld diner. To shop for souvenirs in the busiest parts of town and to eat at the most overrated restaurants. To pay top dollar for an overstuffed pastrami sandwich eight inches high. To indulge in the time-honored tradition of mainstream musical theater. To spend New Year's Eve in Times Square or eat dinner at the Olive Garden. That person is a tourist, and once you live here you must count yourself out of that tiresome brigade, deny yourself these travelers' delights, and consider yourself a resident who has discretion and taste.

With that in mind, we've put together a shortlist of twenty-five things you just don't do now that you live here.

- GO TO THE STATUE OF LIBERTY
- REFER TO THE CITY AS "THE BIG APPLE"
- LINE UP FOR TICKETS IN TIMES SQUARE
- RIDE ONE OF THOSE DOUBLE-DECKER TOUR BUSES
- GET CUPCAKES FROM MAGNOLIA
- HAVE DINNER AT TAVERN ON THE GREEN
- CHASTISE PEOPLE FOR SITTING ON YOUR STOOP
- EXPLAIN NEIGHBORHOOD ACRONYMS OUT LOUD
- EVEN CONSIDER GOING TO TIMES SQUARE FOR NEW YEAR'S
- SHOP AT MACY'S
- TAKE THE STATEN ISLAND FERRY
- RENT BOATS IN CENTRAL PARK
- LOOK UP
- WEAR ANYTHING WITH "I LOVE NY" ON IT
- VISIT GROUND ZERO
- EAT AN OVERPRICED SANDWICH AT THE CARNEGIE DELI OR KATZ'S
- PLAY CARNIVAL GAMES AT THE SAN GENNARO FESTIVAL
- CLIMB THE EMPIRE STATE BUILDING
- TIP LESS THAN 20 PERCENT FOR ANYTHING
- PAY MORE THAN $12 FOR A MANICURE
- BE ON ROOSEVELT ISLAND
- GO ICE-SKATING, ANYWHERE
- LOOK AROUND GRAND CENTRAL INSTEAD OF JUST WALKING THROUGH IT
- WATCH THE THANKSGIVING DAY PARADE IN PERSON
- STOP AND WATCH CREWS FILMING AN EPISODE OF *LAW & ORDER*

EPILOGUE

When I arrived in New York in the fall of 2003, I was lucky enough to have a good friend living here to help me settle into city life. I occupied the living room of a brownstone he shared in Brooklyn, and for the first few weeks of my life as a New Yorker he and his friends—in what I would later understand was an understated enthusiasm endemic among those who grow up here—showed me the ropes. He worked near the Flatiron building and in my first week invited me to lunch by Madison Park—a typical afternoon for him, another new adventure for me. Stepping out of the train at 23rd Street, I saw him waiting for me across Fifth Avenue and strode out confidently through an angry gridlock of honking cabs and sweltering buses. "Look at you," my friend said with a smile when I met him at the sidewalk. "You cross the street like you lived in the city all your life."

Having grown up in London, I thought I *had* lived in the city all my life. There are jams and jaywalkers in London, after all, and music and movies, arts and languages, noise, romance, and the underground. But what New York City has that is unique is the most intense mixture of all these elements, the elements that make living and working in a city so exciting. In some cases, it's less a mixture than a juxtaposition of cultures and ideas that don't coexist in the same way anywhere else: rich and poor, young and old, famous and oblivious, leaves and concrete, Wall Street and Coney Island, Islam and Judaism, galleries and golf clubs, pizza and Peking Duck. New Yorkers are in many ways as free from prejudice and expectation as it's possible for eight million people living in each other's pockets to be. This is because people come to New York to be in New York, to experience something that is at once greater than the sum of its cosmopolitan parts and more tangible and local than any other metropolis in the world.

I still consider myself a Londoner, and—as so many people think of the place where they grew up, and as Caitlin is fortunate to be able to think of New York—I feel that it will always be my home. But after five years, four apartments, three jobs, two books, one dog, and all the experiences of life in this city, I consider myself a New Yorker, too. If there's one thing above all else we hope you can take from this book, it's that whoever you are, wherever you come here from, and whatever you do here, this city can belong to you, too.

—Jacob Lehman, June 2008

GLOSSARY

311: The city's central hotline for non-emergency services. From anywhere in the five boroughs, residents can call 311 to file complaints, make inquiries about city services, and report non-emergency crimes.

ALTERNATE-SIDE PARKING: A set of rules that regulates parking throughout the five boroughs by requiring cars on either side of a street to be moved during certain hours on alternating days each week for street cleaning. The rules are suspended on Sundays, and on more than two dozen legal, religious, and cultural holidays, including Christmas, Independence Day, Washington's Birthday, Lincoln's Birthday, All Saints Day, Diwali, the end of Ramadan, and many Jewish holidays that even many Jewish people have never heard of.

BODEGA: Alternative name for a deli, used particularly to refer to the small freestanding corner stores that sell newspapers, candy, sodas, cigarettes, and pornographic magazines.

BOWERY, THE: A north-south street on the Lower East Side of Manhattan. Always referred to with the definite article, as in "The space on the Bowery where CBGB used to be is now a fancy clothing store."

BQE: The Brooklyn-Queens Expressway, a monstrosity of a highway connecting Brooklyn and Queens. A savior for drivers but a dark and noisy nightmare for residents of any neighborhood it carves through.

BLOOMBERG'S PARKS: Refers to a wild promise made by Mayor Bloomberg in 2007 to green up the streets of the five boroughs until no citizen lives more than a ten-minute walk from a park. As part of his ambitious PlaNYC, he wants to convert every last disused asphalt inch of the city into green space of one kind or another, from community gardens to astro-turf ball fields. As of summer 2008, he has a fair way to go.

BRIDGE-AND-TUNNEL: Derogatory term for people who travel to the city from New Jersey, Long Island, and anywhere far enough from Manhattan to warrant coughing up a toll. Generally used to describe the glitzy crowds who come to party on weekends.

BRONX, THE: One of the five boroughs of New York City. Always referred to with the definite article, as in "the last time I went to the Bronx was for a Yankees game, but I hear the Botanical Gardens are amazing." (See also "the Bowery," above). The Bronx is also the only borough that is actually situated on the mainland United States.

BROWNSTONE: The austere row houses built from dark sandstone that are characteristic of the city's older neighborhoods, from Bedford-Stuyvesant and Park Slope in Brooklyn to Harlem in Manhattan. Brownstones commonly have stoops (see page 275) and are considered hot property by many New Yorkers, often for their beautiful old wooden interiors and because brownstone blocks can be the prettiest in the city.

CENTURY 21: A small chain of department stores that specializes in discount designer clothing, comparable to Loehmann's. The flagship location is in Lower Manhattan, directly across the street from the World Trade Center site. An excellent source for cheap socks and underwear, men's suits, and women's dresses.

"THE CITY": Manhattan, and only Manhattan.

DOWNTOWN: South of 14th Street. Even though it's expensive to live there and it's no longer the mecca of art and rebellion it once was, "downtown" still means young and cool. People like to measure their coolness by how far uptown they roam: some people are so downtown they don't go above Delancey.

FDR: Franklin Delano Roosevelt Drive, the giant road that runs up the east side of Manhattan from the Brooklyn Bridge to Harlem and the bridges to Queens and the Bronx. Some stretches of the FDR are elevated, which makes the neighborhoods beneath less pleasant than Manhattan's Riviera ought to be. Like the West Side Highway, a useful route to know when you're traveling a long distance up- or downtown.

FULTON FISH MARKET: Legendary outdoor seafood market that resided for 180 years at the end of Fulton Street on the far Lower East Side of Manhattan. A traditional dusk-to-dawn fisherman's market, Fulton was picked up in 2005 and moved all the way uptown to its present state-of-the-art facility in the Bronx. It's still the biggest wholesale fish market in America, but it's no longer the lively and atmospheric place to walk around at dawn that it once was.

HIGHLINE, THE: A set of elevated tracks that runs over Tenth Avenue from Gansevoort Street to 34th Street. The tracks were part of a freight railroad that was in use until 1980; then the Highline was abandoned. A section of the Highline is currently being developed for an elevated park; the southern section is being turned into an upscale hotel. Frequently associated with the gentrifying development of the Meatpacking District. Also known as "the Chelsea Highline."

HOUSTON STREET: A major lower Manhattan east-west thoroughfare, and the official boundary of real downtown. Pronounced "house-ton"—*not* like the city in Texas.

LES: Acronym for the Lower East Side, the sprawling area between 14th Street and the Financial District on the East Side of Manhattan that touches on several neighborhoods from the East Village to Chinatown. Once synonymous only with punks, crime, and cheap apartments, the LES is more gentrified now, but is still home to a lot of cheap indie bars and cheap indie clothes.

MAGNOLIA: 1) a bakery in the West Village that specializes in cupcakes, made famous by an appearance on *Sex and the City;* 2) derogative synonym for a local business that has become unpleasantly overrun with tourists after appearing in a popular TV show or movie, or publicized as a celebrity's favorite in a magazine.

NAVY YARD, THE: Formerly the biggest shipbuilding facility in America, the Navy Yard is an industrial space in the quieter half of Dumbo in Brooklyn. The site has remained pretty much the same since its development in 1801—spare, close to the water, and pleasantly unlike the rest of New York—except now the beautiful old industrial buildings are occupied by artists, young businesses, and the occasional lucky resident.

"THE PARK": Central Park, unless you are in Brooklyn, where it's Prospect Park.

P.S.: Acronym for "public school," always followed by a number (e.g. P.S. 40, P.S. 321). Schools referred to with a "P.S." are elementary schools, but not all public elementary schools are called "P.S." (Some are referred to by their official names.) "M.S." refers to Middle School; "I.S." to Intermediate School; and "J.H.S." to Junior High School. High schools rarely are referred to by acronyms. *N.B. Mastering these cryptic naming conventions is not required for admission into these schools.*

"RUNNING IN SECTIONS": The common if unofficial term to describe the unfortunate situation when subways sometimes run in sections while a line is under construction. If a line is "running in sections," instead of running along its entire line, trains in both directions will have as their final stop some station along the line, and each will run back and forth along its track, like a shuttle, so that portions of the track in both directions can be worked on. Passengers trying to get beyond whatever the final stop is of a train running in sections must transfer to the other train across the platform to complete their journeys. Most commonly refers to the G train, which runs in two sections almost every weekend and sometimes during the week.

SAMPLE SALES: Refers to any kind of temporary warehouse or showroom sale where a designer or store sells overstock, end-of-season leftovers, or irregular pieces at a sizeable discount. Most commonly used for clothing, but can also refer to sales of housewares, bedding and home décor, or any kind of accessory. Sample sales last anywhere from a few hours to a week; most last a few days. Also known as "warehouse sales" or "showroom sales." Frequently incredibly crowded, and at any point after the first few hours, disappointingly picked over.

SECOND AVENUE SUBWAY LINE, THE: Mythical subway link for the far East Side of Manhattan that has been notoriously long in development by the MTA. The new T train, should it ever appear, would run from Harlem down to the Financial District—servicing a large part of the city that has never before been tapped by underground transport—east of the 4, 5, and 6 trains. The city's been talking about it for years, and it's scheduled to be completed in 2013.

STOOP: The steps that ascend from the sidewalk to the front door of many of the city's older brownstones and row houses. Stoops were originally constructed to allow people clean entry from the dung-covered streets of the nineteenth century. Now stoops are hangout spots for proud homeowners and weary walkers.

SLICE, A: A piece of pizza that is eaten on the go, as in "I didn't have time for lunch, but I grabbed a slice on the way home from work." Local custom dictates that you fold the slice in half so the crust meets the crust. Never eaten with a knife and fork.

TOWNHOUSE: The brick row houses that characterize the Upper East and Upper West sides of Manhattan, as well as some of the older neighborhoods in Brooklyn and the outer boroughs. Townhouses rank second to brownstones in New Yorkers' affections, and tend to be owned by rich old members of the New York aristocracy.

"THE TRAIN": The subway. Even though there are different kinds of overground trains running in and out of the city, when New Yorkers say they're going to take "the train" they always mean the subway.

TRISTATE AREA, THE: Term referring to the more heavily populated areas of New Jersey, Connecticut, and New York State that are closest to the greater metropolitan area of New York City.

UPTOWN: The opposite of downtown. To a downtown New Yorker, "uptown" can mean anything north of 14th Street. For most of the city's citizens, "uptown" means the Upper East and Upper West Sides, Harlem, and beyond. And to the hip-hop community, "uptown" can mean the Bronx.

INDEX

INDEX BY NEIGHBORHOOD

ABOUT THE AUTHORS

Jacob Lehman is a writer, editor, and Englishman living in New York.
Caitlin Leffel is a writer, editor, and native New Yorker.